The City in Urban Poverty

EADI Global Development Series

Series Editors:

Maja Bucar, Vice-Dean and Professor, Faculty of Social Sciences, University of Ljubljana

Andy Mold, Senior Economic Affairs Officer at the United Nations Economic Commission for Africa

The EADI Global Development series reflects the multi-disciplinary character of EADI member institutes and the association at large. The series seeks to broaden our understanding of the processes that advance or impede human development, whether from a political, economic, sociological or anthropological perspective. EADI's mission is to inform students of development, international relations, and area studies, the academic and policy research and teaching community, development administration, professional training and practice.

Development research is characterised by its interdisciplinary approach and its interest in a strong link between theory, policy and practice. The series invites book manuscripts emanating from EADI working group activities, EADI conferences and EADI research projects, but is also open to external submissions.

EADI Global Development Series
Series Standing Order ISBN 978–1–137–01335–4

You can receive future titles in this series as they are published by placing a standing order. Please contact your bookseller or, in case of difficulty, write to us at the address below with your name and address, the title of the series and the ISBN quoted above.

Customer Services Department, Macmillan Distribution Ltd, Houndmills, Basingstoke, Hampshire RG21 6XS, England

The City in Urban Poverty

Edited by

Charlotte Lemanski
University of Cambridge, UK

and

Colin Marx
University College London, UK

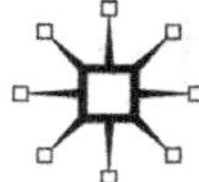

First published 2015 by
PALGRAVE MACMILLAN

Palgrave Macmillan in the UK is an imprint of Macmillan Publishers Limited, registered in England, company number 785998, of Houndmills, Basingstoke, Hampshire RG21 6XS.

Palgrave Macmillan in the US is a division of St Martin's Press LLC, 175 Fifth Avenue, New York, NY 10010.

Palgrave Macmillan is the global academic imprint of the above companies and has companies and representatives throughout the world.

Palgrave® and Macmillan® are registered trademarks in the United States, the United Kingdom, Europe and other countries.

ISBN: 978–1–137–36742–6

This book is printed on paper suitable for recycling and made from fully managed and sustained forest sources. Logging, pulping and manufacturing processes are expected to conform to the environmental regulations of the country of origin.

A catalogue record for this book is available from the British Library.

Library of Congress Cataloging-in-Publication Data

The city in urban poverty / [edited by] Charlotte Lemanski, Colin Marx.
pages cm. — (EADI global development series)
Includes bibliographical references.
ISBN 978–1–137–36742–6
1. Urban poor – Developing countries. 2. Poverty – Developing countries. 3. Sociology, Urban – Developing countries. 4. City planning – Developing countries. 5. Urban policy – Developing countries. I. Lemanski, Charlotte, 1977– II. Marx, Colin, 1967–

HV4173.C45 2015
362.509173'2—dc23 2014049664

Contents

List of Illustrations

Boxes

Figures

Tables

Foreword

One of the many intriguing observations offered to us by Henri Lefebvre is the idea that the city is an impossible object. Of course, this is so in the same way as for any object, as seeking to conceptualise anything reveals its inexhaustibility, the surplus to our attempts to understand. In the case of the city, it is also the immense reservoirs of possibility for the future which are present in the urban that divert our efforts to conceptualise and to contain imaginatively whatever the urban may be. Our hopes for the future of cities, and the dynamic changing nature of the urban, render this object of investigation a possible-impossible (Lefebvre, 2004; Schmid, 2008). Time, then, and the complexities of conceptualisation mean that the city is always slipping away from us, always elsewhere than we imagine it to be (Simone, 2011), creating an atmosphere of impossibility about knowing what the urban is. But it is also the spatiality of the urban itself which unsettles our narratives as we seek to understand aspects of urban life. The processes that shape cities stretch far beyond any semblance of their concentrated urban form, and the impact of urban life is felt across the planet – the limits of the territorialised concept of the city are self-evident (Soja and Kanai, 2007; Merrifield, 2013). As a field of study, in the early twenty-first century, urban studies is embracing a period of theoretical renewal in the search for concepts and insights which are adequate to the shifting nature, extended processes, and expanding form of the urban (Satterthwaite, 2007; Brenner, 2013; Brenner and Schmid, 2013).

It is against this backdrop that this book draws our attention to some essential directions for thinking the urban. In scoping the idea of 'the city and urban poverty', this book delineates both a scholarly and, importantly, political dimension of understanding and acting in the field of the urban. The authors and editors deftly sidestep the limits of thinking with the demarcation, 'development', which has long framed (and limited) ways of approaching the issue of 'urban poverty', in 'developing', 'underdeveloped' or 'low-income' countries. But very importantly, this book clearly signposts the rich analytical resources which emerge from this tradition of urban studies – one which any consideration of the future of cities and the possibility of conceptualising the urban must engage with – and very seldom does. Starting, then, from some of the poorest urban regions, and attending to the political and economic exclusions of the poor, offers an important vantage point for understanding the urban at a planetary scale. Urban development studies bequeaths to the broader traditions of urban studies a strong attentiveness to the production and persistence of poverty in contexts of deep inequality but, at times, also of substantial resources – India's ambitious plans for multiple new smart cities, for example, coexists with some of the deepest urban poverty on the planet. It calls for urban scholars to pay close attention to the kinds of urban futures which are being made through political actions today, including gendered exclusions (Chant and Datu) and brutal state action in displacing (Sanyal), restricting (Goswami), excluding (Lombard) and policing (Jones and Rodgers) the poor in cities across the world.

But one of the most important legacies of the development perspective in writing on poorer cities is the strong attention that has been paid to the 'possibility' of the urban. Whether approached with the significant intellectual resources of Amartya Sen's idea of capabilities which resonates very well with understanding how (informal) spaces of the city both constrain and generate possibilities (Frediani); or through the detailed political analysis of how the patient construction of political voice and agency in settlement after settlement can scale up to transform investments in housing at a city scale, in Levy's important contribution on community organisation and housing finance in Mumbai. Understanding the potential for political organisation to transform the outcomes of state and developer action to make new urban futures now is a powerful contribution to analyses of the urban everywhere. The governmental challenges of poorly resourced urban contexts also reminds urban scholars everywhere of the sometimes taken-for-granted role of co-ordination and knowledge of cities in seeking to shape their futures. States and planning, then, are also sites of potential, where power is a power 'to', and where mapping and statistics (Baud) and the city-wide co-ordination of infrastructural investment (Parnell) are essential to simply sustain urban life today, while plans for investment, funding and location involve future-oriented decisions which powerfully present imaginations of where cities are going, who their future inhabitants will be and the resources they will find to stitch together livelihoods and shelter.

This future-making demonstrates something which has influenced all the chapters in this collection: they perform the connectedness of the urban. If the possibility-impossibility of the urban resides partly in the ways in which we come to know cities (as inexhaustible) and also in the ways in which their futures remain to be crafted (a site of possibility), it is also indexed by the stretched-out and interconnected spatiality of the urban. One of the ways in which the urban slips away from us, then, is that it is literally on the move! Starting anywhere, insights into the creative production of urban life – in this case, through the lens of 'poverty' – are quickly and vitally connected to the wider circulations which produce urban life. The multiplicity of interconnected processes which produce the possibility of the urban can be approached from any starting point but equally lure us away from the specific territorialised context which might constitute our initial standpoint. Thus, in calling for attention to the need for co-ordination and investment in the materiality of the city, at the city-scale, for example, Parnell indexes the circuits of investment and development aid, advice and coercion, geopolitics and trans-frontier trade which will determine the material futures of cities. The World Bank, Cities Alliance, China, Russian and Korean investors, informal traders and armies, barter of minerals for debt by sovereign states and hedge funds alike – the circuits which will shape the futures of the poor in the poorest cities – are deeply enmeshed with globalised circuits of knowledge, power and money. From Luanda to London, or Buenos Aires to Beirut, the futures of cities are certainly intertwined through these and other circuits.

It is in this sense that this book signals an important, if not crucial, moment in shaping the future of urban studies. For the field of 'poverty and "the city"' does not describe a segregated space of analytical endeavour, relevant for only these cities or certain urban populations. Rather, the chapters here index a crucial and arguably central component of the work of understanding and making the impossible future conceptual object of the (multiple, manifold) urban. This book performs the important perforated conceptual geographies which will be needed for that. The chapters build insights from wherever they are needed – drawing on significant approaches in development studies (Frediani), or being inspired to conceptualise urban politics through the innovative and careful achievements of community self-organising (Levy), or drawn to theorise urban economies through legal analysis and detailed attention to street use (Goswami; see also Gidwani, 2014), or placing pragmatic agendas alongside disciplinary theoretical enthusiasms (such as Anglo-American geography's take on 'materialities', in Parnell, or 'place' in Lombard).

The conceptual labour of understanding and trying to fathom the futures of cities, I have argued, needs to be as spatially wide ranging as the urban processes which themselves describe that future (Robinson, 2011). The authors in this book each in their own way move back and forth across different urban experiences in their search for insight; they are eager to find the resources to think the particular urban experience they are concerned with, engaging deeply with scholarship in the cities they work in and on, and reaching out for conceptual insights to thinkers and urban scholars elsewhere. It has long been my consideration that the practices of the field which has been known as 'urban development studies' are exemplary as urban studies, as a whole seeks to transform its geographical referents to produce a more global field of enquiry. The features which I hope will infect the wider field of urban studies include a depth of commitment to particular contexts, matched by a political agenda to enable movements against poverty and for justice, equality and a determined theoretical sophistication which seeks to appropriate inspiration from many different sources.

We might return then to Lefebvre, whose slogan, 'the right to the city' has been appropriated, perhaps in un-Lefebvreian ways, in the worldwide struggle for basic urban rights – to remain, to live in, to survive the city. His deep philosophical work finds a resonance in the pragmatic politics of development rights: an appropriation of his work as politically generative and productive of urban futures as any other, and which speaks to the entwining of the pragmatic and committed inheritance of 'development' representing a productive disturbance in the landscape of urban theory. Maliq Simone (2014) has written evocatively about the impossible inexplicability of the city, circling around a comment he heard, 'it's just the city after all, what do you expect?' Impossible to understand, throwing up obstacles and potential in equal dimensions, a site of intense unpredictability, the cities explored in this book require us to sustain bafflement; but equally to take some certain steps in concert with the efforts to collaborate and co-ordinate urban life which residents of cities are drawn to initiate. This provocative paper from Simone (2014) invites urbanists to learn to think the city from a site which has perhaps been historically similarly segmented and perhaps even more invisible to a wider theorisation of the urban than questions of poverty and development. He starts with the profound inattention to African-American urban experience, shocking the reader with proposing blackness as a theoretical resource to counter an analytical void in the heart of the most common locations of thinking the urban through the twentieth century. As race has been produced and signified through power, exclusion, poverty, violence, he indicates, starting with the specific histories of black urban experience:

> How does one engage the very concrete efforts that constructed the city, with all the layers of physical and cultural memory that new

> regimes usually attempt to cover-up, and all that the city does not show, either because its inhabitants are prohibited from paying attention or because whatever is considered normative or spectacular in city life has to get rid of the messy labor and politics that brought it about. (Simone, 2014)

The potential starting points for rethinking the urban are manifold. They are also political choices, as Simone's tactic makes clear. Starting with questions of poverty, building concepts from the many urban contexts which have not been drawn into some of the wider interpretations of the urban, carving a path across contexts seldom thought together. The moment is open for inventing new geographies of theorising the urban. These would be geographies which certainly dispel the fraught geopolitical projects we might have inherited (of development, of bland bureaucratic imaginations of where or what poverty might be – below a 'line' curving strangely across the globe; having less than an impossible sum to live on); geographies which rather render transparent the power relations and violence which have subtended the analytical disconnections and conceptual voids of urban studies to date. The future of urban studies is to be written from any city. And wherever we work or write from, our conceptual inheritance can be as diverse and wide ranging as the urbanities we explore. This book initiates a conversation about what that could mean, in the tracks of understanding and challenging poverty in urban life.

Jennifer Robinson
Chair of Human Geography
University of London

References

Brenner, N. (2013). Theses on urbanization. *Public Culture*, 25: 85–114.

Brenner, N. and Schmid, C. (2013). The 'urban age' in question. *International Journal of Urban and Regional Research*. Article first published online: 4 December 2013. DOI: 10.1111/1468-2427.12115

Robinson, J. (2011). Cities in a world of cities: The comparative gesture. *International Journal of Urban and Regional Research*, *35*: 1–23.

Satterthwaite, D. (2007). The Transition to a Predominantly Urban World and Its Underpinnings. Human Settlements Discussion Paper Series, Urban Change – 4. London: IIED.

Schmid, C. (2011). Henri Lefebvre, the right to the city and the new metropolitan mainstream, in: N. Brenner, P. Marcuse and M. Mayer (eds), *Cities for People, Not for Profit*. London: Routledge.

Simone, A. (2011). The surfacing of urban life. *City, 15*(3–4): 355–364.
Simone, A. (2014). It's just the city after all!, in: J. Robinson and A. Roy (eds), *Global Urbanisms and the Nature of Urban Theory. International Journal of Urban and Regional Research*. Forthcoming, Debates and Development Symposium.
Söderström, O. (2013). *Cities in Relations: Trajectories of Urban Development in Hanoi and Ougadougou*. Oxford: Wiley-Blackwell.
Soja, E. and Kanai, M. (2007). The urbanization of the world, in: R. Burdett and D. Sudjic (eds), *The Endless City*. New York and London: Phaidon, 54–69.

Preface

The origins of this book are traced to a workshop held in November 2011 at the Development Planning Unit (DPU) at University College London (UCL), funded by a grant from UCL's Grand Challenges Sustainable Cities programme, for which the authors are very grateful.

The workshop was attended by: Pushpa Arabindoo (University College London), Carrie Baptist (London School of Economics), Isa Baud (University of Amsterdam), Sylvia Chant (London School of Economics), Tim Conway (DFID), Kerwin Datu (London School of Economics), Alan Gilbert (University College London), Gareth Jones (London School of Economics), Caren Levy (University College London), Sue Parnell (University of Cape Town), Jenny Robinson (University College London), José Manuel Roche (University of Oxford), Dennis Rodgers (University of Glasgow), Manoj Roy (University of Manchester), Romola Sanyal (London School of Economics), and David Satterthwaite (International Institute of Environment and Development).

We are grateful to all those who participated in the lively discussions at that workshop, which contributed greatly to the themes of this edited collection.

Subsequent to the workshop, three additional authors were invited to contribute to this volume (Alex Frediani, Melanie Lombard and Amlan Goswani).

Acknowledgements

As editors, we are both hugely indebted to our partners, Stuart and Silvia, for allowing us the space and time to complete this book – thank you for getting up with the kids after our successive late-night writing episodes! We are also extremely grateful to Christina Brian and Ambra Finotello at Palgrave Macmillan for all their help and support.

This book is dedicated to our children, two of whom were born during the writing process: Nathaniel, Lucia, Daniel and Sebastian. Thank you.

Notes on Contributors

Isa Baud is Professor of International Development Studies at the University of Amsterdam, Department of Geography, Planning and International Development Studies, where she heads the Governance and Inclusive Development Programme. She has been President of the European Association of Development Institutes since 2011. Her main interests concern issues of urban governance, poverty and inequalities, focusing on the use of ICT and GIS for alternative knowledge to improve urban governance and empower civic organisations. She is scientific coordinator of the EU-funded Chance2Sustain research project, focusing on how cities in emerging economies drive urban development by combined strategies, utilising ICT-GIS-based knowledge processes.

Sylvia Chant is Professor of Development Geography at the London School of Economics, UK. Her research addresses gender, urbanisation and development, including migration, employment, female-headed households and the 'feminisation of poverty', empirically concentrated in Costa Rica, Mexico, the Philippines and The Gambia. Sylvia is Director of the MSc Urbanisation and Development at LSE, and an Associate of the LSE Gender Institute, and has also engaged in consultancy work for agencies such as the World Bank, ILO, UNDP, UNICEF, UNDAW, UN-DESA, UN-HABITAT and the Commonwealth Secretariat. Sylvia is currently completing a co-authored book with Professor Cathy McIlwaine, entitled *Cities, Slums and Gender in the Global South: Towards a Feminised Urban Future* (Routledge).

Kerwin Datu is originally trained in architecture, a field in which he worked in Sydney, Paris and London over nine years, before completing an MSc in Urbanisation and Development in the Department of Geography and Environment at the London School of Economics, during which time he researched the housing and relocation of informal settlers in Manila, Philippines. The MSc inspired the creation of *The Global Urbanist*, an online magazine analysing urban development issues worldwide, of which Kerwin is editor-in-chief. His MSc also led him to do a PhD in the department (awarded in 2014) on global city networks with particular reference to Lagos and West Africa.

Alexandre Apsan Frediani is Lecturer in Community-led Development in the Global South and co-director of MSc (Social Development Practice) at the Bartlett Development Planning Unit, University College London (UCL), UK. His research interests include the application of Amartya Sen's Capability Approach in development practice; participatory planning and design; and squatter settlement upgrading. Alex has collaborated with grass-roots collectives in Kenya, Ghana, South Africa, Brazil, and Ecuador and undertaken consultancies for international development donors and agencies such as Oxfam, Comic Relief, Practical Action and UNDP. Alex is a trustee for Homeless International and an expert affiliate for Architecture Sans Frontières–UK.

Amlanjyoti Goswami heads Law and Regulation, and co-leads the Law and Governance concentration at the Indian Institute for Human Settlements (IIHS), India. He is interested in legality and its relationships with space, politics and culture. His recent work is on the political economy of urban land and land regulation, as well as the legal and regulatory frameworks that govern urban development. He is interested in questions of place and interpretative understandings of everyday life and their epistemic connections with imaginations of law and urban policy. He has more than a decade's experience in domestic and international regulatory, practice and policy matters. He has also worked on Higher Education policy in India. Amlan holds degrees from Harvard Law School and the University of Delhi. He lives in Delhi.

Gareth A. Jones is Professor of Urban Geography at the London School of Economics where he teaches on the MSc (Urbanisation & Development), directs the Latin America and Caribbean Centre, and is founding member of the Institute on Inequalities. His research has focused on access to land for the urban poor, youth and violence, gated communities and comparative urban theory. He is presently involved with an ESRC-NWO-DFG grant with colleagues at universities in Amsterdam and Munich on the commodification of poverty and violence in Brazil, Jamaica, Mexico and the USA.

Charlotte Lemanski is a lecturer in the Geography Department and Fellow of Robinson College at the University of Cambridge, UK. Her research addresses the everyday and structural realities and constraints of inequality within cities of the Global South, focusing specifically on inequalities related to the materiality of housing and land markets, urban governance and citizenship, security and fear, segregation and integration. Her primary empirical focus is South Africa (with a secondary focus on India), and her research has been published in a wide range of international journals. She is also co-editor of the *European Journal of Development Research.*

Caren Levy is Senior Lecturer in the Development Planning Unit (DPU), University College London (UCL), UK. She is Vice Dean International for the Bartlett: Faculty of the Built Environment, UCL, and an urban development planner working on planning and community-led development, with a focus on housing, infrastructure and land in cities of the Global South. She has 30 years' experience in teaching, research, training and consultancy in exploring innovatory approaches to planning methodology; planning education and capacity building; and mainstreaming social justice and diversity, particularly related to the cross-cutting issues of gender and the environment. She works in London and abroad with communities, governments and international organisations. She is a former Director of the DPU.

Melanie Lombard is Lecturer in Global Urbanism at the Global Urban Research Centre, University of Manchester, UK. She has a degree in Political Science, a professional background in the UK social housing sector, and a PhD in Town Planning. Her research interests involve connecting the built environment to social processes through exploring the everyday activities that construct cities, often neglected by formal theories and practices of planning and urbanism. In particular, she is interested in exploring the construction of urban informality, and issues around land and conflict, in cities in Latin America (Mexico and Colombia) and Europe (UK).

Colin Marx is a lecturer in the Development Planning Unit, University College London, UK. His work focuses on reframing questions in relation to land, poverty and informalities in sub-Saharan African cities. His current research focuses on informal land markets in Dar es Salaam and Durban, economic knowledge in the urban informal economy in Nigeria, and the relationships between HIV and AIDS epidemics and informal settlement in eastern and southern Africa. He is interested in developing analyses of cities from the perspective of poor and marginalised groups in order that cities might be more supportive of poor women and men's livelihoods.

Susan Parnell is Professor of Urban Geography at the University of Cape Town (UCT), South Africa. She is a founding member of the African Centre for Cities at UCT and serves on its Executive.

Dennis Rodgers is Professor of Urban Social and Political Research at the University of Glasgow, UK. A social anthropologist by training, he works on issues relating to urban development, conflict and violence in Nicaragua, Argentina, and India. Recent publications include the volumes *Popular Representations of Development: Insights from Novels, Films, Television, and Social Media* (co-edited with David Lewis and Michael Woolcock, 2013), and *Global Gangs: Street Violence across the World* (co-edited with Jennifer Hazen, 2014).

Romola Sanyal is Assistant Professor in Urban Geography at the London School of Economics, UK. Her work intersects political and urban geography and focuses on forced migration, urbanisation and citizenship in the Middle East and South Asia. She has published several articles on this in leading journals such *as Transactions of the Institute of British Geographers, International Journal of Urban and Regional Research* and *Political Geography*. Her co-edited book *Urbanizing Citizenship: Contested Spaces in Indian Cities* was published in 2012. She has a PhD in Architecture from the University of California, Berkeley.

Introduction

Charlotte Lemanski and Colin Marx

This book sets out to explore the reasons why a city-spatial analysis is crucial to contemporary interpretations of, and policy responses to, urban poverty. In recent decades, there has been widespread recognition, within both academic and policy arenas, that the scale of the city is of utmost importance in understanding contemporary social, political, economic and cultural life. This perspective is typically justified by the oft-repeated incantation that more than half of the world's population now live in urban areas (often overlooked in this justification is that urbanisation is not restricted to cities). At the same time, traditional interpretations of poverty as largely rural have lost traction, as aid agencies and scholars alike increasingly recognise the dominance of urban poverty, particularly in the rapidly urbanising Global South. However, whilst the dominance of these two agendas (the city and urban poverty) is now well established, what is striking is the absence of connections between research addressing the spatiality of the city (typically located in geographical approaches) and research exploring the dimensions of urban poverty (situated within poverty studies and development studies).

Essentially, while geographers have critically debated the ways in which the spaces of the city play a role in the formation of urban culture/politics/economics, and poverty scholars have scrutinised the spatial distribution of poverty, very little addresses the ways in which the spaces of the cities themselves are active agents in creating and sustaining unequal distributions. A noteworthy exception is Lakshman Yapa's work that implicates Geography (as a discipline) in the perpetuation of poverty in the Global South. He locates the problem in the basic geographical argument that 'the spatial variation of a problem such as poverty can reveal the intensity of what causes that problem. Presumably areas where the problem is the most experienced must contain a high level of the causative elements' (Yapa, 2002: 44).

The title of this book, *The City in Urban Poverty*, is perhaps a confusing start, and indeed could potentially be criticised as oxymoronic. After all, surely the point of urban poverty is that it exists in cities (and towns)? However, the starting premise of this book is our belief that a rather simplistic approach to urban poverty has historically been taken, one that embraces urban poverty as a process that exists *in* the spaces of the city. Instead, we seek to turn things on their head; arguing that the city itself is also *in* urban poverty, that is to say that the spaces of the city play a crucial role not merely in containing urban poverty (as typically assumed), but also in re-producing and perpetuating processes of exploitation and inequality. So the city is both *in* and *of* urban poverty (and vice versa).

Consequently, this book seeks to explicitly address what are currently implicit spatial aspects of urban poverty, and in doing so, promote the spatial analytical framework that lies at the core of ways of understanding urban poverty.[1] Specifically, it highlights the *dynamics* of interactions between urban spaces and processes of exploitation, rather than merely embracing space (urban or rural) as a static container for poverty. In so doing, the book makes a claim for a new spatial politics of urban poverty and thereby intends to broaden the range of strategies for poverty reduction available to scholars and policy makers. In addition, the book also brings into visibility the ways in which the spaces of cities – particularly in the Global South – are contributing new insights into the dynamics of urban poverty more generally.

This introductory chapter outlines the primary argument upon which the book is grounded (i.e., that attending to the spatiality of urban poverty highlights the dynamics and processes of poverty as well as identifying the location of these processes), as well as providing a brief summary of the chapters that follow. The substantive chapters address a variety of empirical contexts and thematic foci, drawn together by a common recognition of the importance of incorporating the spatiality of the city into analyses of urban poverty. Finally, a summary of the book's cross-cutting arguments as well as lessons for future urban poverty research and policy-based agendas are provided in the conclusion.

What is 'urban' poverty?

In recent decades there have been notable attempts to understand the emergence and perpetuation of urban poverty in cities in the Global

South, countering the long (and ongoing) assumption that poverty in the South is primarily rural. Surprisingly, given the diversity of cities, experiences of poverty, and scholars and policy makers engaged in defining and measuring poverty, there is remarkable consensus on what 'urban' poverty is. Urban poverty is poverty that occurs *in* urban areas. The characteristics that make up the definitions of urban poverty, then, are the characteristics of urban areas and cities. What is far more contentious is which characteristics are appropriate to draw upon in defining and measuring poverty. In this section, we summarise the characteristics of the city that are commonly identified as defining urban poverty, and then move on to the consequences of this definition.

The attempts to define urban poverty – specifically in cities in the Global South – are few and far between. However, before considering definitions of urban poverty it is helpful to remind ourselves of what made it necessary to start defining urban poverty in cities in the Global South. In our view, there were four factors in the late 1980s and early 1990s that made it imperative to begin understanding urban poverty in these cities more clearly. The first was the evidence that general economic growth was not leading to poverty reduction in cities. The second was that the structural adjustment policies imposed on countries in the Global South were having differential impacts on urban and rural populations. The third was the evidence of growing poverty in cities and it was not clear whether this was due to poor people moving to cities and/or cities (further) impoverishing people. The fourth were the initial signs that many countries in the Global South were starting to experience urbanisation at a rapid scale and pace.

In this milieu, Ellen Wratten's (1995) seminal contribution identified four characteristics that have been repeatedly picked up and developed by others (see Table I.1).

Wratten's (1995) contribution has stood the test of time because few would argue with the characteristics that she draws attention to. People come together in cities as environments that are characterised by greater proximities to different land uses, social groups and densities of the built environment. Government is typically more proximate, and it is much more difficult to engage in livelihoods that are not mediated by money. Consequently, individually and in combination, the different characteristics cause, and are symptoms of, various forms of impoverishment in cities. Reflective of the period in which a debate about whether the urban or rural were more important in addressing poverty (see, for example, Lipton's 1977 *urban bias*), the notion of urban poverty has rural poverty as its primary referent (even as Wratten is at pains to sidestep such distinctions).

Table I.1 Wratten's four characteristics of urban poverty

Characteristic	Description
Urban environmental and health risks	Urban poor face environmental health risks relating to their spatial proximity of their residence to harmful industrial processes in relation to competition for land and dense and overcrowded living conditions that are poorly serviced. In short, the externalities of urban industrial production are borne disproportionately by the poor.
Vulnerability arising from commercial exchange	Commercial exchange mediates access to more necessities, commodities and services in urban areas, making people more dependent on access to cash through various forms of employment or control of assets and resources which are irregular, infrequent and/or poorly paid.
Social diversity, fragmentation and crime	Less coherent social bonds, households that are split and/or headed by more vulnerable people, and alienation leading to crime appear more common in urban areas and impoverish people further.
Vulnerability arising from the intervention of the state and police	For many urban poor people, their contact with the state is in negative ways – corruption, confiscation, poor policing and difficulties accessing justice increase poverty.

Source: Adapted from Wratten (1995: 21–26).

In the lineage we are tracing, we identify David Satterthwaite's (2001) contribution as the next seminal attempt to develop an understanding of urban poverty. Synthesising a wide range of literature with his own unique vantage point, he expands on Wratten to identify eight different characteristics of cities that define urban poverty (see Table I.2).

Although the debate about the relative importance of rural versus urban poverty is still ongoing, and the eight aspects have been adapted from a rural poverty frame (drawing on Baulch, 1996), Satterthwaite is more concerned with broadening the understanding of urban poverty per se than whether there are any specific distinctions between urban and rural poverty. Overwhelmingly, the definition of urban poverty that is elaborated builds on the recognition that life in urban areas is mediated by money, and that cities are recognised centres of economic growth and political power, the focus of overlapping state institutions of different kinds and levels, NGOs and international aid organisations. That urban life is mediated by money necessitates access to regular income through employment and/or a secure asset to save or generate

Table I.2 Satterthwaite's eight aspects of urban poverty

Aspects	Description
Inadequate income	Inadequate income (because it is low, irregular, informal and/or infrequent) leads to inadequate consumption of necessities including food and, often, safe and sufficient water; often problems of indebtedness, with debt repayments significantly reducing income available for necessities or for dealing with fluctuating prices.
Inadequate, unstable or risky asset base	Non-material and material assets including educational attainment and housing for individuals, households or communities cannot be converted or are of low value.
Inadequate shelter	Typically poor quality, overcrowded and insecure, which imposes unnecessary expenses and fails to provide a sustainable platform for developing enterprises.
Inadequate provision of 'public' infrastructure	Piped water, sanitation, drainage, roads, footpaths, etc. which increases health burden and often work burden, impoverishing households and communities.
Inadequate provision for basic services	Such as day-care/schools/vocational training, health care, emergency services, public transport, communications, and law enforcement impoverishes because these have to be sought privately or because of unnecessary exposure to risks.
Limited or no safety net	Basic consumption cannot be maintained when income falls; also access to shelter and health care can no longer be paid for imposing additional costs.
Inadequate protection of poor groups' rights through the operation of law	Exclusion from laws and regulations regarding civil and political rights, occupational health and safety, pollution control, environmental health, protection from violence and other crimes, protection from discrimination and exploitation impoverishes by exposing poor people to unnecessary burdensome costs.
Poorer groups' voicelessness and powerlessness	Within political systems and bureaucratic structures, leading to little or no possibility of: receiving entitlements; organising; making demands; and getting a fair response. No means of ensuring accountability from aid agencies, NGOs, public agencies and private utilities to address priorities.

Source: Column 1 reproduced from Satterthwaite (2001: 146).

cash, and/or social policies that underpin different aspects of welfare. That cities are the focus of overlapping institutions invites the questions: Who is responsible for addressing poverty in its different dimensions? Why are these institutions not addressing poverty? Indeed, in the

Table I.3 Additional aspects of urban poverty

High prices paid for many necessities	This is often because of inadequate or no public provision, which means that, for example, water has to be purchased from vendors or kiosks, access to toilets has to be paid for and fees must be paid in order for children to go to school, and these are costs that other wealthier groups do not incur because they are either provided with the service on a different basis or the necessities are purchased in more economical units.

Source: Reproduced from Mitlin and Satterthwaite (2013: 89–90).

most recent contribution to the story we are tracing here, Mitlin and Satterthwaite (2013) develop these themes in-depth with great insight.

In Mitlin and Satterthwaite (2013), a further aspect is added to the eight aspects already listed (see Table I.3). The nine aspects are further elaborated in terms of determinants (op. cit.: 278–280) and associated with particular institutional forms and organisational arrangements in the companion volume of Satterthwaite and Mitlin (2014).

Before considering some of the consequences of this lineage of debate about urban poverty definitions, it is worth briefly turning to other contributions. One example is that of Philip Amis' (1995) contribution. It is useful to consider because, while it cites Wratten, it highlights other factors and draws attention to other strands in the debates about definitions of urban poverty that we are sketching here. It therefore illustrates other issues that we have chosen not to elaborate, but which are important for a broader picture.

For Amis (1995) the discussions of urban poverty miss the point by focusing on urbanisation. For him, the process of proletarianisation or the extent to which people's livelihoods depend on a cash wage determines urban poverty. That is, the problem is not so much specifically 'urban' as related to capitalism (and consequently this type of poverty could potentially exist in cash-based rural economies). Amis identifies nine characteristics of poverty in urban areas – many of which are in common with the dominant lineage traced above. For example, his definitions share a focus on the more commoditised aspects of urban life, insecure and low-value assets, exposure to industrial pollution, little access to alternative 'common' goods when private goods are exhausted, and uneconomical (and hence relatively more expensive) purchasing of commodities, goods and services necessitated by irregular/low incomes.

What is distinctive is his proletarianisation argument that urban poverty is primarily defined by the positions of people in labour markets, which in turn are shaped by the nature of labour markets, market segmentation and levels of casual labour in cities in the Global South. These positions in the labour market are kept in place by rigidities that are determined by education, forms of social discrimination and the location of residential neighbourhoods in relation to employment opportunities. Additional elaborations such as this highlight a broader debate but also serve to underscore the importance of income as a defining element of urban poverty.

Returning to the historicity of urban poverty definitions, rather than synthesising this ongoing and finely nuanced debate, we instead embrace existing definitions (with their complexities and contradictions), in order to concentrate on analysing the purpose of these definitions. In our view, definitions of urban poverty have emerged in response to two of the issues presciently identified by Amis and Rakodi (1994) and a third directly related to the spatial themes of this book. The first is that urban poverty cannot only be defined by income and must include other characteristics. The density of multiple and overlapping aspects of urban life means that there are more chances of processes of impoverishment acting cumulatively and thus requiring action through multiple and simultaneous policies and strategies. The second is that the diversity of life, livelihoods, and aspirations of cities and towns means that it is much more difficult (if it ever were possible?) for experts to define which aspects of poverty to address first and thus, again, it is critical to simultaneously address urban poverty on multiple fronts.

The third overarching goal of urban poverty definitions has been to identify who and where poor people are in cities and towns. Notwithstanding Mitlin's (1995) and Mitlin and Satterthwaite's (2013) evidence that urban poverty continues to be misrepresented and underestimated, what current definitions of poverty are extremely good at is identifying where urban poverty exists within cities and who the people are that live or work in such areas. In this way, the definitions of urban poverty help us with an important aspect of the spatiality of urban poverty by primarily identifying the *distribution* and *location* and then the quantification of women and men, boys and girls, in cities and towns who can be defined as poor, as well as the qualification of this poverty.

The policy consequence of current views of the spatiality of urban poverty

The ability to identify the spatial distribution and location of urban poverty and then quantify and qualify its multiple characteristics is fundamental to poverty reduction or eradication. Consequently, we have a rich spatial vocabulary for analysing urban poverty – notwithstanding distinctions between 'deserving' and 'non-deserving poor' that prefigure any calculations (Dean, 1991). There are the obvious distinctions such as 'urban' and 'rural' poverty that are often drawn upon and sometimes countered (for example, Satterthwaite and Tacoli, 2002). Other spatial referents also yield important insights into urban poverty. For example, notions of 'spatial poverty traps', 'poverty barriers', and 'the urbanisation of poverty' have been operationalised to describe, analyse and respond to poverty and injustice in many cities. In resource-strapped cities of the Global South, indicators for poverty *distribution* and *location* are vital tools for policy makers adjudicating the allocation of scarce resources.

The political consequences that follow existing spatial definitions of poverty are important to consider because they provide the basis for the argument of this book. Current views of the spatiality of urban poverty set up a politics of redistribution that affects both those with the ability to redistribute and those seeking to gain from such redistributions. Once a form of deprivation is located within and across a city, quantified and qualified, it becomes possible for both policy makers and those stigmatised as poor to argue for the redistribution of resources to eliminate the deprivation.

We are clear that redistribution is fundamental to addressing the multiple aspects of urban poverty. Indeed, if resources, opportunities, services, assets, and incomes were more evenly distributed across cities it is arguable whether urban poverty would exist. Without forms of redistribution there is little hope of reducing poverty. But let us return to the politics of redistribution which sets up groups who claim and counter-claim the distribution of urban resources. There are two issues that this politics raises. The first is that, while perhaps successfully addressing the deprivations of a current generation of poor women, men, girls and boys, the politics that come with this view of the spatiality of poverty condemn policy makers to repeat the political struggle for the next generation because any politics surrounding the *causes* of this poverty are not addressed.

The second, following Lakshman Yapa (1998: 99), is that the belief that 'a study of the poor will reveal why they are poor' is to severely limit the politics of addressing urban poverty. What the current spatiality of urban poverty is extremely good at is identifying across and within a city who and how many people, for example, do not have adequate housing. The outcome of this process is that poverty is explained by the incidence of the lack of adequate housing. That is, the cause of poverty is inadequate housing and is located in the identified areas inhabited by the poor. Such a view is not only rather weak at identifying the dynamics of urban poverty, but also results in policies that address only the short-term *outcomes* of poverty (e.g., insecure housing) rather than the long-term inter-generational *causes* of poverty.

Moreover, this specific spatial interpretation of urban poverty essentially interprets poverty as *in* cities. In contrast, we argue in this book that poverty is *of* cities: that is to say that the space of the city itself is dynamic in contributing towards poverty causality and is not merely a static container for poverty (so the city is *in* urban poverty just as much as urban poverty is *in* the city). This notion of (urban) space as dynamic is well established in the geographical literature. Indeed, geographers have long understood space as socially produced (e.g., Unwin, 2000; Massey, 1992; Soja, 1989), and 'the urban' is increasingly understood as the 'co-presence of multiple spaces, multiple times and multiple webs of relations' (Amin and Graham, 1997: 417), meaning that spaces are active in shaping social relations. Consequently, urban geographers conceptualise the city not as a physical space *per se*, but as a relationship between the urban environment (space) and human behaviour (social relations). In other words, whilst the dynamics of urban space are a product of social interactions (between people, institutions, organisations, etc.), these social relations also create distinct urban spaces.

The reciprocal relationship between urban space and social mechanisms is a fundamental foundation of urban geography, as acknowledged by David Harvey's understanding of spatiality as both a consequence and cause of social relations (1973: 10), and Neil Smith's apt recognition that 'society no longer accepts space [solely] as a container, but [also] produces it' (1984: 85). Consequently it is surprising that such a well-established geographical understanding of the spaces of the city as dynamic agents has received so little attention within work on urban poverty, which has instead largely addressed the social and human perspectives of urban life. More recently, geographers have embraced the idea of the city as a site of networks and flows, including infrastructural as well as social elements, exemplified by the ideas of 'splintering urbanism' (Graham and Marvin, 2001), 'urban metabolisms' (Gandy, 2004) and 'urban political ecology' (e.g., Heynen et al., 2006). Although these analytical frameworks are starting to develop a critical Southern perspective amongst geographers (e.g., Lawhon et al., 2014), it is rare to encounter these spatial approaches within analyses of urban poverty.

The aim of the book

We argue that further analyses of the spatialities of urban poverty have the potential to add to the politics of addressing urban poverty and ways of reducing it. The three spatialities that we identify below have all been identified before – sometimes only implicitly – but so far, they have not been adequately analysed and developed.

The first is that the spaces, and space, of cities make a difference to the emergence and perpetuation of urban poverty. Whilst axiomatic that urban poverty is located in cities (in addition to large towns and peri-urban areas), the roles played by the spaces of the city in the emergence and perpetuation of urban poverty go largely overlooked. Whilst the specifically urban characteristics of poverty have been documented and classified (see above), many of which have spatial elements, a conceptualisation of space as having some agency is largely glossed over (with the two notable exceptions of Gotham, 2003, albeit focused on the spatial agency of the poor rather than the spatial agency of the city; and Mabogunje, 2005, who uses space implicitly in interpreting the economic disjuncture between rural and urban areas as a primary (spatial) cause of poverty).

The second is that urban poverty is multi-sited as well as being multi-dimensional. Although this argument is not new (see, for example, Yapa, 1998; Bradshaw, 2002; Chant, 2007), it has yet to gain wider purchase. This perspective highlights how people can experience deprivation and impoverishment in many different spaces of their lives – from the workplace (in terms of low-paying insecure jobs, for example), from the dwelling (in relation to tenure or location or access to services), in educational spaces (in relation to an inability to access quality education), and so on. It is clear that poverty can be compounded across multiple sites. A poor location of residence is likely to mean poor access to educational resources, quality health care and transportation. It could also be that urban space is itself impoverishing.

We identify two possible explanations for why the multi-sitedness of poverty has gained so little traction: firstly, because of the household and settlement focus of typical poverty surveys and analyses; and secondly, because of the sectoral-based nature of research (e.g., housing/health/education), with few studies considering poverty across a broad range of scales and sectors. As some of the contributions in this volume indicate, there is a clear need to start to develop analyses of poverty that take its multi-sited nature into account.

The third is that the spatial positionality of poverty researchers (and potentially organisations representing the urban poor) matters. Ellen

Wratten (1995) drew attention to this early on in the debates noting that it is rarely questioned 'how, and by whom poverty has been defined and measured'. Satterthwaite and Mitlin (2013) also examine how the location of interventions is important. As we write this chapter, two scholars situated in the relative privilege of the ivory towers of the United Kingdom (albeit one of us originally hailing from the Global South), we are intently aware of the implications of our positionalities in seeking to write about a form of urban poverty that neither of us, like the vast majority of poverty scholars, experience in our daily lives. At the same time, the (spatial and other) positionalities of poverty analysts is a virtually unspoken topic, with current urban poverty analyses seemingly written from nowhere and everywhere. Indeed, it is a refreshing contrast that the editors of *The Routledge Handbook on Cities of the Global South* opened the handbook with reference to their spatial location in Cape Town, arguing that 'where one lives and works is crucial' (Parnell and Oldfield, 2014: xx). We certainly do not wish to suggest that only certain types of people living in certain types of spaces are entitled to comment on urban poverty; however, we do argue that the (urban) spaces from which urban poverties are viewed, categorised, calibrated and theorised matter to the understanding of urban poverties that are generated. Consequently, the spaces of the city(ies) from which scholars' perspectives stem, as well as the (urban) spaces in which ideas are debated and distilled, cannot be ignored.

Conclusion

Poverty is an inherently spatial concept, with associated spatial practices. Indeed, this is well recognised in categories such as 'urban' and 'rural', and the politics of (re)distribution that are consequently invoked. Yet, the way in which the space of the city is represented in analyses of urban poverty is surprisingly one-dimensional, overwhelmingly addressing the outcomes of poverty (i.e. distribution), rather than the causes of poverty. Consequently, we argue in this book that the role of space in urban poverty needs more critical debate, and that ultimately, approaching the 'spaces of poverty' from multiple perspectives can aid in the production of more effective and just poverty-reduction policies.

While the urban poverty debates in the Global South have been caught in a partial spatial politics that focuses on the distribution and location of poverty, the rapidly urbanising cities and towns of the Global South are yielding new insights that this book builds on. To summarise, the book's central argument remains that the ways in which we think about space in relation to urban poverty in the Global South must be critiqued in order to broaden the everyday politics of urban poverty and scope for effective poverty-reduction policies.

Summary of chapters

Susan Parnell's chapter highlights the ways in which existing urban poverty research has failed to adequately address the city scale, instead favouring the household and neighbourhood scale. She argues that there is a pressing need, particularly in the Global South, to better understand the role of the material built form and infrastructure of the city (in addition to the existing focus on human agency and communal activity) in the emergence and perpetuation of urban poverty. In essence, Parnell's chapter shifts attention from the current focus on poverty *in* the city, to a consideration of poverty *and* the city.

Sylvia Chant and *Kerwin Datu* provide a comprehensive overview of issues related to gender and urbanisation, particularly highlighting the need to consider both poverty and prosperity within a multi-dimensional and multi-sited analysis. This latter perspective is relatively new, highlighting the ways in which women experience poverty in divergent but related ways across different spaces of the city (e.g. home, work, neighbourhood). This chapter reveals how a multi-sited approach can explore the ways in which diverse intra-urban spaces influence women's relationships to poverty, while also affecting how women contribute to, and benefit from, urban prosperity.

Alexandre Apsan Frediani considers how to integrate spatiality into Amartya Sen's capabilities approach when developing a framework for urban poverty. While Sen's theories have played a significant role in understanding urban poverty, the role of space is often overlooked. Through an empirical analysis of case studies addressing informal settlement upgrading, Frediani's chapter develops a theoretical approach that demonstrates the ways in which space not only creates the context for capabilities, but also the means for addressing urban poverty.

Melanie Lombard explores the socio-spatial role (or 'place') of informal settlements as a method for better understanding the everyday realities of life for the urban poor. By exploring how spatial and social processes interact, her chapter focuses on the construction of urban informal settlements as places. She develops the idea of 'place-making' as an analytical tool that acknowledges the dynamic roles played by both social and spatial processes in creating and perpetuating urban informality and poverty.

Isa Baud explores the ways in which 'mapping' urban poverty can contribute towards more holistic measures of poverty within cities, as well as improved governance processes. Her chapter uses the Indian example to highlight how the spatialisation of knowledge on urban poverty can be used to develop a multiple approach to urban poverty that goes beyond income. Further, she highlights the ways in which the spatial mapping of urban deprivation can play a key role in strengthening claim-making processes in urban governance.

Romola Sanyal's chapter takes a historical perspective, exploring the urban poverty experiences of refugees as an example of a demographic group frequently overlooked in urban poverty analyses. By analysing the position of refugees in late-twentieth-century Calcutta, she develops a critical perspective on the poverty and displacement of refugees as an example that demonstrates the role of the state in producing poverty. This account challenges scholars to develop a broader understanding of urban poverty.

Caren Levy provides an in-depth account of Community-led Infrastructure Finance Facility's (CLIFF) contribution to socio-spatial justice in Mumbai, India. She uses this example to argue that in order for urban planning to address urban poverty (and socio-spatial justice) it must simultaneously prioritise three approaches: material redistribution, inclusive recognition and party political participation. In her chapter, Levy develops the concept of 'room for manoeuvre' as an action space for transformative planning that offers the multiple spaces necessary to achieve the triangulation of redistribution, recognition and parity that underpin socio-spatially just urban development.

Amlanjyoti Goswami explores the relationship between the law and the space of the city in India. He does this by providing a detailed analysis at the scale of the street in Delhi, focusing on the legality and spatiality of street vendors as an example of those marginalised by a contemporary focus on regulation and on a rigid interpretation of (il)legality.

Gareth Jones and *Dennis Rodgers* develop a critical argument around the limited ways in which the city is represented in studies of violence and security. Their chapter highlights the ways in which research on violence and security, especially in relation to development, either ignores the city or assumes it is a necessarily violent place. Using empirical examples from Latin America that explore security governance on the one hand, and gang violence on the other, Jones and Rodgers challenge existing approaches, demonstrating the very spatial nature of violence in cities.

Note

1. It is important to point out that, although not the focus of this book, a similar argument for attending to the spatiality of rural poverty could be made (see, for example, King, 2010).

References

Amin, A. and Graham, S. (1997). The ordinary city. *Transactions of the Institute of British Geographers, 22*(4): 411–429.

Amis, P. (1995). Making sense of urban poverty. *Environment and Urbanization, 7*(1): 145–158.

Amis, P. and Rakodi, C. (1994). Urban poverty: issues for research and policy. *Journal of International Development, 6*(5): 627–634.

Baulch, B. (1996). Editorial: The new poverty agenda: A disputed consensus. *IDS Bulletin, 27*(1): 1–10. Retrieved 7 September 2014.

Bradshaw, S. (2002). *Gendered Poverties and Power Relations: Looking inside Communities and Households*. Puntos de Encuentro, Nicaragua: Middlesex University. http://eprints.mdx.ac.uk/4031/.

Chant, S. (2007). *Gender, Generation and Poverty. Exploring the 'Feminisation of Poverty' in Africa, Asia and Latin America*. Cheltenham: Edward Elgar.

Dean, M. (1991). *The Constitution of Poverty: Toward a Genealogy of Liberal Governance*. London: Routledge.

Gotham, K.F. (2003). Toward an understanding of the spatiality of urban poverty: the urban poor as spatial actors. *International Journal of Urban and Regional Research, 27*(3): 723–737.

Graham, S. and Marvin S. (2001). *Splintering Urbanism: Networked Infrastructures, Technological Mobilities and the Urban Condition*. Routledge, London and New York.

Harvey, D. (1973). *Social Justice and the City*. Baltimore: The John Hopkins Press.

Heynen, N.C., Kaika, M. and Swyngedouw, E. (2006). *In the Nature of Cities: Urban Political Ecology and the Politics of Urban Metabolism*. Abingdon: Routledge.

King, B. (2011) Spatialising livelihoods: Resource access and livelihood spaces in South Africa. *Transactions of the Institute of British Geographers, 36*(2): 297–313.

Lawhon, M., Ernstson, H. and Silver, J. (2014). Provincializing urban political ecology: towards a situated UPE through African urbanism. *Antipode, 46*(2): 497–516.

Mabogunje, A.L. (2005). Global Urban Poverty Research Agenda: The African case. Paper presented at 'Global Urban Poverty: Setting the Research Agenda' seminar (Washington, DC), 15 December.

Massey, D. (1992). *Space, Place and Gender*. Cambridge: Polity Press.

Mitlin, D. (1995). The underestimation and mis-representation of urban poverty. *Environment and Urbanisation, 7*(1): 3–10.

Mitlin, D. and Satterthwaite, D. (2013). *Urban Poverty in the Global South: Scale and Nature*. Abingdon: Routledge.

Parnell, S. and Oldfield, S. (eds) (2014). *The Routledge Handbook on Cities of the Global South*. Abingdon: Routledge.

Satterthwaite, D. (2001). Reducing urban poverty: constraints on the effectiveness of aid agencies and development banks and some suggestions for change. *Environment and Urbanisation, 13*(1): 137–157.

Satterthwaite, D. and Mitlin, D. (2014). *Reducing Urban Poverty in the Global South.* Abingdon: Routledge.

Satterthwaite, D. and Tacoli, C. (2002). Seeking an understanding of poverty that recognises rural-urban differences and rural-urban linkages, in C. Rakodi and T. Lloyd-Jones (eds), *Urban Livelihoods. A People Centred Approach to Reducing Poverty.* London: Earthscan.

Smith, N. (1984). *Uneven Development.* New York: Basil Blackwell.

Soja, E.W. (1989). *Postmodern Geographies: The Reassertion of Space in Critical Social Theory.* London: Verso.

Unwin, T. (2000). A waste of space? Towards a critique of the social production of space. *Transactions of the Institute of British Geographers, 25*(1): 11–29.

Wratten, E. (1995). Conceptualising urban poverty. *Environment and Urbanisation, 7*(1): 11–38.

Yapa, L. (1998). The poverty discourse and the poor in Sri Lanka. *Transactions of the Institute of British Geographers, 23*: 95–115.

Yapa, L. (2002). How the discipline of geography exacerbates poverty in the Third World. *Futures, 34*: 33–46.

1
Poverty and 'the City'

Susan Parnell

Introduction

The twenty-first century is the first truly urban epoch. However, the well-circulated graphs that reveal the inexorable urban transition of past and future decades are only part of the story. Accompanying the headline demographic message, that this is an era where urbanisation is the dominant motif, is the reminder that the locus of the twenty-first century has shifted away from Europe and North America. We not only now live in an urban world but also a Southern world, in which Asia and Africa are numerically dominant. As the absolute epicentres of population, cities and towns are the places and spaces that provide the foundations on which contemporary and emerging global systems and values will be built (Miraftab and Kudva, 2014; Roy and Ong, 2011). There are other substantive ways in which, over the next few decades, what happens in and is exported from 'cities of the South' will come to dominate our collective lives: cities will have massive impact on natural systems changes; the production, distribution and circulation of goods and services; and the experiences of everyday life, health, culture and politics (McGranahan and Martine, 2014; Parnell and Oldfield, 2014; Revi and Rosenwieg, 2013; Elmquist et al., 2013). For the global majority, life will be shaped by urban conditions and expectations. But for all of its centrality, we do not really understand what constitutes 'the city' or how urban form, urban management, urban life and identity interface with the experiences of, or responses to, poverty. For over a decade the ambiguity over how poverty and the city interact has been overlooked, as personalised experiences of poverty in the city have been intellectually and programmatically foregrounded. As we face the post-2015 development challenge, some recalibration is in order.

It is not possible to escape the fact that city in the Global South matters more now than ever before in addressing the perennial issue of poverty. It is this reality that underpinned the push to include an 'urban' goal, targets and indicators in the United Nations' sustainable development goals (Parnell et al., 2014). The demographic and spatial transformation of world populations, not least of which is the massive expansion of the number of people living in poverty in cities (Chen and Ravallion, 2007), raises the question of the intellectual apparatus required in setting out the complex practical and intellectual tasks that lie ahead.

Rather than reiterating the now fairly widespread call for more globally relevant urban theory formation (Watson, 2009; Robinson, 2002), I want to be more specific in my suggestion of a way forward; arguing that to have any resonance at all with the world's wicked problems, like poverty, alternative research perspectives have to either begin from or engage substantively with 'the city' by moving beyond the focus on the individual or micro neighbourhood projects to re-emphasise the materiality of the built form and to explore fundamental urban system reform. The issue of scaling up anti-poverty projects from the neighbourhood scale is a major part of this, but understanding the urban system and the system of cities is more than just expanding micro household- or area-based interventions or even of encouraging national urban strategies or global urban development goals, strategic as those interventions may be.

What has happened over the last decade or so is that the city itself (how it is built, serviced, structured, managed and experienced) has slipped in priority as explanations of urban poverty have placed an increasing emphasis on human agency, livelihood strategies and community mobilisation (Moser, 1998; Rakodi and Lloyd Jones, 2002; Mitlin and Satterthwaite, 2013). The focus on people-centred or bottom-up views of the last two decades are in no way wrong, but the human emphasis has meant that the structural and institutional role of 'the city' in shaping the experiences of poverty and the responses to poverty are now relatively poorly understood (Pieterse, 2008). In the face of the boosterish calls to let the poor take more control of their lives, anti-poverty action at the city scale can (sometimes inadvertently) be reduced to oppressive, invasive or post-political technocratic urban management (Swyngedouw, 2007). This, in my view, is an error.

Failure to fully recognise that how cities are structured physically and organisationally impacts directly on the poor is naïve; a Southern corrective is due that brings 'the city' back into poverty studies, in the same way that the material and ecological understanding of Northern cities saw a resurgence following the work of Marvin and Graham on splintered urbanism (2001). This is not the cry of a lone wolf: there is thankfully a now burgeoning literature focused on urban infrastructure and poverty (Silver et al., 2013; Jaglan, 2013); on the importance of public spaces for the poor (Kaviraj, 1997); and the enduring specialist areas of urban poverty work that are concerned with sectorial elements of the built environment like sanitation, housing or transport. Within the social development and development planning arenas, however, these poverty workstreams have been largely ignored, or alternatively are brought forward as if in response to community demands for local and national governments to address the imperative of scaling up (Tomlinson, 2014; Mitlin, 2014). Rather than this incremental or reformist position that grows out of a participatory planning view, Harrison (2014) argues that what is actually needed is a more fundamental ontological realignment that allows a re-engagement with the materiality of cities and their planning regimes.

Set against Harrison's philosophical challenge, the central argument of this chapter is that the nexus of 'the city' and 'poverty' needs to be reinterrogated from the perspective of the large-scale structural urban realities of the Global South, by which I mean a focus on poverty *and* the city of the Global South, not just poverty *in* the city of the Global South. Crudely, this might be described as a top-down rather than bottom-up perspective; more accurately it is a concern with urban systems and urban form, rather than only urban residents or the urban economy. To achieve this objective of rebalancing the modes through which poverty and the city is constructed, the chapter assumes a Southern perspective; that is, one that takes as the urban norm conditions of urban growth, extreme and pervasive poverty as well as large-scale informality and a fairly weak state (Table 1.1). Clearly there is no neat set of 'Southern urban indicators', and Table 1.1 does not seek to define such a comprehensive list, but it is included to focus discussion on recognisable and often replicable conditions in cities and countries with extreme rates of poverty that must, because of their (often overlooked) structural consequences, have impact in framing the urban poverty challenge.

In building a Southern view on the city and poverty, I begin by defining 'the city' and 'the city scale,' clearing the way to construct the argument that because of the vast numbers involved, thinking about the role of the urban in shaping and ameliorating poverty has not been so important since Engels wrote about deprivation and industrialisation in the late nineteenth century, or the early Chicago School writers put the city at the centre of their explanations for black Americans' disadvantage

Table 1.1 Potentially distinctive characteristics of 'Southern cities' that, individually or collectively, may be significant in assessing poverty profiles, dynamics and responses

1. A history of colonialism, conquest, or a recent experience of war or natural disaster.
2. Inadequate bulk infrastructure (public or private) to meet the needs of all residents and businesses.
3. Higher than average rates of urban growth (caused by a combination of high fertility rates that drive natural urban population growth, in-migration from rural areas and from other urban areas).
4. A workforce with a high percentage, especially, of young people without the necessary skills to compete competitively in the global, national and local economy.
5. Extreme levels of chronic income poverty, with higher than global averages of households living under a $1 a day. This is the product of both low wages and high unemployment.
6. Large-scale 'informality' – in the workplace, transport, housing and land ownership.
7. Complex *and often competing* systems of urban regulation (traditional, elected, corporate, informal, etc.).
8. A fairly weak local state that is unable to collect taxes, target resource allocation or redistribute to the poorest sections of the population.

in the early twentieth century. I then move to reflect critically on the urban poverty research that has current academic and policy currency, demonstrating that the work on urban demography and gender in the city, livelihoods and rights-based analyses made significant advances in understanding urban poverty from the perspective of individuals and communities. Conceptually, however, this emphasis obscures the way poverty is located in the wider workings of the city and does not do justice to the scale of the urban poverty problems outlined in the first section. In seeking alternatives to the micro-scale lived experiences, I revisit important urban poverty work on 'gender and the city'. Like both Chant and Datu (in this volume) and Moser (2014), I suggest that the older literature on gender included a valuable structural interpretation of urban poverty that has been diluted in recent decades. Reprioritising the more material mode of thinking in the gender and the city writing provides a corrective to inform a framework of 'poverty and the city' that gives weight not just to areas of overtly city-scale anti-poverty action, but also to understanding the underlying governmentality, regulatory, natural resource and technical systems that underpin the urban system. Viewed alongside existing knowledge, this more structural, institutional or political economy view provides both an intellectual and political case from which to better understand and advance the fight against urban poverty.

What is 'urban' poverty?

This chapter rests on the notion that poverty in an urban world is somehow constituted differently from that of a rural world. This is not just an issue of settlement scale, density or function. Moreover, appropriate poverty responses that are grounded in the building and running of the city and which meet basic needs as perceived by urban citizens are essential if global sustainable development goals (SDGs) are to be met and if the globally unacceptably high levels and rates of poverty are to be pushed back. For individual cities, accepting that there is a great deal that can and must be achieved at the sub-national or city scale, puts the political focus of anti-poverty action on actors both within and outside of national government.

Describing the ways that urban poverty is distinct from national rates of deprivation is not simple. Scholars like Moser (1998) and Gilbert (2002) have helpfully and clearly expressed how, in the absence of subsistence livelihoods and access to land, cash or assets become the means for securing rent, transport and food in the city – making income a poor basis of urban-rural comparisons. Mitlin and Satterthwaithe (2013) moreover provide an authoritative account of why urban poverty is consistently underestimated and misrepresented because the specificities of cities (crucially, the dominance of cash-based economies and high levels of inequality) are overlooked. Emphasising the central role of cash in the city has its own dangers and much of the influential new work on urban poverty data, including efforts to move beyond GDP measures, seek to quantify non-subsistence and extra-income variables that determine well-being for urban contexts (c.f. Kanbur, 1987; Kubiszewski et al., 2013). Acknowledging the differential characteristics and measurements of urban poverty in this way is a start to rethinking the city/poverty nexus – but it is far from the whole, not least because the nature and quality of the physical fabric remains an underappreciated or enumerated driver (or ameliorator) of poverty.

The most obvious manifestation of a definitional ambiguity of urban poverty is the reluctance of quantitative poverty specialists, who have just acclimatised to using multi-definitional approaches to poverty, to enter the definitional mire of 'the urban' even though, as several chapters in this book suggest, identifying or 'seeing' the urban poor is critical for both state and civil society (see also Scott, 1998; Beall and Fox, 2011; Mitlin and Satterthwaite, 2013). Recognising that poverty is not a uniform or singular experience means not only embracing multiple livelihood strategies, but also conceding poverty will vary in its manifestation over time and space (Bradshaw, 2002). The problem is that an inability to define 'the urban' means that innovations in measuring chronic and transient poverty at the city scale have lagged behind national and global assessments (c.f. Hume, 2005; Hume and Sheppard, 2003). The weak analytics for urban poverty in turn detract from sustained analysis of specific urban, place-based, drivers of poverty.

The absence of a global working definition of cities/towns/villages is especially tricky when the point is to talk about a physical form and scale of experience and not an administrative entity. Understanding what is meant by the city or urban scale is also complicated by the fact that in many parts of the world, especially Africa and South Asia, it is very difficult to distinguish peri-urban or low-density areas that either have no formal governance or where some form of subsistence livelihood prevails (Simon, 2008; Bryceson and Potts, 2006; Montgomery, 2008). Given that the informal or peri-urban fringe is often where the majority of poor residents live, it would seem logical to use the most inclusive and expansive definition of cities/towns/villages. If drawing the line between rural and urban is hard, so too is it difficult to distinguish the boundaries of cities – as inevitably large cities like Rio, Cairo, or Seoul sprawl way beyond their formal edge. Moreover, new city regions or conurbations, such as that of greater Lagos, are in formation (UN-Habitat, 2014). In the case of big cities it is especially hard to distinguish who actually runs the greater urban area, as it is rare that the metropolitan authority is the sole or even the most important political player in the city region. Despite the slippage in defining what an urban area is or who controls cities, the notion that the sub-national or urban scale is one of increasing significance is widely accepted by policy makers and urban analysts in the Global South (UN-Habitat, 2009; WDR, 2009; McGranahan et al., 2014), as most recently evidenced by the adoption of an 'urban' Goal (#11) as a milestone for the post-2015 development agenda.

Notwithstanding all the technical definitional problems, or the numerous warnings to be mindful of urban rural linkages on which the poor depend (c.f. Potts, 2012), the overarching point that urban poverty can be distinguished from rural poverty is well taken (Mitlin and Satterthwaite, 2013). But the absence of clarity on what makes a city (i.e., what defines the urban condition) means that the specificities of urban poverty remain elusive, too (Fox, 2013); though few with any experience of Southern urbanism would go so far as Scott and Storper (2014), who misguidedly suggest that cities and industrialisation are interconnected states, (inadvertently?) implying that the swathes of poverty in the dense non-industrial settlements of Africa or Asia are not truly urban.

Putting cities at the centre of the fight against poverty and social exclusion is even more difficult than making the case that 'the urban' matters – political opposition, ignorance and institutional inertia combine with the difficulties of operating across large and ill-defined areas to create an anti-urban ethos (UN-Habitat, 2011; Corbridge and Jones, 2008). Yet because something is hard to define does not mean its impact cannot be felt. In the case of cities it is their embodied presence, how and by whom they are run and how people identify themselves with the urban place that makes 'the city' an independent variable in the experience of poverty and in the fight against it (Simone, 2014). Moreover, the material experience of the organisation of streets, the physical distribution of urban services, and the natural and built terrain of cities establish the canvas on which and through which profiles of poverty are etched – an idea already that has gained traction in the safer city and healthy city literatures (Capon, 2007; Smit and Parnell, 2012). Regardless of whether one is born rich or poor, 'the city' is the material, operational and ideological scale that mediates contemporary humans' identity, economy and investment. The territory, scale and governmentality we are speaking of here is not the plot or the street or even the neighbourhood, but that of 'the city'.

Operationally, the city or urban scale I refer to is the sub-national sphere of government associated with cities and towns and the extra-neighbourhood scale of administration or government (and, as per Table 1.1, in the Global South this often involves multiple, overlapping and contradictory governments and administrations plus 'tribal authorities' who may be less formally constituted). This urban scale is typically the preserve of formal local government, which outside of Western Europe is a notoriously weak or nominal sphere of the state. This is in part because colonial governments did little to establish local regulatory and administrative systems beyond the very limited areas in which they lived and worked, and in part because it has not been in the interests of new national elites to encourage the devolution of power necessary to foster strong urban government (Mamdani, 1997). It is also true that local elites often secure their own interests through the fragmentation of local governance arrangements – the classic case being Los Angeles or Sao Paulo (Soja, 2011), but this is also evident in African cities (Goodfellow,

2012). It is not only local elites that seek to influence the sub-national or local political agenda. For mega cities like Jarkata or Mexico City, the poor can increasingly access resources that will determine their future well-being by their positioning themselves within their city regions as much as they can through their national governments (Mathur, 2013). Overall, though, the fragmented nature of urban governance in cities with large proportions of poor people militates against the sorts of big interventions in the built form (such as improved design or better public transport) that could create poverty-ameliorating spaces, and the focus has tended to fall on social policy as the way to address urban poverty.

Historically weak, the urban scale has, however, also been adversely affected by decades of neo-liberal emphasis on reducing or limiting the role of progressive, socially protecting functions of the state, thereby forcing/allowing civil society to fill the social vacuum (Ballard, 2013). The city become a site of political struggle as decentralisation and privatisation eroded what, in some places, were fairly comprehensive urban spending programmes within government (Miraftab, 2013). In other contexts comprehensive urban-scale, state-sponsored social protection is almost unknown and the city-scale impact of neo-liberalism has been more muted (Parnell and Robinson, 2012; Davila, 2013). The absence of detailed case studies of citywide poverty interventions from the Global South makes it difficult to generalise, but it would appear that regardless of whether there was always a weak state or if the capacity of the state has been denuded by neo-liberal forces, the overtly urban applications of social policy seem implicit rather than prominent in the minds of policy makers (Table 1.2). This is not to say that there is no wider awareness of how to end poverty in cities, especially cities of the Global South. Satterthwaite and Mitlin, two of the most influential voices in the field, have recently undertaken an assessment of the field in their twin volume works on urban poverty (2013; 2014). These are comprehensive works and the next section rests on the Satterthwaite and Mitlin texts, but gives much stronger prominence to the spatial question and the problem of how cities and city-ness are formative of the condition and responses to poverty.

Reasserting 'the city' in urban poverty research and action

Across the social sciences, there is a dangerous tendency to dismiss or undermine past theoretical and conceptual approaches in order to clear the way for big new ideas and/or to adjust to changing circumstances such as neo-liberalism. On some occasions this is essential, as in the insertion of a greater ecological sensitivity in the recent SDG formulation

Table 1.2 Social policy approaches and their relevance to poverty in cities

	Typical usage of the concepts and terms	**The relevance of the concept in cities**
Social welfare	State-funded transfers to the poor such as unemployment benefits, child grants and pensions. Associated with Europe rather than North America and almost always absent from the Global South – though some nations have embryonic welfare systems. Although in many advanced capitalist societies social welfare payments have been under significant threat from neo-liberal reforms and fiscal austerity, there has been an expansion of social welfare payments such as state pensions and housing grants in middle- income countries.	Because very few local governments generate enough revenue to operate costly social welfare programmes like schooling or health-care programmes, urban social welfare policy is not typically autonomous of national government. Some cities do have powers and budget devolved to them to deliver social welfare services; but over the last few decades, the argument has been that the devolution of responsibility for social spending has not been accompanied by adequate funding. Many richer cities have created independent welfare systems, for example, through rates rebates and service subsidies.
Social protection	Widely used by international comparative public policy analysts to compare the cost and institutional mechanisms used by governments to deliver the suite of social interventions aimed at protecting poor and vulnerable people, mitigating inequality and ensuring the social reproduction of the dominant values of the society. Social protection includes both direct welfare payments and indirect measures aimed at enhancing the public good.	Tends to describe national or very local policies, although there is no reason why government programmes at the urban scale may not be included in the cluster of social protection activities, especially as many social protection programmes operate across different scales (e.g., crime prevention, child protection, etc.).
Social development	Social development refers as much to the manner in which public policy is executed as it does the funds that are expended in the hope of improving the social welfare of citizens. Unlike the terms 'social protection' and 'social welfare', it is not generally restricted to the work of governments and often includes NGOs and faith-based organisations.	Public participation and projects that aim to build the skills and capacity of the beneficiaries of urban social development programmes have been popular alternatives to the direct transfer of funds to the poor in cities across the world since the mid-1980s.

Continued

Table 1.2 Continued

	Typical usage of the concepts and terms	**The relevance of the concept in cities**
Social exclusion/inclusion	Social exclusion refers to people who are not able to participate fully in social, economic and political life in a particular context for various reasons including poverty and prejudice. Analytically the emphasis is on who is excluded, by whom, and through which institutional mechanisms. Social inclusion is the set of policy actions introduced to reverse or mitigate exclusionary dynamics.	The focus on the scale where macro-economic and micro-community dynamics come together means social inclusion is an approach that is often adopted at the urban scale. As social exclusion can be *area-based* (people living in a stigmatised, isolated or distantly located area) or *identity-based* (age, gender, sexuality or religion), patterns of exclusion vary within and between cities.
Social capital	Social capital refers to the social support structures and networks and the capabilities that give access to further resources. It is useful to make a distinction between *bonding* capital (when group membership gives you a sense of belonging, security and capability it can lead to enhanced civic engagement) and *bridging* social (connections who introduce you to outside opportunities).	Social capital has tended to be understood at a household or group (neighbourhood, ethnic group) level and not at a city scale. For urban policy makers there is also a tension between fostering in group cohesion or bonding and promoting integration and social mixing.
Social safety nets	The social safety net that any individual, group or city will be able to draw upon (in good times and in bad) will be a product of all of the above forms of social assistance and social development. In counties where there are significant financial resources available to the state, public policy decisions are made about what form of social safety net to foster and what the different roles of government, the private sector and civil society might be. In poorer contexts, civil society is of necessity a more dominant force shaping the social safety net.	The social safety net of urban residents draws from all available sources of social support. The urban contribution to a social safety net includes direct and indirect interventions that uphold the rights of citizens and enhance their individual and collective social well-being in the city. Strong social safety nets operate across global, national, *city*, neighbourhood, family and individual scales.

(Pelling, 2003; Revi and Rosenwig, 2013), and it is always important to reflect on the ground clearing that may be necessary to insert alternative ways of thinking and acting. Ideological positions will also make some anti-poverty agendas more appealing than others. But this kind of paradigmatic clarification is not what I have in mind here. Rather, by setting out the genealogy of urban poverty thinking by specialist Southern urbanists, I wish to show that, while over the last two decades significant advances have been made in approaches to, and understandings of, the problem of poverty *in* an urban context, we remain limited in what we imagine the appropriate interventions to be because of the failure to adequately or consistently engage the Southern city itself.

We have already seen that the city is an elusive concept, but the 'city gap' in development thinking that we see today is also the fault of poverty researchers who appear unable/unwilling to define what a top-down or inter-generational, urban anti-poverty agenda would include. Notwithstanding Pieterse's (2008) macro overview of the ideological underpinnings of urban policy in the South, scholars working at the city scale have tended to take refuge in critique (e.g., of the World Bank or of neo-liberalism) and have shied away from taking responsibility in actually setting out new policy agendas for large-scale and enduring urban anti-poverty action (Parnell and Robinson, 2012). When clear policy positions are adopted, as in the World Bank's effort (2009) to address the spatial dimensions of urban poverty and growth in the *World Development Report*, there was, understandably, a very lukewarm reception because of the over-dependence on old-fashioned, neo-classical thinking, even while the focus on the city was lauded (c.f. Turok and McGranahan, 2013; Turok, 2013; Rigg et al., 2009). Interesting examples of work can be found that do affirm innovation at the city scale: Bunnel et al. (2013), Davila (2013) and Beall et al. (2014), for example, trace pro-poor interventions in Indonesia, Colombia and South Africa to reveal the impact of city-scale coalitions that brokered innovative solutions in city structure and management that enhanced the lives of the poor. Overall, though, it would be true to assert that the last 20 years, urban research has failed to adequately illuminate the macro-political economy of inequality in the Global South because of a general inattention to the operational site and scale of the city. In other words, we have lots of work on poverty in urban places, some good work on inclusive urban governance, masses of work on how the poor help themselves, but a very modest platform that engages the city itself as an (inter-generational) poverty actor.

Retrieving and giving greater emphasis to more structural aspects of poverty and the city itself does not imply a rejection of the lived experiences of the poor; rather it calls for a conceptual and political rebalancing to ensure that, in the fight against urban poverty, appropriate energy is committed to issues of maximum possible reach and impact. This means ensuring that the city scale and the inter-generational temporal impacts of urban form for the poor are promoted, rather than only focusing on the intellectual advances that saw a focus on the everyday, assets, livelihoods and civil society capacity and organisation. In the spirit of clearly understanding the issues before us, I suggest it is time not so much for a paradigm shift but for a recalibration and rescaling in urban poverty studies. Such a shift implies, alongside a greater focus on the political ecology of urban poverty, giving less weight to livelihoods and participation and more weight to the production and management of the built form over time and at different scales. To help reset (not reformulate) the poverty focus, I look back to the now somewhat dated urban development literatures of the 1980s and 1990s to refresh an especially innovative mode through which scholars and implementers usefully analysed the dynamics and dimensions of urban poverty, illuminating linkages between poverty and the material attributes of the city and its urban form: gender. Unlike Chant and Datu's Chapter 2 in this volume, which provides a parallel focus on gender in the city and highlights the enduring experience of discrimination and exclusion of woman, the follow section draws attention to the analytical power of the gender mainstreaming analysis for revealing the city/poverty nexus.

Lessons from the gender, poverty and 'the city' literature

Perhaps the most significant pro-poor urban transformation of the late twentieth century had to do with the gains of the feminist movement and the emergence of gender-based planning. The utopian nature of the movement's claim was not simply that women, who make up half the urban population, should be given greater profile in planning, but rather that gender-based differences should no longer negatively impact on urban service provision, urban livelihood opportunities or urban quality of life indicators and that to achieve this a paradigm shift was necessary. Although no longer in fashion, the legacy of gender-based planning still holds the most substantive pathways to thinking about the city in ways that seek to minimise discrimination (Moser, 2014). Incorporating these gendered principles into the resurgent demand for city planning in the Global South (Watson, 2009; UN-Habitat, 2009) would seem a reasonable way to ensure that poverty is kept at the heart of planning practices.

The gender-based planning movement was promoted by international development agencies and NGOs in the 1980s, and although undoubtedly a product of Western feminist thought, it was quickly embraced by activists in many cities of the Global South. In practice the patriarchal nature of many poor societies meant that the endorsement of a vision of a gender-equitable city would only be palatable if coupled with the challenges of fighting urban poverty. In translating the gender and development perspective into a blueprint for action, Moser (1998) led the way in her piece in *World Development* that invoked the notion of the triple oppression of women (where women work at home, at the workplace and in the community). Gender planning was never presented as a utopian movement, but in retrospect the transformative capacity of the gender movement, that shaped city policies and programmes across the world in ways that removed discrimination and defied traditionalism, was among the most radical and effective of the entry points intended to induce transformative change in cities of the Global South (Watson, 2014; Tacoli and Chant, 2014).

In the mid-1990s, after the Beijing conference, the prevalence of poverty among women (and children) meant that the strategy of 'gender mainstreaming' assumed widespread purchase as the single, most important proxy for poverty, including among urbanists. The notion was that to address the needs of the poorest and most vulnerable, governments and other actors should promote an active and visible gender perspective in all city policies and programmes.

For gender and development specialists, like Beall (1997), Kabeer (2005) and Moser (1998), applying gender-mainstreaming strategies to the urban arena moved far beyond ensuring equal numbers of women and men in decision-making structures and involved rethinking and influencing all methods, processes, analyses, policies and institutions with a gendered perspective – paying attention to and reflecting over women's and men's different roles, responsibilities, needs and priorities. Levy's (1996) systematic 'Gender Web' (which was not designed for cities but did deal with complex institutions) included detailed institutional guidance on the mainstreaming process. What Levy's Web, which traced key decision-making nodes of the state, implied was an engagement with, rather than the rejection of, the structures of authority. She warned that deep institutional knowledge was a prerequisite for successfully achieving gender mainstreaming and poverty reduction. The other critical point Levy made was that not all individuals, groups or organisations could influence every part of the 'Web' – hence the need of understanding one's role, position and power in a system (Levy, 1996). The city-scale framing of Cole et al. drew on this logic (Table 1.3) to reveal how the varied aspects of poverty and urban development reflected a gendered set of relationships (2000).

Table 1.3 The gendered interface of poverty and the city

Urban development	
Migration pattern	• If the percentage of men and women who work in the city is distorted a number of problems emerge (e.g., 1. money is spent on travelling between urban and rural homes, 2. men especially are inclined to establish two households – and this has many problems, not least being the double expenditure on housing – and household effects). • Generally men make the decisions about who will migrate to urban areas. This dramatically affects what work women can do and how they live their lives.
Urbanisation pattern	Generally men and women migrate to urban areas in response to jobs, they do not therefore go simultaneously. Differential timing of urbanisation causes split families.
Urban growth rate	Cities with high fertility rates will have large numbers of small children, with all the implications for child care and service expenditure. Alternatively, those with low growth rates are likely to have a greater proportion of older people and generally these populations are biased towards women.
Planning fundamentals	
Zoning	The separation of home and work makes life very difficult for women who generally have to move between the two more often than men because of domestic responsibilities.
Decentralisation of retail and office space	Although putting the shops and offices closer to residential areas may seem a good idea for women there are generally no public transport links in highly decentralised cities thus making it difficult, especially for the poor, to access malls.
Suburbanisation/ urban sprawl and compaction	Increasing the distances (measured in time spent getting to places) people travel has a gender-differentiated impact, especially as women tend to do more trips per day than men. Reducing costs of servicing cities through greater density tends to benefit the poor who gain the most from services delivered by governments or supported by subsidies.
Using the household as the basic unit of planning	• Very few households are nuclear; most have only one breadwinner, and this is not always the man. • Men without dependants are often left out of the household planning equation.
Urban finance	
Costing of different services (revenue and expenditure)	• If car licences are cheap but public transport is expensive, the poor and women will suffer. Policies which favour the rich are less sensitive to the needs of women, especially female-headed households, who tend to be poorer. • Tariffs which encourage off-peak usage may simply extend the working day.

Continued

Table 1.3 Continued

Service payment procedures	• How often households pay for services is in part a product of where the office is, how much it costs to get there and what times it is open. As women are more commonly involved in this activity it should suit their schedules.
City construction	
Electricity and other energy sources	• Electrification changes peoples' lifestyles which varies according to gender-determined activity patterns; evidence from South African cities suggest that gender dynamics within the household, not cost, prevent women from maximising the labour saving and safety benefits of electricity.
Water	• Without access to piped, potable water, women spend huge amounts of time cooking and cleaning. As a result, women suffer unduly water-borne diseases.
Signs	• We need to ask what is on the sign? For example, reduce speed, warning of children ahead or directions to the town centre and sport facilities. • Policies on public advertising can reinforce or undermine gender stereotypes.
Lighting	• Women seem to prefer high mast lighting because it cannot be vandalised. Lighting generally reduces crime.
Pavements	• Walking, especially with a pram or pushing a wheelchair is much easier with even-graded pavements. As looking after the sick and the young tends to be done by women, this impacts more directly on them.
Roads	• Tarred roads do reduce dust, but they also increase speeds in residential areas.
Sewerage	• Because of greater involvement in domestic chores women are much more susceptible to water-borne diseases.
City economies	
Informal sector/SMME policy	• This sector is dominated by women who have special needs. • Not all city management facilitates informal sector activity. • There may be a tendency to target unemployed women for informal work or SMME, thus ignoring male unemployment.
Formal sector	• Wages continue to be higher on average for male workers.
Changes in the labour market	Changing sectoral patterns of employment often impact more directly on either a predominantly male or female workforce.
Local economic development	Small flexible incentives and local initiatives may be more readily embraced by women than large-scale sector support. How enforcement is imposed has a big impact on women in informal and irregular activities.

Source: Adapted from Cole et al. (2000) and Levy (1996).

The logic of the gender planning work of the 1980s and 1990s, which placed an overt focus on the institutional nexus of the way the city worked and the distribution of disadvantage and discrimination, provided a city-scale entry point overlooked by conceptual approaches to urban poverty that focus on individuals and communities. Cole et al.'s (2000) conceptual logic of working systematically through the variables that impoverished some and not others identified the structural instruments of exclusion, including the organisation, variable quality and costs to users of the urban form, in much the same way as the later social exclusion literature did (De Haan, 2011; Beall, 1997). The analytic put forward by Chant and Datu in Chapter 2 has echoes of this, except that there the logic is to explore the essential elements of woman's life in the city. Whether the differentiating dimensions were founded in gender, race, ethnicity, age or religion, attention was drawn to the materiality of the city and the way that formal or informal urban management entrenched power and inequality through the city form (Levy, 1996). The power of the gender and the city writing was that it identified multiple drivers and expressions of urban poverty and, as such, was the intellectual force that opened up the space to think about the multiple dimensions and sites of poverty, an idea that is now widely taken for granted (Moser, 2014; Chant and Datu, Chapter 2).

The recognition of the gendered (or racialised) experience of poverty and the inability to identify poor individuals, households, and neighbourhoods with standard income criteria on which most poverty targeting depends was, alongside a widespread distrust of income-based measures of poverty, an explanation for why many in cities of the Global South adopted more differentiated anti-poverty strategies. Wratten's (1995) seminal piece on urban poverty consolidated the nascent acceptance in the WDR (World Bank, 1990), that there were multiple layers to the experience of urban poverty, and set out systematically the differential conceptual understandings of poverty and how these played out in the city. Just to remind us, she traced fundamentally conflicting conceptions of poverty from income-based assessment, the basic needs approach and the much less tangible human development approach. As Wratten (1995) was at pains to point out, however, one potential problem of an unspecific or all-embracing framing of the problems of poverty in the city is that it failed to make explicit the hard policy choices implied by acknowledging the very theoretically different view on the experiences and responses to social inequality and deprivation. The fact that there has been so little discussion about the conflicting rationalities (or potential impacts) of investment in different forms of urban anti-poverty action is in part because the focus in poverty research has largely turned away from material investments for the poor of the city (where these contradictions manifest in budgets and planning codes) to the impoverished residents themselves.

Provincialising livelihoods, assets, and participation and (re)centring the city

Building on the logic of the multi-dimensionality of the poverty experience, several players (e.g., DFID) used a multi-dimensional framing of poverty, most obviously through the livelihoods conceptions. Unlike the urban demographic and enumeration thrusts that highlighted the city as a new and important site for anti-poverty action, or the gender-mainstreaming work that exposed the dynamics of power in the city so as to influence the equal allocation of goods, services and opportunities for women and men, the livelihoods cluster of work was defined by its focus on how poor people actually got by in the city through adopting differentiated or multiple livelihood strategies. Livelihoods and assets frameworks tried to rethink sector analyses by working backwards from the perspective of poor people (i.e., taking their lives as the integrated whole of the lived experience of poverty). Moving beyond a static consumption-based understanding of poverty, Moser's work on asset accumulation (Moser and Felton, 2007) was especially helpful in defining how the urban poor gather financial, social and natural resource assets to improve their livelihoods as well as passing on assets across generations of urban households. The logic of the poor drawing on multiple assets and capabilities gained further credibility through the work of Nobel laureates Sen (1999) and Ostrom (1990) and has dominated the last two decades of poverty work. Much of the current vulnerability work of the climate change and food security literatures draws directly from this thinking – and the broad family of livelihood-inspired work is arguably still an influential mode for framing assessments of urban poverty in the Global South (Frayne et al., 2012; Bickman et al., 2009).

The focus on poor people's livelihoods in urban contexts was, pretty much from the outset, expanded to include the institutions of the poor as part of the social capital through which poor households survived (Rakodi and Lloyd-Jones, 2002). Given the rich tapestry of civic mobilisation in cities, especially in poor areas, this made obvious sense. In both the Global North and South, however, civil society organisations tend to have greater strength in individual, household or neighbourhood mobilisation and are largely unable to effectively navigate the more complex structures of city government, where populist participatory mechanisms are ill-suited to achieving representation and influence (Tendler, 1997). By implication, the state and large-scale institutions that fail to reach the poor were (consciously and unconsciously) de-prioritised, and in the first wave of research there was less concern with the city scale; the assumption was that the poor knew better than large, cumbersome institutions what worked for them and that they would (and should) find ways to realise these needs and aspirations. Interestingly, the intellectual shift from household livelihood improvement to collective action at the city scale followed practice, as scholars tracked the scaling up of community organising to access the resources of the state not through household livelihood diversification but through direct engagement with local authorities, the best-known example being that of SDI (Mitlin and Satterthwaite, 2013).

With a careful reading of the literatures on livelihoods, assets and participation it is possible not only to see the immense resourcefulness of the poor but also to uncover what about the city had to be navigated (physically and institutionally) in order to survive. It is this focus on city-scale blockages or the institutional barriers to equity that provided the focus of the social exclusion tradition that was so influential in urban poverty debates in the Global North (see Table 1.2). In the Global South, attention focused less directly on the institutional barriers to urban inclusion, maybe because many states had so little to offer. Instead the stress fell both on defining the urban entitlements that might be claimed by the poor (Bahn, 2009) and the city-scale reforms that would be necessary to enable institutions to give effect to universal urban rights (Parnell and Pieterse, 2010). Thus, the discourse of the right to the city began to replace livelihoods as the most prevalent reframing of the urban poverty agenda.

Note

Funding for this paper draws from my South African National Research Foundation grant and the support of Mistra Urban Futures on Fair Cities.

References

Albertyn, C., Beall, J. and Parnell, S. (2014). Conflicts between tradition and modernity: African city regional dynamics. *International Journal of Urban and Regional Research,* in press.

Ballard, R. (2013) Geographies of development: Cash transfers and the reinvention of development for the poor. *Progress in Human Geography, 6*: 811–821.

Beall, J. (ed.) (1997). *A City for All: Valuing Difference and Working with Diversity.* London: Zed.

Beall, J. and Fox, S. (2011). *Cities and Development*. London: Routledge.
Bhan, G. (2009). This is no longer the city I once knew: Evictions, the urban poor and the right to the city in millennial Delhi. *Environment and Urbanization, 21*: 127–142.
Bicknell, J., Dodman, D. and Satterthwaite, D. (eds) (2009). *Adapting Cities to Climate Change: Understanding and Addressing the Development Challenges*. London: Earthscan.
Bradshaw, S. (2002). *Gendered Poverties and Power Relations: Looking Inside Communities and Households*. Mangua: Punto de Encuntro.
Bryceson, D. F., Gough, K. V., Rigg, J. and Agergaard, J. (2009). Critical commentary. The World Development Report 2009. *Urban Studies, 46*: 723–738.
Bryceson, D. F. and Potts, D. H. (eds) (2006). *African Urban Economies: Viability, Vitality, or Vitiation?* London: Palgrave Macmillan.
Bunnell, T., Miller, M. A., Phelps, N. A. and Taylor, J. (2013). Urban development in a decentralized Indonesia: Two success stories? *Pacific Affairs, 86*: 857–876.
Capon, A. G. (2007). Health impacts of urban development: Key considerations. *New South Wales Public Health Bulletin, 18*: 155–156.
Chen, S. and Ravallion, M. (2007). Absolute poverty measures for the developing world, 1981–2004. *Proceedings of the National Academy of Sciences, 104*(43): 16757–16762.
Cole, J. and Parnell, S. (2000). *A Report on Poverty, Gender and Integrated Development Planning in South African Municipal Practice*, Western Cape Department of Provincial Local Government, Cape Town.
Cook, S. and Kabeer, N. (2009). Socio-economic Security Over the Life-course: A Global Review of Social Protection. Prepared as the final report of a Social Protection Scoping Study funded by the Ford Foundation, Centre for Social Protection.
Dávila, J. (ed.) (2013). *Urban Mobility and Poverty: Lessons from Medellin and Soacha, Colombia*. Development Planning Unit, UCL and Universidad Nacional de Colombia.
De Haan, A. (2011). *Social Exclusion and the Road Not Taken: An Insider Account of Conceptual Travel within Development Practice*. Manchester: Chronic Poverty Research Centre.
Elmqvist, T. et al. (eds) (2013). *Urbanization, Biodiversity and Ecosystem Services: Challenges and Opportunities: A Global Assessment* (SpringerOpen).
Fernandes, E. (2007). Constructing the right to the city in Brazil. *Social & Legal Studies, 16*: 201–219.
Fox, S. (2012). Urbanization as a global historical process: Theory and evidence from sub-Saharan Africa. *Population and Development Review, 38*: 285–310.
Frayne, B., Moser, C. O. and Ziervogel, G. (2012). *Climate Change, Assets and Food Security in Southern African Cities*. London: Earthscan.
Gilbert, A. (2002). On the mystery of capital and the myths of Hernando de Soto: What difference does legal title make? *International Development Planning Review, 24*: 1–19.
Goodfellow, T. (2012). *State effectiveness and the politics of urban development in East Africa: A puzzle of two cities, 2000–2010*. Doctoral dissertation, The London School of Economics and Political Science (LSE).
Graham, S. and Marvin, S. (2001). *Splintering Urbanism: Networked Infrastructures, Technological Mobilities and the Urban Condition*. London: Routledge.

Harrison, P. (2014). Making planning theory real. *Planning Theory, 13*: 65–81.
Huchzermeyer, M. (2003). Housing rights in South Africa: Invasions, evictions, the media, and the courts in the cases of Grootboom, Alexandra, and Bredell. *Urban Forum, 14*: 80–107.
Hulme, D. and McKay, A. (2005). *Identifying and Measuring Chronic Poverty: Beyond Monetary Measures*. Indian Institute of Public Administration.
Hulme, D. and Shepherd, A. (2003). Conceptualizing chronic poverty. *World Development, 31*: 403–423.
Jaglin, S. (2013). Networked services and features of African urbanization: Other paths toward globalization, *L'Espace géographique (English edition), 41*: 51–66.
Jones, G. A. and Corbridge, S. (2010). The continuing debate about urban bias the thesis, its critics, its influence and its implications for poverty-reduction strategies. *Progress in Development Studies, 10*: 1–18.
Kabeer, N. (2005). Gender equality and woman's empowerment: A critical analysis of the third Millennium Development Goal. *Gender and Development, 1*: 13–14.
Kanbur, S. R. (1987). Measurement and Alleviation of Poverty: With an Application to the Effects of Macroeconomic Adjustment (Evaluation quantitative de la pauvreté et remèdes possibles: analyse des effets d'un ajustement macroéconomique)(Medición y alivio de la pobreza, con una aplicación a los efectos del ajuste macroeconómico). *International Monetary Fund Staff Papers*, 60–85.
Kaviraj, S. (1997). Filth and the public sphere: Concepts and practices about space in Calcutta. *Public Culture, 10*: 83–113.
Kubiszewski, I., Costanza, R., Franco, C., Lawn, P., Talberth, J., Jackson, T. and Aylmer, C. (2013). Beyond GDP: Measuring and achieving global genuine progress. *Ecological Economics, 93*: 57–68.
Lefebvre, H. (1968). *Le Droit à la ville*. Paris: Anthropos.
Levy, C. (1996). *The Process of Institutionalising Gender in Policy and Planning: The Web of Institutionalization*. London: DPU.
Lipton, M. (1997). *Why Poor People Stay Poor: Urban Bias in World Development*. Cambridge, Mass.: Harvard University Press.
Mamdani, M. (1996). *Citizen and Subject*. Princeton: Princeton University Press.
Marcuse, P. (2009). From critical urban theory to the right to the city. *City, 13*: 185–197.
Martine, G. and McGranahan, G. (eds) (2014). *Urban Growth in Emerging Economies: Lessons from the BRICS*. London: Routledge.
Mathur, O. (ed.) (2013). *State of the Urban Poor Report, 2013: Inclusive Urban Planning*. India: Oxford University Press.
Miraftab, F. and Kudva, N. (eds) (2014). *Cities of the Global South Reader*. London: Routledge.
Mitlin, D. (2004). Civil society organisations: Do they make a difference to urban poverty, in N. Devas (ed.), *Urban Governance, Voice and Poverty in the Developing World*. London: Earthscan, 123–144,
Mitlin, D. and Satterthwaite, D. (2013). *Urban Poverty in the Global South; Scale and Nature*, London: Routledge.
Montgomery, M. R. (2008). The urban transformation of the developing world. *Science, 319*: 761–764.
Moser, C. O. (1989). Gender planning in the Third World: Meeting practical and strategic gender needs. *World Development, 17*: 1799–1825.

Moser, C. O. (1998). The asset vulnerability framework: Reassessing urban poverty reduction strategies. *World Development, 26*: 1–19.
Moser, C. O. and Felton, A. (2007). *The Construction of an Asset Index: Measuring Asset Accumulation in Ecuador*. Manchester: Chronic Poverty Research Centre.
Moser, C. (2014). *Gender Planning and Development: Revisiting, Deconstructing and Refecting*. DPU-Associates Working Paper, DPU, London.
National Research Council (ed.) (2003). *Cities Transformed: Demographic Change and Its Implications in the Developing World*. Washington, DC: National Academies Press.
Ostrom, E. (1990). *Governing the Commons: The Evolution of Institutions for Collective Action.*, Cambridge: Cambridge University Press.
Parnell, S. and Oldfield, S. (eds) (2014). *The Routledge Handbook on Cities of the Global South*. London: Routledge.
Parnell, S. and Pieterse, E. (2010). The 'right to the city': Institutional imperatives of a developmental state. *International Journal of Urban and Regional Research*, 34: 146–162.
Parnell, S. and Pieterse, E. (eds) (2014). *Africa's Urban Revolution*. London: Zed.
Parnell, S. and Robinson, J. (2012). (Re)theorizing cities from the global south: Looking beyond neoliberalism. *Urban Geography, 33*.
Parnell, S., Siri, J., Elmqvist, T., Marcotullio, P., Capon, A., Revi, A., Pelling, M. and Ivey Boufford, J. (2014). Making the Sustainable Development Goals operational through an urban agenda: Perspectives from science. *Solutions,* in press.
Patel, S., Baptist, C. and d'Cruz, C. (2012). Knowledge is power – informal communities assert their right to the city through SDI and community-led enumerations. *Environment and Urbanization, 24*: 13–26.
Pelling, M. (2003). *The Vulnerability of Cities: Natural Disasters and Social Resilience*. London: Earthscan.
Pieterse, E. A. (2008). *City Futures: Confronting the Crisis of Urban Development*. London: Zed.
Pieterse, E. and Simone, A. (2013). *Rogue Urbanism: Emergent African Cities*. Cape Town: Jacana Media.
Potts, D. (2008). Displacement and livelihoods: The longer term impacts of Operation Murambatsvina, in: M. Vambe, *The Hidden Dimensions of Operation Murambatsvina in Zimbabwe*, 53–64, Oxford: African Books Collective.
Potts, D. (2012). Viewpoint: What do we know about urbanisation in sub-Saharan Africa and does it matter? *International Development Planning Review, 34*: v–xxii.
Pouw, N., Baud, I. and Dietz, T. (eds) (2012). *Local Governance and Poverty in Developing Nations*. London: Routledge.
Rakodi, C. and Lloyd-Jones, T. (eds.) (2002). *Urban Livelihoods: A People-Centred Approach to Reducing Poverty*. London: Routledge.
Revi, A. and Rosenzweig, C. (2013). *The Urban Opportunity: Enabling Transformative and Sustainable Development.* Background research paper submitted to the High-level Panel on the Post-2015 Agenda.
Rigg, J., Bebbington, A., Gough, K. V., Bryceson, D. F., Agergaard, J., Fold, N. and Tacoli, C. (2009). The World Development Report 2009 'reshapes economic geography': Geographical reflections, *Transactions of the Institute of British Geographers, 34*: 128–136.
Robinson, J. (2002). Global and world cities: A view from off the map. *International Journal of Urban and Regional Research, 26*: 531–554.

Robinson, J. (2008). Developing ordinary cities: city visioning processes in Durban and Johannesburg, *Environment and Planning, A, 40,* 74–85.

Roy, A. and Ong, A. (eds) (2011). *Worlding Cities: Asian Experiments and the Art of Being Global*: Oxford: John Wiley & Sons.

Satterthwaite, D. and Mitlin, D. (2013). *Reducing Urban Poverty in the Global South.* London: Routledge.

Scott, A. J. and Storper, M. (2014). The nature of cities: The scope and limits of urban theory. *International Journal of Urban and Regional Research,* in press.

Scott, J. C. (1998). *Seeing Like a State: How Certain Schemes to Improve the Human Condition Have Failed.* New Haven: Yale University Press.

Sen, A. (1999). *Commodities and Capabilities.* Oxford: Oxford University Press.

Seto, K. C., Fragkias, M., Güneralp, B. and Reilly, M. K. (2011). A meta-analysis of global urban land expansion, *PloS one, 6*: e23777.

Silver, J., McEwan, C., Petrella, L. and Baguian, H. (2013). Climate change, urban vulnerability and development in Saint-Louis and Bobo-Dioulasso: Learning from across two West African cities. *Local Environment, 18*: 663–677.

Simon, D. (2008). Urban environments: Issues on the peri-urban fringe. *Annual Review of Environment and Resources, 33*: 167–185.

Smit, W. and Parnell, S. (2012). Urban sustainability and human health: An African perspective. *Current Opinion in Environmental Sustainability, 4*: 443–450.

Soja, E. W. (2011). Regional urbanization and the end of the metropolis era, in: G. Bridge and S. Watson (eds), *The New Blackwell Companion to the City.* Hoboken, NJ: Wiley-Blackwell, 679–689,.

Swyngedouw, E. (2007). Impossible sustainability and the post-political condition, in: R. Krueger and D. Gibbs (eds), *The Sustainable Development Paradox: Urban Political Economy in the United States and Europe.* New York: Guilford Press, 13–40.

Tendler, J. (1997). *Good Government in the Tropics,* Baltimore: Johns Hopkins University Press.

Tomlinson, R. (2013). Dentists, politicians and policy professionals: The prescriptive character of best practice 'knowledge products' for slum upgrading. *International Development Planning Review, 35*: 353–369.

Turok, I. (2013). People-based versus place-based policies: The 2009 World Development Report. *Local Economy, 28*: 3–8.

Turok, I. and McGranahan, G. (2013). Urbanization and economic growth: The arguments and evidence for Africa and Asia. *Environment and Urbanization, 25*: 465–482.

UN-DESA [United Nations, Department of Economic and Social Affairs, Population Division]. (2012). *World Urbanization Prospects: The 2011 Revision.* Population Division of the Department of Economic and Social Affairs of the United Nations Secretariat, New York.

UN-Habitat. (2009). *Global Report on Human Settlements: Planning Sustainable Cities.* Nairobi: UN-Habitat.

UN-Habitat (2014). *The State of African Cities 2014.* Nairobi: UN-Habitat.

Watson, V. (2009). Seeing from the South: Refocusing urban planning on the globe's central urban issues. *Urban Studies, 46*: 2259–2275.

Watson, V. (2014). Co-production and collaboration in planning – The difference. *Planning Theory & Practice,* 1–15.

Winkler, T. (2011). On the Liberal Moral Project of Planning in South Africa. *Urban Forum, 22*(2): 135–148.

World Bank (1990). *World Development Report: Poverty*. Washington, DC: World Bank.

World Bank (2009). *World Development Report: Reshaping Economic Geography*. Washington, DC: World Bank.

Wratten, E. (1995). Conceptualizing urban poverty. *Environment and Urbanization*, *7*: 11–38.

2
Women in Cities: Prosperity or Poverty? A Need for Multi-dimensional and Multi-spatial Analysis

Sylvia Chant and Kerwin Datu

Introduction and background

Urbanisation is often celebrated as a gateway to expanded economic, social and political opportunities for women, as well as greater possibilities for independent upward mobility. This is one plausible reason why, in the context of increased fetishisation of the city as a generator of wealth and well-being, the issue of gender and urban prosperity has come to the fore, being the theme of UN-Habitat's *State of Women in Cities 2012/13* (UN-Habitat, 2013). Yet while not denying that urban women enjoy some advantages over their rural counterparts, barriers to female 'empowerment' remain widespread in towns and cities of the Global South, especially among the urban poor. Indeed, that several gender inequalities and injustices persist in urban environments is highlighted all the more when considering prosperity in conjunction with poverty. An analysis encompassing both phenomena reveals the frequently stark contrasts between what women contribute to wealth in cities through their paid and unpaid labour, their endeavours in building and consolidating shelter, and their efforts to work around shortfalls in essential services and infrastructure, and the often limited rewards they reap in respect of equitable access to 'decent' work and living standards, human capital acquisition, physical and financial assets, personal safety and security, and representation in formal structures of urban governance (Chant, 2013).

Recognising that it is useful to think about how wealth accumulates in cities, and who is responsible in this process, rather than simply focusing on poverty per se, it is important to bear in mind that despite growing emphasis on 'holistic' notions of urban prosperity and urban poverty, income remains a dominant marker in the conceptualisation and measurement of both. For example, proof of the wealth-producing capacity of urban areas is almost invariably linked to stylised mantras, such as 'Cities and towns are hubs of prosperity' (WB/IMF, 2013: 8). To some extent, and in strictly material terms, this is borne out by estimations that cities contribute around 70–80 per cent of global GDP, despite containing only 50 per cent of the world's population (ibid.). Yet although at a macro scale statistical data reveal a broadly positive correlation between national levels of urbanisation and per capita GDP (Dobbs et al., 2011; UN-Habitat, 2012; World Bank, 2009), suggesting that cities are not just the outcome of 'development' but 'engines of growth' in their own right (Satterthwaite, 2007; UNFPA, 2007), there is rather less evidence of this in developing regions, especially in Africa (UN-Habitat, 2012).

Prosperity is not an inevitable outcome of urbanisation, and in the absence of appropriate management, cities can become sinkholes of poverty and inequality. Persistent poverty and poor living standards when compounded by glaring socio-economic disparities and lack of decent work opportunities are often associated with violence, crime, insecurity, and mental and physical ill health (Krujit and Koonings, 2009; Jones and Rodgers, 2009; Mitlin and Satterthwaite, 2013; Rakodi, 2008; Rodgers et al., 2011). Although the United Nations Fund for Population Activities notes that 'no country in the industrial age has ever achieved significant economic growth without urbanisation', it also concedes, in particular relation to the Global South, that '[t]he current concentration of poverty, slum growth and social disruption in cities does paint a threatening picture' (UNFPA, 2007: 1).

Such portents are particularly applicable to urban poverty when viewed through a 'gender lens' (Chant, 2013). While eschewing the oversimplified and frequently unsubstantiated notion that the 'feminisation of poverty' translates into a growing gap in income-based poverty between women and men, and that this is largely due to a 'feminisation' of household headship (see Chant, 2007a, 2008; and below), it is clear that urbanisation does not necessarily favour greater gender equality. Indeed, while broad correlations are observable at a regional level between urbanisation, wealth and a lower incidence of poverty, there is no systematic relationship between these and major quantitative gender indices (Chant, 2011, table 1.5; Chant and Datu, 2011).

This is not to deny a view – particularly favoured by advocates of 'smart economics' (for example, Buvinic and King, 2007) that 'economic development and growth are good for gender equality, and conversely, that greater gender equality is good for development' (Morrison et al., 2010: 103) – and that in 'prosperous' cities, women will benefit in various ways. As postulated by the World Bank and International Monetary Fund in their 2013 *Global Monitoring Report*, for example: 'The potential of urbanisation to close the gender gap in earnings and enhance women's empowerment is enormous' (WB/IMF, 2013: 101). Yet cautions have been raised with regard to the 'asymmetrical' relationship between gender equality and economic growth. Naila Kabeer and Luisa Natali (2013: 3), for instance, indicate that gender equality in education and employment contributes much more systematically to economic growth than economic growth does to reducing gender gaps in such arenas as health, well-being and rights. In turn, while the space of the city in general might be regarded as presenting a series of opportunities for women to exit poverty and enjoy more gender-equitable shares of prosperity, this is difficult to countenance for all women (Khosla, 2009: 7).

In addition to heeding heterogeneity among women, how gendered 'poverty' and 'prosperity' are approached analytically is also vital. In line with Sarah Bradshaw's (2002: 12) contention that women's poverty is 'not only multidimensional but is also multisectoral' and 'is experienced in different ways, at different times and in different "spaces"', it is necessary to recognise different dimensions of poverty such as income, assets, time and power, as well as to address how different, albeit porous and interconnected, urban spaces – at domestic, community, citywide and national levels – combine to disadvantage particular constituencies of women (UNRISD, 2010: 108). Indeed, despite the de facto continuum of 'private' and 'public' spaces, and the fact that the former may actually present more risks for women than the latter (Tankel, 2011; Valentine, 1989), Tovi Fenster (2005) among others has drawn attention to the gender-blindness of Lefebvre's (1986) formulation of 'rights to the city', in which the 'private space' of the home, frequently infused by patriarchal power relations, has been comparatively neglected.

Such issues have long been recognised in feminist analyses of the city and undergirded by the call to acknowledge that the built environment in general, and its multiple component spaces, are typically constituted by, as well as constitutive of, gender-discriminatory processes (Jarvis et al., 2009; Massey, 1994, 1995; McDowell, 1999). As eloquently articulated by Linda Peake and Martina Rieker (2013: 2): '[W]omen are an important node in the constellations of power, and thus in the production of centre and margins, in imaginaries of the urban'.

In the sections which follow we attempt to flesh out some of the most pertinent intersecting demographic, economic, social and political phenomena affecting women in cities in developing regions, at various scales and in different spaces, with particular attention to their interrelations with poverty and prosperity.

Feminising urban demographies

Urban populations across the Global South appear to be undergoing a process of 'feminisation'. This partly owes to female-selective migration, which in regions such as Latin America has been pronounced for several decades (Chant, 2013). In the period 1965–1975, for example, it is estimated that 109 women moved to towns and cities in Latin America for every 100 men (Gilbert and Gugler, 1982: 59). In sub-Saharan Africa, alternatively, the ratio during the same period was only 92 female rural-urban migrants per 100 males (ibid.).

In several Latin American countries, and in some Southeast Asian nations too, female bias in rural-urban movement in the second half of the twentieth century was stimulated by increased employment opportunities for women in towns and cities, including in domestic service and export manufacturing (see Chant and McIlwaine, 2009; Tacoli, 2012). In sub-Saharan Africa and South Asia, by contrast, such openings were rarer. In combination with a range of moral and physical restrictions on independent female movement, virilocal marriage, and the encouragement of young men to gain experience in the city as a form of masculine 'rite of passage', this acted to depress women's mobility, and in turn, proportions of urban-resident women (Chant and McIlwaine, 2009; Tacoli and Mabala, 2010).

Yet even if in countries such as Kenya, where there are still only 68 women per 100 men in urban areas, and in India where the urban sex ratio of 90 women per 100 men is lower than the all-India figure of 93.3 (and in the largest ['million-plus'] cities drops to only 86.1; see Gupta et al., 2009: 24; Khosla, 2009: 18), there is evidence to suggest that male selectivity in rural-urban movement is on the wane. This appears to be particularly notable in slums, which in India are characterised by less masculinised sex ratios than non-slum areas (Khosla, 2009: 25).

The rising tide of women's urbanward migration in sub-Saharan Africa, and especially South Asia, owes in part to recent increases in possibilities for female wage labour in services, public sector employment, and industry. However, other factors include 'distress-driven' movement provoked by rural women's cumulative disadvantage in land acquisition and inheritance, economic deterioration in the countryside and pressures on households to spread risk (Tacoli, 2010). Additional factors contributing to women's urban drift in countries such as Tanzania include the need for HIV-positive women to obtain medical treatment, as well as to avoid stigma and ostracism in close-knit rural communities (Hughes and Wickeri, 2011: 837–838).

Despite inter-regional variations in urban sex ratios deriving from the different historical legacies described above, the generally female-positive skew in life expectancy in a global context of demographic ageing appears to be exerting an across-the-board effect in terms of feminising sex ratios among 'older' cohorts of urban inhabitants (>60 years) and especially among the 'older old' (>80 years). 'Older old' women not only outnumber their male counterparts by nearly two to one in Latin American countries such as Argentina and Chile, for instance, but also in sub-Saharan African countries such as Botswana and South Africa (UNSD, 2008: 155–173, table 7). In East Asian countries such as China and Malaysia, the female-to-male ratio among the older old is around 150 to 100, and even in India, where urban sex ratios overall remain distinctively masculine, there are 116 women for every 100 men in the over-80 cohort (ibid.; see also Chant and Datu, 2011).

That with few exceptions senior female citizens far outnumber their male peers raises questions as to the possibilities for greater female shares of urban prosperity now and in the future. In many contexts advanced age is associated with greater poverty, especially among women. Many older women may not only be widowed and in a situation of living alone, or heading their own households, but slip under the radar of mainstream – or even gender-specific – anti-poverty interventions (see Varley, 2013: 131–132). In turn, younger women may bear the fallout due to their routine position in the frontline of duties of care for elderly (and infirm) relatives.

Cities of female-headed households?

Sex-selective demographic ageing, and its association with widowhood, has undoubtedly contributed to upward trends in female-household headship in recent decades. In urban Latin America, for example, households headed by women rose by an average of nearly 10 per cent between the late 1980s and the end of the first decade of the twenty-first century (Chant, 2013). Other reasons commonly mooted for rising proportions of female-headed households in towns and cities not only in Latin America but further afield include greater access by urban women to employment and independent earnings, and to land and property, and partly as a result of this, dwindling control by patriarchal kinship systems (see Bradshaw, 1995; Chant, 1997; Folbre, 1991; Safa, 1995).

Cities, gender and fertility

While declining fertility is an integral aspect of the demographic transition, and is regarded by some as conducive to women's progressive 'emanicipation' as well as fundamental to urbanisation (Dyson, 2010), spatial and social differences among urban-resident women are immensely significant. Although in general urban women have lower fertility than their rural counterparts, total fertility rates (TFRs) are routinely higher among groups living in poor as opposed to wealthier urban neighbourhoods (Chant and McIlwaine, 2013). In urban Bangladesh, for example, the TFR in slums is 2.5 compared with 1.9 in non-slum settlements (Schurmann, 2009). Such disparities are commonly attributed to uneven information and access to family planning, and can have far-reaching implications. Early fertility is frequently associated with school dropout among adolescent girls (see Figure 2.1) which has knock-on effects on their prospects of jobs and lifetime earnings, and accordingly for female shares of 'urban prosperity'. These phenomena intersect with a suite of widespread gender gaps in the acquisition of 'human capital' such as education, vocational skills and training.

Gender and education in cities and slums

Education is not only critical in terms of women's participation in labour markets and economic growth overall (Arbache et al., 2010; Klasen, 2002; World Bank, 2006), but is also an integral aspect of 'personhood', affecting women's general capacities, their self-esteem and their ability to exert agency. Educated women, on average, delay marriage and childbirth, are less vulnerable to HIV/AIDS, enjoy more power in their homes and in public arenas, and have fewer children, who are also likely to be healthier and better educated themselves (Plan International, 2009; Tembon and Fort, 2008). Yet despite closing gender gaps in education, women still constitute approximately two-thirds of 774 million adult illiterates worldwide (UN-DESA, 2010: 43). And among contemporary generations of girls, completion of education (especially at secondary and tertiary levels) is often disproportionately low (Morrison et al., 2010; Tembon and Fort, 2008; Yadav and Srivastava, 2006).

Although urban girls tend to be somewhat more advantaged than their rural counterparts, this is not always the case in urban slums, as noted previously (Figure 2.1). In major Indian cities, for example, differences in

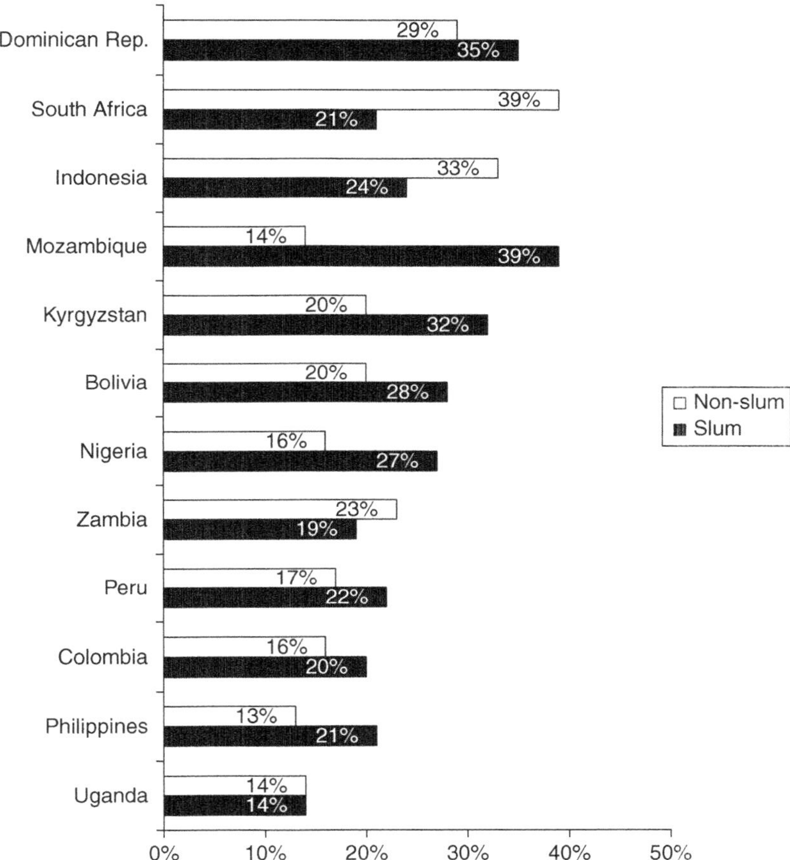

Figure 2.1 Female school dropout due to pregnancy and early marriage, slum and non-slum residents in selected countries (%)

Source: Adapted from UN-Habitat (2010b, figure 2.9, p. 23).

education among women according to place of residence are striking. In Kolkata and Delhi, for example, only 28 per cent of women in non-slum areas have no education or less than five years of schooling, whereas in slums the proportions rise to 51 per cent and 57 per cent, respectively (Gupta et al., 2009, figure 2.11, p. 32).

Among the many reasons for educational disadvantage among slum-dwelling girls is that private study may be constrained by lack of space, light, tranquillity, security or basic infrastructure, or because during girls' time out of school they are recruited into domestic chores (see Chant and Touray, 2012; Hughes and Wickeri, 2011: 889). Several young women may also be withdrawn from school (if they are actually enrolled in the first place) because parents or guardians deem their education unimportant, or because their labour is needed from an early age to help out with household finances, even if there is considerable evidence that young women can and do combine paid and unpaid work and schooling (see for example, De Vreyer et al., 2013; Jones and Chant, 2009). Such barriers to female education not only affect girls directly but as Stephan Klasen (2002) argues, can impede the prosperity of all.

Gendered divisions of paid and unpaid labour in cities

Leading on from this, gendered divisions of labour constitute another crucial dimension in conceptualising gendered poverty and prosperity in cities. Gendered divisions not only apply to the paid labour force, but also to the unpaid 'care economy', a sector which, in including routine domestic tasks as well as more specialised care work, plays a crucial role in producing 'surplus value', even if it remains conspicuously absent from GDP and the System of National Accounts (SNA) (see Budlender, 2008; Elson, 1999; Folbre, 1994; Razavi, 2007: 4–5; UNRISD, 2010).

While men's labour is largely concentrated in 'productive'/income-generating work, women undertake the major role in 'reproductive', unpaid labour, and although women across the Global South are increasingly engaged in remunerated activities, this does not seem to have been accompanied by a commensurate 'masculinisation' of domestic labour and care work (see for example, Chant, 2007a; ECLAC, 2004; McDowell et al., 2006). Such inequities reinforce if not exacerbate a female-biased 'reproduction tax' (Palmer, 1992) which, despite the stretching of women's overall working hours, combines with other discriminatory processes within the home and in the labour market, to impinge upon the type of income-generating activities available to women, as well as leading to downgraded value of women's market work regardless of what the work actually entails (Perrons, 2010; Perrons and Plomien, 2010).

Thus while, nominally, rising levels of engagement in economic activity are 'good' for women, gender gaps remain significant in terms of how far and where women and men are engaged in urban labour markets (for example, in industry and services), and on what basis, notably 'formal' or 'informal' (Chen et al., 2004; Kabeer, 2008a, 2008b).

Gender divisions in 'formal' employment in the city

Formal urban employment is generally better protected and better paid than informal work but is predominantly an employer of men. Women tend to be underrepresented in formal occupations overall, as well as confined to 'feminised' sectors or segments in which gender stereotypes remain deeply engrained. In large-scale manufacturing, for instance, women tend only to be recruited in labour-intensive assembly work, commonly in 'offshore' multinational branch plants where female preference is predicated on women's assumed docility, reliability and capacity to work more efficiently than men for lower rates of pay (Elson and Pearson, 1981; also UN Women, 2011: 35).

Although new economic sectors such as information and communications technology (ICT) nominally offer scope for a more level playing field, there is little evidence that women are making as much headway as their male counterparts. Although some women, especially those who are educated and able to speak English, have been able to secure niches in relatively well-remunerated occupations in the digital economy, such as in call centre work (see Patel, 2010), the bulk of female workers are concentrated in basic, low-paid occupations such as data entry (Lugo and Sampson, 2008; UNRISD, 2010: 119).

For the many women who are excluded from the 'formal' economy, the only option is 'informal' employment which has conventionally encompassed own-account entrepreneurship, subcontracted labour, and work in small-scale 'family' businesses, sometimes on an unpaid basis. Informal workers generally operate beyond the remit of labour and social security legislation and endure precarious working conditions. This situation has arguably worsened since the debt crisis of the 1980s during which the 'feminisation of labour' appears to have run parallel to an 'informalisation of labour' across the Global South.

Gender dimensions of informal urban employment

Although men also work informally, women are not only disproportionately engaged in this sector but typically confined to its lower echelons. This owes variously to a lesser repertoire of skills and work experience, limited access to start-up capital, and under- or unpaid roles in 'family enterprises' (Chant and Pedwell, 2008; Chen et al., 2004; see also Figure 2.2). As a result of additional constraints on women's spatial mobility arising from moral and social norms, not to mention reproductive ties, their informal economic activities are commonly based at home.

Figure 2.2 Segmentation by sex within the informal economy

Women's home-based enterprises encompass the preparation and/or sale of food or drinks, the fabrication of crafts or household goods, laundry work, seamstressing, hairdressing, the operation of small general stores, and in some instances, the running of eateries, diners, bars, gaming parlours, or tiny neighbourhood cinemas. Added to this is a wide range of subcontracted piecework for formal factories engaged in the production of fireworks, footwear, costume jewellery and so on. Yet despite the diversity, and often considerable ingenuity, characterising women's own-account domestic-based ventures, it is also important to recognise the constraints to scale and profitability posed on female slum dwellers, whose frequently peripheral locations – compounded by inaccessible or unaffordable transport – hamper access to wider and more remunerative markets. In turn, the financial turnover of home-based businesses is held in check by reproductive burdens which are made especially heavy by inadequate space, services and infrastructure (Chant, 2007b, 2013; see also below).

Gender gaps in urban assets

Pursuant to the above, gender-differentiated access to housing (a 'private' asset) along with the gender-differentiated impacts of deficient services and infrastructure (public assets) constitutes a further assemblage of household/community spaces which act as 'spatial poverty traps' (Unterhalter, 2009: 16) for poor and/or slum-dwelling urban women.

Land and housing

Housing is critical to women not only because it is often the basis of informal businesses, and therefore crucial to their economic status, but also because it serves as a key resource in their social and psychological identity, well-being, security and mobility (Miraftab, 2001; Moser, 2009).

Yet despite a plethora of national and international policy and legislative instruments to promote women's human rights to shelter, gender remains a major axis of discrimination (COHRE, 2008; Varley, 2013: 132). While urban women are often thought to have better access to land and property than their rural counterparts, partly on account of more favourable earning opportunities, and partly because property is more likely to be acquired through the market rather than inheritance (UNFPA, 2007: 19), this does not seem to lead to an appreciable shift in respect of gender-equal shares. For example, a UN-Habitat survey of 16 low-income urban communities in Ghana, Senegal, Tanzania, Uganda, Zambia, Sri Lanka, Colombia and Costa Rica revealed that only one-third of owner-occupiers were female (Miraftab, 2001). Even where formal housing interventions aim to grant women equal or preferential access, as in Senegal, property titles in male-headed households still tend to go to men (Rakodi, 2010: 355).

Since access to land and housing by women in many parts of the world is filtered through male kin (especially husbands or fathers), those who are divorced or deserted commonly face eviction and/or homelessness in the event of conjugal breakdown. The same applies to widows who may be subject to 'property grabbing' by in-laws, as noted in India (Nakray, 2010), as well as in many parts of sub-Saharan Africa (Rakodi, 2010; Sweetman, 2008). Even where still-married women may be de jure owners of land or property, this may mean little in respect of their de facto rights over control, sale, transfer or utilisation (Chant, 2007b; Varley, 2007). This is all the more unjust given women's major roles in generating 'urban prosperity' through contributions of time, money and labour to the urban housing stock, especially in slums in which 'self-help' is the prevalent mode of provision (Chant, 2013).

Gender disparities in urban shelter and the tendency for land and housing to be registered in the name of (male) 'household heads' are often attributed to women's limited access to stable employment and earnings, finance and credit (COHRE, 2004). Additional factors are that women may be dissuaded from claiming title for fear of property taxes (Khosla, 2009: 39), or succumb to socio-cultural pressures to defer to men's prerogatives in respect of ownership and management of household assets (Hughes and Wickeri, 2011: 847).

While women within male-headed households share many of the barriers to effective property ownership with those who head their own households, it is important to bear in mind that female-household heads may self-select to rent for reasons of security, as is the case in the slums of Luanda, Angola, where such women commonly opt for dwellings annexed to landlord-occupied housing (see Ducados, 2007). Yet there is also gender discrimination in rental tenure. In some instances, lone women or female heads of household lack sufficiently regular or well-paid employment to secure rental contracts, particularly where these involve substantial down payments. Additional factors, noted by Penny Vera-Sanso (2006) for southern Indian cities, is that rental accommodation may be hard to obtain in the face of aspersions about the sexual propriety of women without male 'guardians'. This may be compounded by stigma against HIV/AIDS-affected women (Hughes and Wickeri, 2011: 859–860), or lesbians (Benavides Llerena et al., 2007).

Urban services

Safe drinking water and sanitation were both established as human rights by the UN Human Rights Council in 2010. This undoubtedly lent impetus to the objective of reducing by half the proportion of the population without sustainable access to safe drinking water and basic sanitation by 2015, as exhorted by Target 10, Millennium Development Goal 7. Yet although there has been some progress, especially in urban areas and with respect to water (see WB/IMF, 2013), major shortfalls remain. Over and above the fact that the water target does not extend beyond that which is fit to drink, to include an adequate supply for bathing, washing and cleaning (Joshi et al., 2011: 102), nor take stock of reliability and proximity of supply (Mitlin and Satterthwaite, 2013), advances in sanitation have been tardier still, and are particularly lagging in slums. In India, for example, not even one-quarter of slum households in Chennai, Delhi, Mumbai and Kolkata avail of improved toilet facilities (Gupta et al., 2009: 20), forcing many households to resort to 'open defecation'.

Lack of access to decent or affordable services forces women into heavy loads of compensating labour. Where dwellings lack domestic mains-supplied water, for instance, women have to collect it from public standpipes, wells, boreholes, rivers, or storage drums served by private tankers, a task which may be both arduous and time-consuming, especially where women have to compete with one another at communal sources (see Thompson et al., 2000 on Kenya). The costs of informally supplied water may also be prohibitive. In Niger, for example, the mean price of a cubic metre of water from a piped network is only around one-quarter of that provided by water vendors (WB/IMF, 2013: 9; see also Chant, 2007b: 62).

Where there is no electricity, time must be spent collecting or buying fuel and making fires to cook and heat water, and to shop on a daily basis. Where there is no rubbish collection, women themselves have to dispose of solid waste (Khosla, 2009). And in a number of South African cities, where waste management has been privatised, women are now devoting more time to keeping streets clean in their communities (Samson, 2003).

Lack of services not only impacts women's and girls' workloads but their dignity and self-respect. Having to use communal toilets and washblocks when experiencing menstruation or pregnancy can be extremely stressful, especially when for reasons of propriety women have to restrict the times they use or accompany their children to shared facilities (Joshi, 2013). On top of this, fear of violence en route or at destination may dissuade women from using community services at all (Amnesty International, 2010; Chant and McIlwaine, 2013; McIlwaine, 2013).

Gender and violence in cities

Urban women have been identified by the World Health Organisation (WHO) as being at particular risk of gender-based violence, leading, inter alia, to the establishment in 2009 of the Global Programme on Safe Cities Free from Violence Against Women by UN-Habitat and UNIFEM (UN-Habitat, 2010a: 13). Although data remain sparse and uneven (see OECD, 2013), domestic violence added to other forms of violence allegedly makes urban women twice as likely as men to suffer acts of aggression (UN-Habitat, 2006). Moreover, in cities such as Delhi and Chennai, where the estimated rate of physical and/or sexual violence against ever-married women aged 15–49 years ranges from 15 per cent to 41 per cent, respectively, levels are commonly twice as high in slums than in non-slum areas (Gupta et al., 2009: 62).

The extent to which urban violence affects women has arguably been somewhat sidelined in the literature on cities given the 'predominance and visibility of male-on-male violence and consequent masculine homicide and incarceration statistics' (Wilding and Pearson, 2013: 165). Men are clearly at high risk in regions such as Latin America where an estimated three out of four young people who die from violence are male (Figueroa Perea, 1998), and where premature male mortality is often most pronounced in slums where becoming part of a youth gang – often associated with drugs and other forms of crime – is the only viable means of livelihood (see Jones and Rodgers, 2009; McIlwaine and Moser, 2004). Yet as Polly Wilding and Ruth Pearson (2013: 165) remind us in the context of Rio de Janeiro, 'gang members do not operate in male-only spaces, so the impact of gang activity (and corresponding police interventions) is felt not just by men and boys, but also by the women and girls who live in these areas' (see also Kern and Mullings, 2013: 36 et seq. on 'garrison communities' in Kingston, Jamaica). Indeed, the very real threat of 'street violence' for women is perhaps most graphically evidenced in the phenomenal rates of abduction, rape and/or murder ('femicide') which have occurred in cities such as Ciudad Juárez on Mexico's northern border with the USA in recent years (Jarvis et al., 2009: 112).

Yet if by the same token 'public space' is often uppermost in discourses of 'safe cities' for women, it is paramount to acknowledge that there are 'connections and continuums between the public and private, and how they are socially constructed and habitually entwined' (Tankel, 2011: 353). Taking on board the exhortation that 'A gendered analysis of urban violence has to explore the two-way links between the private and public sphere and spaces' (Wilding and Pearson, 2013: 159), it is crucial to stress that women are often as much at risk of violence in their own neighbourhoods as in cities at large, especially where they have to venture out of their homes to collect water, or to use communal sanitation facilities, and where basic infrastructure such as adequate street lighting and effective policing are lacking (Chant and McIlwaine, 2013; Moser and McIlwaine, 2004).

Young women are frequently regarded as at greatest risk of sexual violence, including gang rape; but frail, elderly women may also be vulnerable along with women who 'transgress' heteronormative boundaries such as those who live 'independently'. Where dwellings are precariously built and there are no security patrols, women may also be vulnerable to break-ins, theft and rape in their own homes (Chant and McIlwaine, 2013; McIlwaine, 2013). The relative anonymity of some female urban dwellers, especially recent migrants, may make them more vulnerable to attack from strangers, or in cases of intimate partner abuse, less able to seek protection from kin or neighbours – the latter often exacerbated where women lack personal property rights (COHRE, 2008). Beyond this, there may be little in the way of locally accessible institutional support services for women suffering violence in slums (Wilding and Pearson, 2013: 172).

Gender and health in urban areas

Now recognised as a major health issue affecting women (WHO, 2009), gender-based violence compounds a host of problems related to physical and mental well-being in cities and slums, which have major ramifications for gender, poverty and prosperity.

The 2013 *Global Monitoring Report* identifies that urban health conditions in general compare favourably with those in rural areas (see WB/IMF, 2013). However, conditions in slums are often so poor that the notion of an 'urban penalty' in health has been widely debated (for example, Harpham, 2009; Montgomery et al., 2004; Satterthwaite, 2011). Evidence from eight large Indian cities, for example, shows that slum dwellers suffer a disproportionate risk of communicable diseases such as tuberculosis (Gupta et al., 2009: 43 et seq.). This compounds conditions linked with inadequate diet and health care, such as anaemia, to which women and young children are particularly prone (ibid.; see also Mitlin and Satterthwaite, 2013: ch. 3).

The risks to women's health in slums are aggravated by a range of 'stressors' attached to their routine household labour (see Chant, 2007b; Ekblad, 1993; WHO, 2009). For example, the use in cooking of solid fuels such as wood, coal and charcoal is not only more harmful to the environment but to people's health than 'cleaner', more expensive, alternatives such as kerosene, liquid petroleum, gas and electricity. This is especially the case in cramped, poorly ventilated spaces, such that 'indoor air pollution' has been termed a 'quiet and neglected killer' of poor women and children (UN-Habitat, 2008).

Mental health is also a concern. On top of the general observation that women and the poor worldwide are particularly prone to depression (Patel, 2001; Spitzer, 2005), evidence from São Paulo, Brazil, reveals that common mental diseases (CMDs) are almost twice as high (at 21 per cent) in the poorest socio-economic district of the city than in the wealthiest (at 12 per cent) (Blue, 1996: 95). This resonates with recent research on Cape Town, South Africa, which reveals a higher prevalence of CMDs in peri-urban slums (35 per cent) compared with rural areas (27 per cent), and that being female, unemployed and/or engaging in substance abuse are the most common correlates (Harpham, 2009: 112).

Gender dimensions of intra-urban mobility and connectivity

Women's access to different spaces in the city – especially public spaces – is frequently more limited than men's, not only due to the domestic-based time and resource constraints associated with reproductive labour, but because of strong symbolic dimensions surrounding the 'forbidden' and 'permitted' use of spaces governed by patriarchal power relations and norms of female propriety – factors which may require certain modes of dress and/or behaviour to render women 'invisible' or unapproachable (Fenster, 1999, 2005; Jarvis et al., 2009).

On top of this, women's intra-urban mobility is constrained by male-biased transport planning which prioritises travel from peri-urban areas to city centres during 'peak hours' at the expense of non-peak 'trip chaining' (multi-purpose, multi-stop excursions which relate to domestic labour, care work, and informal, part-time employment in non-centralised zones) (Kunieda and Gauthier, 2007). Low-income women also face challenges with respect to the affordability of public transport and personal safety, with elderly and differently abled women often suffering most (Jarvis et al., 2009; Peters, 2001).

Restricted spatial mobility can seriously jeopardise women's prospects of exiting poverty and gaining in prosperity through disadvantages in completing school, entering the labour force and social networking (Kantor, 2002; Lessinger, 1990; Vera-Sanso, 1995; Weiss, 1994). This is aggravated further by a gendered 'digital divide' in an era in which technology has the potential to diminish the constraints posed by physical limitations (Buskens and Webb, 2009; ESCAP, 2002; Perrons, 2004). In Indonesia, for example, girls are only half as likely as boys and young men aged 15 to 24 to use the Internet (Plan International, 2010: 19), with parental restrictions on girls' use of public space acting to depress their access to Internet cafés. The gap is even greater in Ghana where only 6.6 per cent of female youth use Internet cafés compared with 16.5 per cent of their male counterparts (ibid.: 114).

Gendered divisions in political power and urban governance

A final component critical in the analysis of interrelationships between gender, poverty and prosperity in urban areas relates to gender differences in power and rights which apply at all scales – from the personal, through household, community, citywide, and ultimately national and international levels.

Major disparities persist in the formal political realms of civic engagement and governance (UN-Habitat, 2008: 3; see also Patel and Mitlin, 2010), which is not to deny evidence of increased mobilisation and organisation of women at the grass roots, as well as a mounting female presence in urban bureaucracies.

In the city of Porto Alegre, Brazil, for example, which has been a pioneer in inclusive urban governance, women are the majority of participants in budgetary assemblies. In India, there has been an unprecedented representation of women in local government following the 74th Constitutional Amendment Act of 1992, which requires 30 per cent of seats on local councils (*'panchayati raj'*) to be occupied by women (Khosla, 2009). South Africa, too, has enjoyed among the highest increases in women's representation in local government across developing regions since the mid-1990s, all of which undoubtedly helps to prioritise matters of importance in women's daily lives (see Beall, 2010). However, it is also crucial to remember that local government bodies are often under-resourced, and that women's contributions are frequently unpaid and/or confined to rank-and-file rather than leadership positions. As Jo Beall (2010: 636) further cautions: '[I]t is important that the pursuit of decentralisation and women's rights does not become a vehicle for putting a human face on neo-liberal preoccupations with privatisation, deregulation and cost recovery at the expense of poor women'. Indeed, in contexts such as in Ecuador and Venezuela, where, despite transitions to more left-wing governments in the last two decades, the maternalist framing of women as 'problem-solvers' for poverty in their communities has changed little, with Amy Lind (2010) contending that the 'institutionalisation of women's struggles' has effectively served to compensate for weak welfare states. A related problem is that women's engagement in movements and programmes around basic services and poverty reduction tend to feminise responsibility in ways that burden women even more, sideline men further, and neglect 'strategic gender interests' in favour of 'practical gender needs' (Molyneux, 1984, 2001; also Moser, 1989, 1993).

Despite some undoubted spin-offs for women from formal and informal modes of civic participation, one major concern is how the general instrumentalism of state (and NGO) initiatives that court their engagement plays out in terms of their shares of urban prosperity. Although women's efforts in urban political and policy terrains can undoubtedly help to reduce income poverty and other gendered deprivations common, one also has to ask about the cost at which this comes. If women's engagement is sought primarily in the interests of creating wealth for all, then one of the biggest questions is where they stand in relation to others in the queue for benefits.

In the short term, and possibly in the longer term, too, to enlist poor women in the largely unpaid, and fundamentally altruistic, work of creating better cities arguably entrenches and entraps them in roles which go against the grain of transforming gender, or effecting more equal allocations of urban wealth. By the same token, as asserted by Khosla (2009: 10), without women's engagement – especially in decision-making positions – there is little likelihood of granting gender issues a seat at the political and policy table.

Concluding comments

Women's disadvantage in cities occurs at a number of interconnected scales, which both reflect and reinforce gender divisions of labour, discrimination, notions of female 'propriety', and gender-differentiated autonomy in, and access to, 'private' and 'public' spaces. It is accordingly necessary to analyse gendered urban poverty (and prosperity) from a multi-dimensional and multi-spatial vantage point. This entails considering gendered inputs, as well as outcomes across an array of issues (such as housing, service provision, productivity, politics) and sites (home, neighbourhood/community, city, nation), with due regard to the varied nature of spaces therein and to their intersectionalities with other axes of social difference such as class, 'race', age and migrant status.

Given the plethora of socio-spatial processes responsible for gender inequalities in urban environments, clear or comprehensive pro-female urban policies are likely to remain elusive. By the same token, the very diversity of factors involved in perpetuating male bias in cities potentially offers a number of 'entry points' through which to move towards greater gender equality in the future, and to increase urban women's prospects of exiting poverty – and achieving prosperity.

Notes

We have borrowed part of our title from Rakodi (2008). This chapter draws substantially on the draft lead chapter prepared by Chant for UN-Habitat's *State of Women in Cities 2012/13* (Chant, 2011), as well as associated papers, notably Chant (2013), Chant and Datu (2011) and Chant and McIlwaine (2013).

1. 'Garrison communities' are described by Kern and Mullings (2013: 36) as 'ghettoised spaces of poverty and violent political sectarian control'.

References

Amnesty International. (2010). *Insecurity and Indignity: Women's Experiences in the Slums of Nairobi, Kenya*. London: Amnesty International. (http://www.amnesty.org/en/library/asset/AFR32/002/2010/en/12a9d334-0b62-40e1-ae4a-e5333752d68c/afr320022010en.pdf)

Arbache, J. S., Kolev, A. and Filipiak, E. (2010). *Gender Disparities in Africa's Labor Market.* Washington, DC: World Bank.

Beall, J. (2010). Decentralisation, women's rights and poverty: Learning from India and South Africa, in: S. Chant (ed.), *The International Handbook of Gender and Poverty: Concepts, Research, Policy.* Cheltenham: Edward Elgar, 633–637.

Benavides Llerena, G., Sánchez Pinto, S., Chávez Nuñez, G.;, Solesdipa Toro, A. and Sol Paredes, M. (2007). *Diagnóstico de la Situación del Derecho de las Mujeres a la Vivienda Adecuada desde una Perspectiva de Género en Ecuador.* Quito: Comité de América Latina y El Caribe para la Defensa de los Derechos de la Mujer [CLADEM Ecuador].

Blue, I. (1996). Urban inequalities in mental health: The case of São Paulo. *Environment and Urbanization, 8*(2): 91–99.

Bradshaw, S. (1995). Female-headed households in Honduras: Perspectives on rural-urban differences. *Third World Planning Review, 17*(2): 117–131.

Bradshaw, S. (2002). *Gendered Poverties and Power Relations: Looking Inside Communities and Households.* Managua: Puntos de Encuentro.

Budlender, D. (2008). *The Statistical Evidence on Care and Non-Care Work Across Six Countries.* Programme Paper No. 4. Geneva: UNRISD. (www.unrisd.org)

Buskens, I. and Webb, A. (eds) (2009). *African Women and ICTS: Investigating Technology, Gender and Empowerment.* London: Zed Books.

Buvinic, M. and King, E. M. (2007). Smart economics: More needs to be done to promote the economic power of women. *Finance and Development, 44*(2). (http://www.imf.org/external/pubs/ft/fandd/2007/06/king.htm)

Centre on Housing Rights and Evictions (COHRE). (2004). *Bringing Equality Home: Promoting and Protecting the Inheritance Rights of Women: A Survey of Law and Practice in Sub-Saharan Africa.* Geneva: COHRE. (http://www.cohre.org/)

Centre on Housing Rights and Evictions (COHRE). (2008). *Women, Slums and Urbanisation: Examining the Causes and Consequences.* Geneva: COHRE. (http://www.cohre.org/)

Chant, S. (1997). *Women-headed Households: Diversity and Dynamics in the Developing World.* Basingstoke: Palgrave Macmillan.

Chant, S. (2007a). *Gender, Generation and Poverty: Exploring the 'Feminisation of Poverty' in Africa, Asia and Latin America.* Cheltenham: Edward Elgar.

Chant, S. (2007b). *Gender, Cities and the Millennium Development Goals in the Global South.* LSE Gender Institute, New Series Working Paper, Issue 21, London. (http://www.lse.ac.uk/collections/genderInstitute/pdf/CHANT%20GI.pdf)

Chant, S. (2008). The 'feminisation of poverty' and the 'feminisation' of anti-poverty programmes: Room for revision? *Journal of Development Studies, 44*(2): 165–197.

Chant, S. (2011). Gender and the prosperity of cities. First draft of chapter in preparation for UN-Habitat. *State of Women in Cities 2012/13.* Nairobi: UN-Habitat.

Chant, S. (2013). Cities through a 'gender lens': A golden 'urban age' for women in the Global South? *Environment and Urbanization, 25*(1): 9–29.

Chant, S. and Datu, K. (2011). Urban prosperity doesn't automatically mean gender equality. *The Global Urbanist,* September. (http://globalurbanist.com/2011/09/27/urban-prosperity-doesnt-automatically-mean-gender-equality).

Chant, S. and McIlwaine, C. (2009). *Geographies of Development in the 21st Century: An Introduction to the Global South.* Cheltenham: Edward Elgar.

Chant, S. and McIlwaine, C. (2013). Gender, urban development and the politics of space. *e-International Relations*. (http://www.e-ir.info/2013/06/04/gender-urban-development-and-the-politics-of-space/).

Chant, S. and Pedwell, C. (2008). *Women, Gender and the Informal Economy: An Assessment of ILO Research, and Suggested Ways Forward*. Geneva: International Labour Organisation. (http://www.ilo.org/wcmsp5/groups/public/ – -dgreports/ – -dcomm/documents/publication/wcms_091228.pdf)

Chant, S. and Touray, I. (2012). *Gender in the Gambia in Retrospect and Prospect*. GAMCOTRAP Working Paper 1. Kanifing, The Gambia: GAMCOTRAP. (http://www.gamcotrap.gm/content/images/stories/documents/Chant_Touray.pdf)

Chen, M. A. (2010). Informality, poverty, and gender: Evidence from the Global South, in: S. Chant (ed.), *The International Handbook of Gender and Poverty: Concepts, Research, Policy*. Cheltenham: Edward Elgar, 463–471.

Chen, M. A., Carr, M. and Vanek, J. (2004). *Mainstreaming Informal Employment and Gender in Poverty Reduction: A Handbook for Policymakers and Other Stakeholders*. London: Commonwealth Secretariat.

De Vreyer, P., Gubert, F. and Rakoto-Tiana, N. (2013). The work school trade-off among children in West Africa: Are household tasks more compatible with school than economic activities?, in: P. De Vreyer and F. Roubaud (eds), *Urban Labor Markets in Sub-Saharan Africa*. Washington DC: World Bank, 349–372.

Dobbs, R., Smit, S., Remes, J., Manyika, J., Roxburgh, C. and Restrepo, A. (2011). *Urban World: Mapping the Economic Power of Cities*. Seoul, London and New York: McKinsey Global Institute. (http://www.mckinsey.com/mgi/publications/urban_world/index.asp)

Ducados, H. (2007). Women in War-torn Societies: A Study of Households in Luanda's Peri-urban Areas. Unpublished MPhil dissertation, Gender Institute, London School of Economics and Political Science.

Dyson, T. (2010). *Population and Development: The Demographic Transition*. London: Zed Books.

Economic Commission for Latin America and the Caribbean (ECLAC). (2004). *Roads Towards Gender Equity in Latin America and the Caribbean*. Santiago de Chile: ECLAC. (www.eclac.org)

Economic and Social Commission for Southeast Asia (ESCAP). (2002). *Issues, Policies and Outcomes: Are ICT Policies Addressing Gender Equality?* New York: United Nations. (http://www.unescap.org/esid/gad/Publication/Issues.pdf).

Ekblad, S. (1993). Stressful environments and their effects on the quality of life in Third World cities. *Environment and Urbanization, 5*(2): 125–134.

Elson, D. (1999). Labour markets as gendered institutions: Equality, efficiency and empowerment Issues. *World Development, 27*(3): 611–627.

Elson, D. and Pearson, R. (1981). 'Nimble fingers make cheap workers': An analysis of women's employment in Third World export manufacturing. *Feminist Review, 7*: 87–107.

Fenster, T. (1999). Space for gender: Cultural roles of the forbidden and the permitted. *Environment and Planning D: Society and Space, 17*: 227–246.

Fenster, T. (2005). The right to the gendered city: Different formations of belonging in everyday Life. *Journal of Gender Studies, 14*(3): 217–231.

Figueroa Perea, J. G. (1998). Algunos Elementos para Interpretar la Presencia de los Varones en los Procesos de Salud Reproductiva. *Revista de Cadernos de Saúde Pública, 14*: suplemento 1, 87–96.

Folbre, N. (1991). Women on their own: Global patterns of female headship, in: R. Gallin and A. Ferguson (eds), *Women and International Development Annual Vol. 2*, 89–106, Boulder: Westview,

Folbre, N. (1994). *Who Pays for the Kids? Gender and the Structures of Constraint*. London: Routledge.

Gilbert, A. and Gugler, J. (1982). *Cities, Poverty and Development: Urbanisation in the Third World*. Oxford: Oxford University Press.

Gupta, K., Arnold, F. and Lhungdim, H. (2009). *Health and Living Conditions in Eight Indian Cities*. National Family Health Survey (NFHS-3), India, 2005–06, Mumbai and Calverton, Maryland: International Institute for Population Sciences/ICF Macro. (http://www.measuredhs.com/pubs/pdf/OD58/OD58.pdf).

Harpham, T. (2009). Urban health in developing countries: What do we know and where do we go? *Health and Place, 15*: 107–116.

Hughes, K. and Wickeri, E. (2011). A Home in the city: Women's struggle to secure adequate housing in urban Tanzania. *Fordham International Law Journal, 34*(4): 788–929 (Special Report). (http://law.fordham.edu/publications/index.ihtml?pubid=300)

Jarvis, H., with Cloke, J. and Kantor, P. (2009). *Cities and Gender Critical Introductions to Urbanism and the City*. London: Routledge.

Jones, G. A. and Chant, S. (2009). Globalising initiatives for gender equality and poverty reduction: Exploring 'failure' with reference to education and work among urban youth in The Gambia and Ghana. *Geoforum, 40*(2): 84–96.

Jones, G. A. and Rodgers, D. (eds) (2009). *Youth Violence in Latin America: Gangs and Juvenile Justice in Perspective*. New York: Palgrave Macmillan.

Joshi, D. (2013). Apolitical stories of sanitation and suffering women, in: T. Wallace and F. Porter with M. Ralph-Bowman (eds), *Aid, NGOs and the Realities of Women's Lives: A Perfect Storm*. Rugby: Practical Action, 215–226.

Joshi, D., Fawcett, B. and Mannan, F. (2011). Health, hygiene and appropriate sanitation: Experiences and perceptions of the urban poor. *Environment and Urbanization, 23*(1): 91–112.

Kabeer, N. (2008a). *Paid Work, Women's Empowerment and Gender Justice: Critical Pathways of Social Change*. Pathways Working Paper 3, Institute of Development Studies, University of Sussex, Brighton. (http://www.pathwaysofempowerment.org/PathwaysWP3-website.pdf).

Kabeer, N. (2008b). *Mainstreaming Gender in Social Protection for the Informal Economy*. London: Commonwealth Secretariat.

Kabeer, N. and Natali, L. (2013). *Gender Equality and Economic Growth: Is There a Win-Win?*, IDS Working Paper, No. 417. Brighton: Institute of Development Studies.

Kantor, P. (2002). Female Mobility in India: The Influence of Seclusion Norms on Economic Outcomes, *International Development Planning Review, 24*(2): 145–159.

Kern, L. and Mullings, B. (2013). Urban Neoliberalism, Urban Insecurity and Urban Violence, in: L. Peake and M. Rieker (eds), *Rethinking Feminist Interventions into the Urban*. London: Routledge, 23–40.

Khosla, R. (2009). *Addressing Gender Concerns in India's Urban Renewal Mission*. New Delhi: UNDP. (http://data.undp.org.in/dg/pub/AddressingGenderConcerns.pdf).

Klasen, S. (2002). Low schooling for girls, slower growth for all? Cross-country evidence on the effect of gender inequality in education on economic development. *World Bank Economic Review, 16*(3): 345–373.

Kruijt, D. and Koonings, K. (2009). The rise of megacities and the urbanisation of informality, exclusion and violence, in: D. Kruijt and K. Koonings (eds), *Megacities: The Politics of Urban Exclusion and Violence in the Global South*. London: Zed Books, 8–26.

Kunieda, M. and Gauthier, A. (2007). *Gender and Urban Transport: Smart and Affordable*. Eschborn: GTZ. (http://www.itdp.org/documents/7aGenderUT(Sept).pdf)

Lefebvre, H. (1986). *Writings on Cities*. Oxford: Blackwell.

Lessinger, J. (1990). Work and modesty: The dilemma of women market traders in Madras, in: L. Dube and R. Palriwala (eds), *Structures and Strategies*. New Delhi: Sage, 129–150.

Lind, A. (2010). Gender, neoliberalism and post-neoliberalism: Reassessing the institutionalisation of women's struggle for survival in Ecuador and Venezuela, in: S. Chant (ed.), *The International Handbook of Gender and Poverty: Concepts, Research, Policy*. Cheltenham: Edward Elgar, 649–654.

Massey, D. (1994). *Space, Place and Gender*. Minneapolis: University of Minnesota Press).

Massey, D. (1995). Reflections on Gender and Geography, in: T. Butler and M. Savage (eds), *Social Change and the Middle Classes*. London: UCL Press, 330–344.

McDowell, L. (1999). *Gender, Identity and Place: Understanding Feminist Geographies*. Minneapolis: University of Minnesota Press.

McDowell, L., Ward, K., Fagan, C., Perrons, D. and Ray, K. (2006). Connecting time and space: The significance of transformations in women's work in the city. *International Journal of Urban and Regional Research, 30*(1): 141–158.

McIlwaine, C. (2013). Urbanisation and gender-based violence: Exploring the paradoxes in the Global South. *Environment and Urbanization, 25*(1): 65–79.

McIlwaine, C. and Moser, C. O. N. (2000). Violence and social capital in urban poor communities: Perspectives from Colombia and Guatemala. *Journal of International Development, 13*(7): 965–984.

Miraftab, F. (2001). Risks and opportunities in gender gaps to access shelter: A platform for intervention. *International Journal of Politics, Culture and Society, 15*(1): 143–160.

Mitlin, D. and Satterthwaite, D. (2013). *Urban Poverty in the Global South: Scale and Nature*. London: Routledge.

Molyneux, M. (1984). Mobilisation Without Emancipation?, *Critical Social Policy, 10*(4): 59–71.

Molyneux, M. (2001). *Women's Movements in International Perspective: Latin America and Beyond*. Basingstoke: Palgrave Macmillan.

Morrison, A., Raju, D. and Singa, N. (2010). Gender equality, poverty reduction, and growth: A Copernican quest, in: R. Kanbur and M. Spence (eds), *Equity and Growth in a Globalising World*. Washington DC: World Bank on behalf of the Commission on Growth and Development, 103–129, (http://www.growth-commission.org/storage/cgdev/documents/volume_Equity/equityandgrowth-sansch8.pdf).

Moser, C. O.N. (1989). Gender planning in the Third World: Meeting practical and strategic gender needs. *World Development, 17*(11): 1799–1825.

Moser, C. O. N. (1992). Adjustment from below: Low-income women, time and the triple role in Guayaquil, Ecuador, in: H. Afshar and C. Dennis (eds), *Women and Adjustment Policies in the Third World*. Basingstoke: Palgrave Macmillan, 87–116.

Moser, C. O. N. (1993). *Gender Planning and Development*. London: Routledge.

Moser, C. O. N. (2009). *Ordinary Families, Extraordinary Lives: Assets and Poverty Reduction in Guayaquil, 1978–2004*. Washington, DC: Brookings Institution Press.

Moser, C. O. N. and McIlwaine, C. (2004). *Encounters with Violence in Latin America*. London: Routledge.

Nakray, K. (2010). Gender, HIV/AIDS and carework in India: A need for gender-sensitive policy, in: S. Chant (ed.), *The International Handbook of Gender and Poverty: Concepts, Research, Policy*. Cheltenham: Edward Elgar, 333–338.

Organisation for Economic Cooperation and Development (OECD). (2013). *Transforming Social Institutions to Prevent Violence Against Women and Girls and Improve Development Outcomes*. Paris: OECD Development Centre.

Palmer, I. (1992). Gender, equity and economic efficiency in adjustment programmes, in: H. Afshar and C. Dennis (eds), *Women and Adjustment Policies in the Third World*. Basingstoke: Palgrave Macmillan, 69–83.

Patel, R. (2010). *Working the Night Shift: Women in India's Call Center Industry*. Stanford: Stanford University Press.

Patel, S. and Mitlin, D. (2010). Gender Issues and Shack/Slum Dweller Federations, in: S. Chant (ed.), *The International Handbook of Gender and Poverty: Concepts, Research, Policy*. Cheltenham: Edward Elgar, 379–384.

Patel, V. (2001). Cultural factors and international epidemiology. *British Medical Bulletin, 57*: 33–45.

Peake, L. and Rieker, M. (2013). Rethinking feminist interventions into the urban, in: L. Peake and M. Rieker (eds), *Rethinking Feminist Interventions into the Urban*. London: Routledge, 1–22.

Perrons, D. (2010). Gender, Work and Poverty in High-income Countries, in: S. Chant (ed.), *The International Handbook of Gender and Poverty: Concepts, Research, Policy*. Cheltenham: Edward Elgar, 409–414.

Perrons, D. and Plomien, A. (2010). *Why Socio-Economic Inequalities Increase? Facts and Policy Responses in Europe*. EU Report Commissioned by DG Research, European Commission, Brussels. (http://ec.europa.eu/research/social-sciences/pdf/policy-review-inequalities_En.pdf)

Peters, D. (2001). *Gender and Transport in Less Developed Countries: A Background Paper in Preparation for CSD-9*. Background Paper for the Expert Workshop 'Gender Perspectives for Earth Summit 2002: Energy, Transport, Information for Decision-Making'. Berlin. (http://www.earthsummit2002.org/workshop/Gender%20%26%20Transport%20S%20DP.pdf).

Plan International. (2009). *Because I Am a Girl: The State of the World's Girls 2009: Girls in the Global Economy*. London: Plan International. (http://plan-international.org/files/global/publications/campaigns/BIAAG%202009.pdf)

Plan International. (2010). *Because I Am a Girl. The State of the World's Girls 2010: Digital and Urban Frontiers: Girls in a Changing Landscape*. London: Plan International. (http://plan-international.org/girls/resources/digital-and-urban-frontiers-2010.php)

Rakodi, C. (2008). Prosperity or poverty? Wealth, inequality and deprivation in urban areas, in: V. Desai and R. Potter (eds), *The Companion to Development Studies, 2nd ed*. London: Hodder Arnold, 253–257.

Rakodi, C. (2010). Gender, poverty and access to land in cities of the South, in: S. Chant (ed.), *The International Handbook of Gender and Poverty: Concepts, Research, Policy*. Cheltenham: Edward Elgar, 353–359.

Razavi, S. (2007). *The Political and Social Economy of Care in a Development Context: Conceptual Issues, Research Questions and Policy Options*. Geneva: UNRISD. (www.unrisd.org)

Rodgers, D., Beall, J. and Kanbur, R. (2011). *Latin American Urban Development into the 21st Century: Towards a Renewed Perspective on the City*. Working Paper 2011/05. Helsinki: UNU-WIDER.

Safa, H. (1995). *The Myth of the Male Breadwinner: Women and Industrialisation in the Caribbean*. Boulder, Colorado: Westview.

Samson, M. (2003). *Dumping on Women: Gender and Privatisation of Waste Management*. Woodstock, Cape Town: Municipal Services Project and the South African Municipal Workers' Union. (http://www.gdrc.info/docs/waste/005.pdf)

Satterthwaite, D. (2007). *The Transition to a Predominantly Urban World and Its Underpinnings*. Human Settlements Discussion Paper Series, Theme: Urban Change-4, International Institute for Environment and Development, London. (www.iied.org)

Satterthwaite, D. (2011). Why is urban health so poor even in many successful cities? *Environment and Urbanization, 23*(1): 5–11.

Spitzer, D. L. (2005). Engendering health disparities. *Revue Canadienne de Santé Publique*, 96(2): 578–595.

Tacoli, C. (2010). Internal mobility, migration and changing gender relations: Case study perspectives from Mali, Nigeria, Tanzania and Vietnam, in: S. Chant (ed.), *The International Handbook of Gender and Poverty: Concepts, Research, Policy*. Cheltenham: Edward Elgar, 296–300.

Tacoli, C. (2012). *Urbanization, Gender and Urban Poverty: Paid Work and Unpaid Carework in the City*. Urbanization and Emerging Population Issues Working Paper 7, London: International Institute for Environment and Development (IIED)/United Nations Fund for Population Activities (UNFPA). (http://pubs.iied.org/10614IIED.html?k=Tacoli)

Tacoli, C. and Mabala, R. (2010). Exploring mobility and migration in the context of rural-urban linkages: Why gender and generation matter. *Environment and Urbanization, 22*(2): 389–395.

Tankel, Y. (2011). Reframing 'safe cities for women': Feminist articulations in Recife. *Development*, 54(3): 352–357.

Tembon, M. and Fort, L. (eds) (2008). *Girls' Education in the 21st Century: Gender Equality, Empowerment and Economic Growth*. Washington, DC: World Bank.

Thompson, J., Porras, I., Wood, E., Tumwine, H., Mujwahusi, M., Katui-Katua, M. and Johnstone, N. (2000). Waiting at the tap: Changes in urban water use in East Africa over three decades. *Environment and Urbanization, 12*(2): 37–52.

United Nations Department for Economic and Social Affairs (UN-DESA). (2010). *The World's Women 2010: Trends and Statistics*. New York: UN.

United Nations Fund for Population Activities (UNFPA). (2007). *State of the World's Population 2007: Unleashing the Potential of Urban Growth*. New York: UNFPA. (www.unfpa.org)

UN-Habitat. (2006). *The State of the World's Cities 2006/2007: The Millennium Development Goals and Urban Sustainability – 30 Years of Shaping the Habitat Agenda*. London: Earthscan.

UN-Habitat. (2008). *The State of the World's Cities 2008/2009: Harmonious Cities*. London: Earthscan.

UN-Habitat. (2010a). *Gender Equality for Smarter Cities: Challenges and Progress*. Nairobi: UN-Habitat. (http://www.unhabitat.org/pmss/listItemDetails.aspx?publicationID=2887)

UN-Habitat. (2010b). *State of the Urban Youth 2010/2011 – Levelling the Playing Field: Inequality of Youth Opportunity*. London: Earthscan.

UN-Habitat. (2012). *State of the World's Cities 2012/13*. Nairobi: UN-Habitat.

UN-Habitat. (2013). *State of Women in Cities 2012–13*. Nairobi: UN-Habitat.

United Nations Research Institute for Social Development (UNRISD). (2010). *Combating Poverty and Inequality: Structural Change, Social Policy and Politics*. Geneva: UNRISD. (www.unrisd.org)

United Nations Statistics Division (UNSD). (2008). *Demographic Yearbook*. New York: UN. (http://unstats.un.org/unsd/demographic/products/dyb/dyb2008.htm)

Unterhalter, E. (2009). Gender and poverty reduction: The challenge of intersection. *Agenda: Empowering Women for Gender Equity, 23*(81): 14–24.

Valentine, G. (1989). The geography of women's fear. *Area, 21*(4): 385–390.

Varley, A. (2007). Gender and property formalisation: Conventional and alternative approaches. *World Development, 35*(10): 1739–1753.

Varley, A. (2013). Feminist perspectives on urban poverty: De-essentialising difference, in: L. Peake and M. Rieker (eds), *Rethinking Feminist Interventions into the Urban*. London: Routledge, 125–141.

Vera-Sanso, P. (1995). Community, seclusion and female labour force participation in Madras, India. *Third World Planning Review, 17*(2): 155–167.

Vera-Sanso, P. (2006). Conformity and contestation: Social heterogeneity in South Indian settlements, in: G. de Neve and H. Donner (eds), *The Meaning of the Local: Politics of Place in Urban India*. London: Routledge/Cavendish, 125–141.

Weiss, A. (1994). Challenges for Muslim women in a postmodern world, in: A. S. Ahmed and H. Donnan (eds), *Islam, Globalisation and Postmodernity*. London: Routledge, 123–136.

Wilding, P. and Pearson, R. (2013). Gender and violence in Maré, Rio de Janeiro: A tale of two cities?, in: L. Peake and M. Rieker (eds), *Rethinking Feminist Interventions into the Urban*. London: Routledge, 159–176.

World Bank. (2006). *Gender Equality as Smart Economics: A World Bank Action Plan (Fiscal Years 2007–10)*. Washington, DC: World Bank. (www.worldbank.org)

World Bank. (2009). *World Development Report 2009: Reshaping Economic Geography*. Washington, DC: World Bank. (www.worldbank.org)

World Bank and International Monetary Fund (WB/IMF). (2013). *Global Monitoring Report 2013: Rural Urban Dynamics and the Millennium Development Goals*. Washington, DC: World Bank.

World Health Organisation. (2009). *Women and Health: Today's Evidence, Tomorrow's Agenda*. Geneva: WHO. (www.who.org)

Yadav, A. K. and Srivastava, M. (2006). *Primary Education in Delhi Slums: Access and Utilisation*. Delhi: Institute of Applied Manpower Research in association with Manak Publications.

3

Space and Capabilities: Approaching Informal Settlement Upgrading through a Capability Perspective

Alexandre Apsan Frediani

Introduction

Definitions around the concept of poverty have fundamental implications as to how the role of space is understood in shaping and tackling deprivations in the urban context. The capability approach has emerged as a prominent evaluative framework in the redefinition of poverty as a multi-dimensional, dynamic and socially constructed phenomenon. However, there has been very limited interrogation of how such an understanding of poverty takes into account the role of space and how it could therefore contribute to discussions exploring the relationship between space and poverty. This chapter draws on different case studies to explore how capabilities are conditioned by spatial arrangements and imaginaries, but also how the expansion of capabilities of the urban poor can contribute towards a more socially just production of space.

Drawing from the work of Amartya Sen (1999) and Martha Nussbaum (2011), capabilities are understood as people's freedom to achieve the values they have reason to value. The notion of 'capabilities' differs from the notion of 'capacities', as it makes reference to a wider set of issues shaping people's freedom to pursue the aspired dimensions of well-being. Instead of focusing on life satisfaction, writers within the capability-approach literature have been calling for studies not to focus merely on individuals' well-being achievements, but most importantly on the options, abilities and opportunities of individuals and groups to pursue well-being dimensions. Options are the available strategies to expand well-being aspirations. Abilities refer to the set of skills and capacities individuals and groups have access to which would mediate the achievement of a certain dimension of well-being. Meanwhile, opportunities are the structural elements conditioning the availability and use of abilities and options (see Box 3.1 for an illustration of this definition). A capability analysis requires therefore a dynamic assessment of the relationship between options, abilities and opportunities to achieve well-being outcomes. By exploring freedoms as well as well-being achievements, capability-led studies would require an engagement with the exploration of the structural processes conditioning people's freedom to pursue social change.

Box 3.1 The bicycle example

In the capability literature, the relationship between a bicycle (an example of a commodity) and capabilities are often utilised to illustrate Amartya Sen's concepts with more clarity. To examine the success of an initiative that has focused on the distribution of bicycles to reduce poverty, one would have to firstly question the purpose for using a bicycle: for enhancing mobility, generating income opportunities, leisure, etc. Such outcomes, are the multiple dimensions of well-being associated with cycling. There are a series of factors conditioning people (individuals and groups in all of their diversity) in their use of the bicycle for achieving their valued aspirations. Such social, economic, environmental, political and physical elements are defined as conversion factors (Robeyns, 2005). These factors can be understood as individual abilities (i.e., skills to cycle or physical impairment), collective abilities (i.e., mobilisation capacities to push for legislations that will protect cyclists), or opportunities (i.e., social norms constraining some social groups from using bicycles). Meanwhile, a capability analysis would require engaging also with the alternative options for achieving people's valued aspirations, to allow the examination if people are using bicycles because of a lack of options, or based on choice to do so (for more on this, see Oosterlaken, 2009 or Frediani, 2010).

Thus, there is a more fundamental question concerning issues of justice and equity underlying the debates on how capabilities are understood and pursued. Amartya Sen and Martha Nussbaum's works have contributed to the ongoing debates to push current understandings of justice beyond utility maximisation, and to interrogate questions of equity in the distribution of capabilities. The understanding of social diversity present in the capability approach has contributed to emphasising how difference is constructed and how it shapes groups' capabilities. As with other debates in this field (White, 2010), the capability approach has the potential to bring together material, relational and subjective components of well-being, directly referring to issues of recognition and distribution present in preoccupations with justice. The capability approach is not about exploring levels of satisfaction or happiness; it positions well-being within debates of social change and justice, emphasising the importance of the enabling or disabling environment for the pursuit of well-being.

Nevertheless, most of the advancements in the capability literature focusing on its operationalisation have been around measurement and how data can capture the multi-dimensional aspects of poverty. The limited work so far exploring issue of space and the urban context in the capability literature has evolved in two ways. The first approach has focused on how the availability of infrastructure or characteristics of the built environment might compromise or facilitate individuals' abilities to enhance their well-being. The second trend in this field has focused on attempting to measure the diverse levels of quality of life spread across the urban territory, making use of GIS mapping and visualisation techniques to express urban inequalities in terms of distribution of resources.

The first area of work in this field draws on discussions about the functioning of the built environment to explore how individuals in all of their diversity make use of particular urban facilities. The capability-approach literature is used in this context to stress the importance of looking not only at the availability of certain urban infrastructure facilities, but of who uses them and for what purposes (i.e., Lewis, 2012, Oosterlaken, 2009; Talu and Blečić, 2012). The concept of 'conversion factors' within the capability-approach literature resonates particularly well with the preoccupations in this field, as it highlights the importance of exploring a series of factors that mediates the availability and use of commodities (i.e., personal, environmental and social factors) (Robeyns, 2005). Such tendencies have often reduced notions of capabilities and freedom to mere usability of space, without sufficiently addressing the wider social, political and economic trends underpinning the production of such spaces.

The second trend linking space and capabilities explores the measurement of quality of life in urban territories. Such studies address important questions of how public resources are distributed in the city and thus have the potential to generate important evidence on spatial segregation (i.e., Blečić, Cecchini and Talu, 2013; Fancello, 2011). Such preoccupations are present in many urban sociology studies, which have brought together data around the availability of infrastructure and levels of vulnerability to produce maps of deprivations in cities. Baud's

Chapter 5 in this volume on mapping spaces of deprivation is a particularly useful contribution in this field, articulating the added value of a multi-dimensional understanding of poverty to the identification of spots of deprivation in cities. While arguing for a more comprehensive data set, the potential contribution of the capability approach in such studies is still inconclusive. The focus on measurement within these initiatives runs the risk of establishing reductionist assumptions about the relationship between the availability of and proximity to urban facilities and the reduction of poverty that contradicts some of the underlying notions of capabilities. Thus, so far in the capability-approach literature the links between concepts of space and poverty have been done in a limited, instrumental and localised manner.

On the other hand, the literature on critical urban theory has focused on examining space to understand structural causes of injustices and inequalities in cities. Although not tackling poverty per se, various writers have elaborated on the dialectical relationship between the *spatiality of injustice* and the *injustice of spatiality* (Dikeç, 2009). The former concept relates to how injustices are manifested in space, while the latter explores how space and the way in which it is produced relates to social, political and economic dynamics structuring injustice. In particular, studies from the critical urban theory perspective explore the linkages between material (distribution of goods and resources) and relational (set of relationships governing distribution of opportunities) aspects of justice in the city, but often neglect the subjective (multiple imaginaries and values associated with lifestyle options) implications of such debates. While Fainstein (2010) recognises the potential of the capability approach in contributing to this articulation of the material, relational and subjective dimensions of justice from a critical urban theory perspective, little has been done to advance this front.

This chapter argues that relating notions of capabilities to debates emerging from critical urban theory can make a valid contribution to reflections on the linkages between poverty and space. This contribution can be elaborated by exploring the relationship between space and the three core concepts articulated by the capability approach on the examination of poverty: abilities, opportunities and aspirations. However, in this chapter, they are positioned in relation to discussions from the literature on critical urban theory. Thus, 'abilities' is understood as agency to pursue social change; 'opportunities' are the structural conditions governing the set of relationships that produces (in)justice; and 'aspirations' are the imaginaries and values associated with various lifestyles that people pursue in the city.

This chapter draws on reflections from three case studies to illustrate these three components of analysis. Firstly, the relationship between space and 'abilities' is interrogated through the exploration of the impacts of a housing typology implemented in an informal settlement-upgrading programme in Salvador da Bahia (Brazil) called Ribeira Azul. Secondly, the relationship between space and 'opportunities' is examined through the analysis of the impact of a delegated management model implemented in an informal settlement-upgrading project in Kisumu, Kenya. Finally, the relationship between space and 'aspirations' is explored through the findings and reflections from a participatory design workshop undertaken with the community of Los Pinos in the periphery of Quito, Ecuador.

Space and abilities

As articulated by Lefebvre, the ways in which spaces are conceived, perceived and lived has a direct relationship with how urban citizens have access to entitlements in the city. Urban citizens' entitlements are shaped by their access to political, social, natural, physical, financial and human assets that can be facilitated or constrained due to how space is produced and experienced. Informal settlement upgradings are examples of spatial welfare programmes, targeting a certain territorial locality with the objective of enhancing local residents' access to assets and thereby reducing poverty. However, underlying such programmes is a complex set of relationships between urban design, delivery strategies, social relations, political structures and economic opportunities that mediate their success in terms of poverty reduction.

The exploration of the impacts of the Ribeira Azul informal settlement-upgrading programme in Salvador da Bahia (Frediani, 2007a) emphasises the linkages between space and the ability of local residents in accessing assets. This research focused on a housing estate called Nova Primavera, which was part of a multi-stage programme called Ribeira Azul, implemented by the state government of Bahia in collaboration with the Italian Associazione Volontari per il Servizio Internazionale (AVSI) and supervised by the Cities Alliance. Implementation took place between 2001 and 2006 with funding of US$80 million from a variety of sources, including a World Bank loan and a grant from the Italian government. Nova Primavera was implemented in 2001, which relocated residents living on stilts from the Cabrito Cove into an adjacent housing estate of nearly four hectares, targeting 312 households. Each housing unit is of around 44 square metres and the design of the housing estate resembles a village, with many open spaces and courtyards, which aims to encourage sociability.

The research focused on the identification of housing aspirations of local residents targeted by the programme, and explored its impact on residents' capability to achieve them. Through focus group activities and semi-structured interviews with local residents, five key housing aspirations were identified and described in Table 3.1 below. Such housing aspirations are associated with the everyday housing practices of local residents, revealing the underlying intentions and values embedded in the way local residents interact with their dwelling spaces.

After identifying the dimensions of housing, the research aimed to explore the impacts of the upgrading programme on residents' freedom to achieve these housing aspirations. One of the main findings of the research revealed that the typology of the design of the housing estate

Table 3.1 Dimensions of housing

Housing aspirations	Definitions
Individualise and expand	Freedom to interact with one's environment as a way of reflecting one's cultural, social, economic and political interests. This dimension was articulated as a mechanism of social mobility by investing in one's property.
Maintain social networks	Freedom to maintain and expand bonds of relationships that are valued as a positive for the housing process. Such networks were articulated as crucial elements to foster a sense of belonging and enhance support systems in their neighbourhoods.
Healthy environment	Freedom to have secure tenure, sustainable access to infrastructure and services, resilience against environmental threats, access to health care and education, and safety.
Participate in decision-making	Freedom to participate in the spaces of decision-making in communities and in the city. This aspect was brought up as an important issue not only in the implementation of upgrading projects, but more widely as a goal of democratisation in the city.
Afford living costs	Freedom to afford the living costs where one lives. This dimension was particularly emphasised due to the fear of upgrading programmes generating costs that households would not be able to cope with, and therefore pushing most vulnerable groups to move into more peripheral and affordable areas.

Source: Compiled from Frediani (2007b).

and the process of designing it compromised residents' freedom to pursue their housing aspirations. In the previous stilt houses, residents felt a strong sense of ownership of their space, as they actively engaged in the incremental process of consolidating their dwelling environment. Teixeira (2002) shows the self-help practices of consolidation by local residents, where initial stilt settlement was originally designed with the intention of construction of future roads and verticalisation of houses. Teixeira's (2002) research showed that apart from building on local and embedded norms of urbanisation, such incremental practices allowed local residents to strengthen social networks and practices of solidarity with family members as well as among neighbours. This was confirmed in the research in Nova Primavera, as local residents stressed the importance of making extensions to their houses as a means of maintaining tight family support systems, especially in a locality where there is a substantial number of single mothers working long hours, and where family members provide crucial support for the upbringing of children.

In contrast to such incremental practices, at Nova Primavera residents were not permitted to expand and individualise their living environment. Such a break from familiar processes of incremental improvement has led to a general detachment from their dwelling spaces. Residents argued that they do not feel a sense of ownership of their houses as they cannot change it as they please, and therefore feel as though they are temporary occupants.

Meanwhile, those that have expanded their houses have experienced unanticipated physical and social consequences. Following ground-

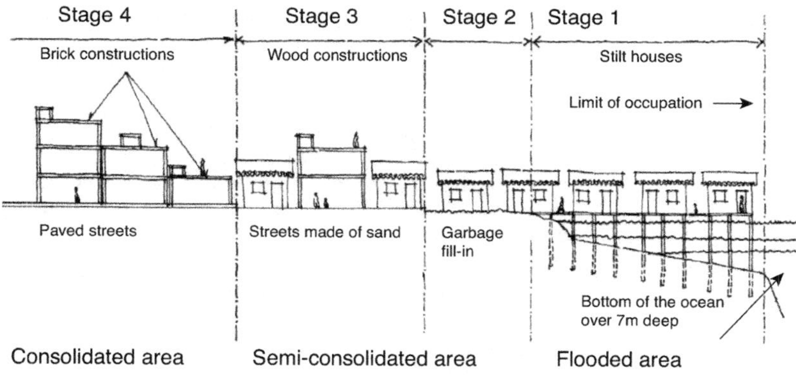

Figure 3.1 Stages of consolidation of stilts
Source: Adapted from Teixeira (2002).

floor extensions, many walls of the houses started to crack. The bottom household argued that it was their space for future growth, while the upper household claimed that it was now their terrace for their own future extension. The design of water and sanitation system also added further tensions between upper and ground floor neighbours. Water tanks of the ground floor households were placed inside a room of the upper flat. To reduce costs of installation, sanitation was based in an interconnected system, meaning that if there were blockages or damages in one of the pipes, both flats would experience disruptions. All these factors combined meant a profound change in social relations, turning bonds of solidarity into feelings of competition and conflict, thereby causing community fragmentation.

Figure 3.2 Vertical terrace units of the Nova Primavera Estate
Source: Picture by Eduardo Teixeira.

This case study highlights the importance of engaging with the relationship between dwelling practices of local residents and their strategies for poverty reduction. Spatial productions that fail to recognise this relationship can potentially create new obstacles and reproduce cycles of marginalisation. In the case of Nova Primavera, it has meant that most vulnerable households ended up selling informally the flats acquired through the upgrading programme and settling in even more peripheral locations of the city (Soares and Espinheira, 2006).

Space and opportunities

Apart from a series of reflections on people's ability to bring about social change, Sen's writings have been particularly important in highlighting the structural conditions causing inequality and poverty. Sen's (1981) examination on the causes of famine were particularly important in shifting a debate focusing merely on the production and availability of food to one focusing on the processes shaping the inequitable distribution of food. Similarly, critical urban theorists (i.e., Harvey, 2009; Marcuse et al., 2009; Soja, 2010) have also articulated the importance of engaging with the structuring processes shaping the production of spaces in the city and consequences in terms of justice. Instead of merely outlining the availability of resources in the city, this literature emphasises that it is fundamental to understand the underlying processes producing unjust geographies.

An examination of a delegated management model (DMM) of water delivery in the informal settlement of Manyatta B in Kisumu, Kenya, reveals the importance for urban poverty-oriented interventions to engage with the underlying processes of production of spaces in the city. Manyatta B contains a population of nearly 30,000 people, with a high-density mix of structure owners and rental tenants. Over 65 per cent of its residents have access to water through communal stand pipes, which experience high risk of contamination, causing frequent incidences of water-borne diseases such as typhoid and dysentery.

With the objective of generating a more effective and efficient water system, the 2002 Kenya Water Act encouraged a move from state-led provision of water to a privately run system, managed and maintained by water service providers (WSPs). In Kisumu, the managing WSP is the Kisumu Water and Sewerage Company Limited (KIWASCO). Within this context, the DMM has been put forward as a strategy for delivering water in informal settlements in Kisumu. This entails the formation of community groups known as 'master operators', who manage the master meter that accounts for the connection between the community facility and KIWASCO's main water pipes. The community groups are responsible for the maintenance and running of water connections within the informal settlement.

In 2013, a group of students from the masters programme in Social Development Practice at the Bartlett Development Planning Unit carried out a four-month research project on the impacts of the DMM on the well-being of local residents in Manyatta B, which included a two-week field trip to Kisumu. In this particular case, the DMM was part of a wider participatory planning project led by international NGO Practical Action, called People's Plans into Practice. The project's objective was to strengthen the capacity of residents of informal settlements in Kisumu and Kitale to participate in decision-making processes in the city. The findings from the students' report revealed that while access to water at Manyatta B has increased, this process of water delivery has not challenged underlying power imbalances shaping the production of the urban environment in Kisumu. Whilst new spaces of participation have been created, and communities' abilities to negotiate with the government and KIWASCO have improved, the DMM has transferred new burdens and responsibilities to local groups without the necessary conditions to cope with these sustainably and equitably (Martinez Cure et al., 2013).

Based on the analysis of water policy documents in Kenya, the students identified six relevant dimensions of well-being that have been impacted by the DMM of water delivery: security of livelihoods, bodily health, water security, safety, empowerment and community cohesion. The evidence of their research in Manyatta B shows that through this model, new water kiosks have been installed in the neighbourhood, which has generated many positive impacts on the well-being of local residents around these dimensions (See Table 3.2 below).

However, the DMM simultaneously reproduced a market logic for service delivery which devolves new responsibilities and risks to communities. This logic is potentially viable in contexts where local groups are resourced and well-organised, but it leaves behind localities and residents that are more vulnerable. KIWASCO requires a series of criteria and fees for the management of a master meter, which presents a series of challenges to community groups identified by NGOs working in this context. Community groups find it challenging to keep records of their accounts and to cope with the maintenance costs caused by theft of the master meter, leakages, bursts and illegal connections. Furthermore, while the intention of increased privatisation was to allow 'water-users' to regulate water service providers, in reality community groups

Table 3.2 Summary of findings of impact of DMM on well-being dimensions

Dimensions	Findings
Security of livelihoods	DMM offered increased opportunities for income generation through the running of water kiosks and points, while also reducing water prices (20-litre jerrycan bought from water vendors reduced from 20 Ksh to 3 Ksh bought from kiosks and water points).
Bodily health	DMM facilitated a reduction in the physical effort required by water fetcher (primarily women and children) and increased consumption of clean water through improved proximity to water points and better affordability.
Water security	Residents expressed that they felt they could rely on the quantity and quality of water provided through the DMM.
Safety	Personal safety for water operator and consumers is perceived to have improved, particularly for women.
Empowerment	DMM project has opened new spaces for dialogue between community residents and the government and KIWASCO.
Community cohesion	Residents expressed that DMM activities facilitated new spaces of interaction, improving local networks and forging bonds of solidarity among residents.

are unable to exert any influence in KIWASCO practices. The government authorities do not mediate this relationship which, due to lack of bargaining capacity of local communities, results in the devolution of risks to community groups as well as in assuring that greater benefits are accrued by KIWASCO, which is able to tap into a vast informal market with little investment and responsibilities.

Although the DMM has the potential to enhance the authority of local residents over their water services, the lack of management support, unequal distribution of risks and limited government mediation has compromised the impact of this model of service delivery on the set of relations governing the distribution of resources in the city. Therefore, the study argues that this mode of public-private partnership reinforces a mode of production in the city that commodifies the delivery and access to resources in a way that can reproduce inequalities, leaving behind the most vulnerable. Despite improvements in particular well-being dimensions due to better access to water, Martinez Cure et al. argue that 'the model as it currently exists serves as a mechanism to cope with the current system of entitlements, rather than working to contest the unequal distribution of resources and recognition' (2013: 34).

Space and aspirations

By approaching poverty as deprivation of capabilities, the literature on the capability approach emphasises the importance of revealing and examining aspirations. Understanding poverty as deprivation of capabilities requires recognising it as a process that relates not only to material and relational aspects of well-being, but also to people's values, informing their visions of the future and lifestyle options. Appadurai's work on 'capacity to aspire' (2004) makes the important distinction between 'wants' being a set of immediate desires, and 'aspirations' which are of 'higher order normative contexts' as part of 'wider ethical and metaphysical ideas which derive from larger cultural norms' (2004: 67–68). Building on Appadurai's definition of aspirations, White (2010) defines this subjective aspect of well-being as

> much more than a random selection of individual perceptions or preferences. Instead these perceptions are seen as constituted in culture and ideology, which in turn structure the material, social, and personal through a cascade of associations that makes them meaningful and designates some as pressing (White, 2010: 162).

Conradie and Robeyns (2013) have explored the role of aspirations in the expansion of capabilities and argue that it has two potential roles: firstly, voicing and reflecting about aspirations can help in prioritising capabilities that are most valued or important for people; secondly, talking and reflecting collectively about aspirations can unlock agency, especially when reflection is associated to action.

Similar interrogations between aspirations and process of change have been unfolding within critical urban theory literature, where the role of space has been explored in unleashing new urban imaginaries. Lefebvre's (1991) writings articulate the importance of thinking about space in contesting the reproduction of the contemporary city, where market-driven hegemonic structures have conditioned all areas of social life, including the ability to envision alternative futures. Thus, a key form of contestation in urban areas has been conflicts over differing spatial imaginaries in the city, where critical urban theorists call for imaginaries to be driven on the vision of the 'city for people, and not for profit' (Brenner, Marcuse and Mayer, 2011). Within such a context, spatial imaginaries are seen as a mechanism to encourage utopian thinking, which is defined by Friedmann (2000) as:

> the capacity to imagine a future that departs significantly from what we know to be a general condition in the present. It is a way

> of breaking through the barriers of convention into a sphere of the imagination where many things beyond our everyday experience become feasible. All of us have this ability, which is inherent in human nature, because human beings are insufficiently programmed for the future. We need a constructive imagination that we can variously use for creating fictive worlds (2000: 463).

A series of participatory design workshops entitled 'Change by Design', run by Architecture Sans Frontières (ASF) – UK, in recent years have focused on how discussions about space can be used to capture the aspirations of urban dwellers. Such aspirations are related to values associated with living in the city. Following Bourdreau's definition, such spatial imaginaries 'are collectively shared internal worlds of thoughts and beliefs that structure everyday life' (Bourdreau, 2007: 2596). Two-week workshops took place in 2009 and 2010 in Salvador da Bahia (Brazil), in 2011 in Nairobi, Kenya, and in 2013 in Quito, Ecuador. The activities of the workshops were designed to contribute to the upgrading of the informal settlements where the activities took place through the elaboration of community plans.

The methodology of the Change by Design process is underpinned by a desire to interrogate spatial imaginaries whilst acknowledging three main concerns: 1) the diversity of interests and identities of local communities; 2) the asymmetries of power between stakeholders in the process of informal settlement upgrading; and 3) the need to unpack issues associated with the various scales of urban interventions. To address such concerns the workshops have partnered with local social movements and grass-roots networks, and focused their activities on the urban experience, identifying linkages between local processes and wider issues associated with urban trends. Activities during the workshop included a series of spatial action research and visioning exercises as well as design charrettes between workshop participants, local residents and key informants. These activities exposed, integrated and overlaid systematisations of various everyday practices of appropriation of the urban environment. Through the discussions, diagnoses were aimed at moving from merely describing the manifestation of injustices, towards reflections that addressed trends and processes driving current living conditions (Frediani, French and Nunez Ferrera, 2011).

After the initial diagnosis, activities focused on the production of design principles[1] based on the aspirations of local residents. For the Change by Design methodology, it is important to position the debate about aspirations in the process of critical engagement with current conditions and urban trends. As articulated by Jacques (2001), the search for such spatial principles aims to establish a bridge between the wider processes of urban change to the everyday manifestations and meaning expressed in and by the production of space. In the context of Salvador da Bahia, the concept of dignified housing emerged as a prominent vision, linking the material, relational and subjective components of housing. In Quito, the process of articulating such spatial imaginaries in the site of Los Pinos (see Box 3.2 below) emerged out of the values associated with different scales (dwelling, community and city) and policy and planning processes. Local residents and activists were interested in linking the localised spatial imaginaries to the broad development agenda of 'buen vivir'.[2] Thus, activities aimed to capture and reveal principles associated with the spaces of 'buen vivir' in the city. Table 3.3 below shows the integrated principles and how they relate to the principles emerging from each scale.

Box 3.2 A brief description of Los Pinos

Los Pinos is a peri-urban site, located on agricultural land owned by the Ministry of Agriculture (MAGAP) in the municipality of Mejia, bordering Quito. The site is an area of approximately 13 hectares, and was previously considered unsuitable for urban use. It was occupied through an 'invasion' seven years ago when over 300 people settled on the plot of unused public land at once.

Instead of building shacks in a disorderly fashion, residents decided to plan the process of occupation. Firstly, the area was divided into plots, and a small number of houses were built through collective self-help strategies (known as *mingas*). An improvement committee was set up, where representatives were elected every two years. New houses were built progressively with the slow upgrading of services. Occupiers have a very strong position against densification, as they do not want to duplicate extremely precarious conditions. Currently, only 62 families are living in their plots. In order for them to stay in the plot and be able to apply for some kind of regularisation, they have to generate a management plan to demonstrate to MAGAP and governmental authorities that the intended use of the area responds to MAGAP requirements as well as to the land use regulations of local municipality. The Change by Design workshop intended to support local residents in developing such a plan. At the same time, it hoped to contribute to the ongoing debates about democratising the production of spaces in Quito and therefore support the realisation of the 'buen vivir' development agenda in an urban context as well as pursue goals expressed by the 'Contrato Social por la Vivienda' (Social Contract for Housing), set up between civil society organisations and the municipality of Quito in 2005.

Table 3.3 Design principles

Integrated principles	Dwelling	Community	City	Policy and planning
Promote socially inclusive processes			Participation in the improvement of environmental conditions	Adaptable processes and product
Articulate relations with external actors			Reinforce existing knowledge networks; increase relations among neighbourhoods	Reinforce existing networks
Strengthen community organisation				Strengthen the organisational structures of the community
Inclusive design of the built environment	Respond to the cultural diversity through multiple housing typologies	Accessible design of the neighbourhood	Integrate urban and rural agendas	Equitable spatial opportunities
Right of permanence			Stability in short and long term in space	Security of tenure
Respond to generational changes	Provide the freedom to expand and adapt according to changing needs	Ability to maintain proximity to family and social networks	Intergenerational solidarity	Intergenerational equity
Economic security	Affordability in the short and long term	Creation of economic opportunities in community spaces	Increase of income-generation opportunities	Integrated development; secure and sustainable provision of services

Live according to one's possibilities		Utilise available resources in its full potential		Strengthen community's capacity to resist shocks, stresses and trends
Basic qualities for dignified housing	Allow the opportunity for independent housing environment; provide quality and comfort for a dignified way of living	Adequate response to the conditions of the locality; ability to maintain proximity to family and social networks		
Access to dignified public services			Equitable access to the city	Dignified quality of spaces and services
Adequate balance between rural and urban lifestyles	Provide an appropriate balance between urban and rural conditions	Appropriate balance between urban and rural conditions	Live in an urban-rural area	
Responsible management of natural resources		Sustainable design of infrastructure and neighbourhood; equal access to resources in the community	Inhabit an environment of healthy lifestyle	

Source: Adapted from Frediani et al. (2014: 88–89).

Some key reflections on the relationship between aspirations and space arose from the workshop in Los Pinos. Firstly, it is interesting to note that while activities were focused on the spatial imaginaries from the territory of Los Pinos, issues discussed were associated not only with that space, but were more broadly concerned with the municipality/region within which the community is located and the wider processes of urbanisation. The focus on aspirations opened up the possibility of a dialogue that engages with multiple scales. Secondly, while the principles identified were cross-scalar, it was difficult to discuss actions that were of the same nature. Participatory design activities ended up generating a rich diagnosis and brought to the table a deliberation of wider contextual issues. However, the localised nature of the participatory process (circumscribed by the boundaries of Los Pinos) made it challenging to deliberate on actions that went beyond the area defined by the community management plan. As a consequence, cross-scalar principles were mainly used to inform localised actions. Nevertheless, the activities generated a set of contextualised aspirations, which were in line with the broad visions of 'buen vivir', but with much clearer resonance to the urban environment, its opportunities and challenges.

While it is not possible to draw any conclusions about how reflecting about aspirations unlocked agency, as articulated by Conradie and Robeyns (2013), according to local partners of the workshop from the Universidad Politecnica Salesiana, this synergy between local and wider development plans generated the potential to enhance communities' leverage to bring about local change. Furthermore, the partners of the workshop[3] also aim to contribute to the realisation of the 'buen vivir' goals by setting precedents that can illustrate the potentials of such collaborative efforts.

Furthermore, the workshop revealed that the focus of the community plan on design principles as opposed to concrete physical interventions had the potential to mediate tensions within the community of Los Pinos without homogenising identities, and at the same time building bonds of solidarity. This potential of the link between space and aspirations has also been articulated by Miessen's (2010) work on 'conflictual participation'. By making reference to Derrida's (1997) work on the politics of friendship, Miessen argues that for constructive conflict to generate critical engagement there is a need to engage with 'friendly enemies' who share a symbolic space: 'they [friendly enemies] agree on the ethnic-political principles that inform the political association, but they disagree about the interpretation of these principles, a struggle between different interpretations of shared principles' (2010: 102).

Thus, the 'Change by Design' work has been interested in finding mechanism through participatory informal-settlement upgrading to construct collaboratively such symbolic meanings of space, while at the same time reveal different ways through which they can be materialised in the built environment through concrete physical and social interventions. The alternatives for the materialisation of the design principles are summarised through a 'portfolio of options' exercise. Through debates elicited by negotiations among concrete design and planning options, this exercise is approached not as mediation or resolution of conflicts, but rather as a mechanism to discuss trade-offs, priorities, differences and values. This resonates with Till's (2005) reflections on transformative participation, when he quotes Forester (1985) to argue that design should move away from a problem-solving approach towards one that focuses on a process of making sense of realities:

> If form giving is understood more deeply as an activity of making sense together, designing may then be situated in a social world where meaning, though often multiple, ambiguous and conflicting, is nevertheless a perpetual practical accomplishment. (Forester, 1985: 14)

In this manner, this spatially led participatory engagement stimulates imaginaries about the type of city one wants to live in, while at the same time, constructs concrete alternatives to materialise aspirations. From this perspective, the outcomes of design are then not purely associated with its product, but also with the process of deliberating, reflecting, and therefore enhancing collective capabilities to bring about change. From this perspective, space acquires an instrumental role in instigating and constructing the multiple dimensions of well-being in the city and unleashing collective agency to make localised improvements while opening up avenues to struggle towards addressing the structural drivers of urban poverty.

Conclusions

The three case studies explored in this chapter aim to illustrate some of the linkages between the concept of poverty and space when analysing informal settlement-upgrading initiatives through a capability perspective. When evaluating the impacts of the upgrading programme in Salvador, the relationship between space and abilities highlights the importance of engaging with the impact of physical interventions on residents' agency. Instead of minimising the side effects of upgrading programmes, this research calls for a reorientation of upgrading processes, moving away from a physical deterministic approach, to one that understands space as a social product. The research calls for approaches that can recognise local spatial practices as a key component in the reduction of poverty, as they mediate social networks, support systems and sense of belonging as well as economic opportunities.

The case study of Kisumu, exploring the relationship between space and opportunities reveals the importance of engaging in the various scales of the processes of urbanisation when tackling poverty. The case study illustrates how localised approaches might not necessarily provide mechanisms to address structural drivers reproducing injustices in the city. In such contexts, the reflections highlight the limitations of spatially targeted welfare approaches and call for an upgrading process that is based on setting precedents in terms of a new set of relationships governing the production of spaces in the city. The renegotiation of relationships means engaging with not only the ways in which responsibilities are shared but most importantly who absorbs risks. The role of the state is emphasised, supporting communities in their negotiation with the private sector and creating the conditions for more equitable partnerships.

Finally, the reflections from the Change by Design workshops on participatory design highlight the importance of space in the debate about aspirations and the multiple dimensions of poverty. Spatially based participatory approaches, focusing on values and imaginaries have the potential to stimulate agency and bonds of solidarity while recognising multiple forms of living in the city. In this sense, spaces of participation in urban interventions are located not only in forum and focus group discussions, but also in the practices of everyday life, where spatial production has a symbolic meaning related to how people value living in the city. The role of such participatory initiatives becomes to support the reading of such meanings, and to generate alternative options to bring about positive change. This chapter hopes to engage in the debate on how capabilities are contested in spaces, whilst also showing how spaces are mediators of capabilities, unleashing imaginaries, conditioning opportunities and shaping agency.

Notes

1. The concept of design principles is drawn from Boano et al. (2013).
2. 'Buen vivir' is literately translated as 'good living'. This agenda emerged from indigenous movements as an alternative to market-driven development

plans by articulating the need to address social, cultural, environmental and economic issues in an interconnected manner.

3. Workshop partners included Universidad Politecnica Salesiana, Instituto de Altos Estudios Nacionales, neighbourhood committee of Los Pinos as well as the National Confederation of Neighbourhoods of Ecuador (Confederacion Nacional de Barrios del Ecuador, CONBADE).

References

Appadurai, A. (2004). The capacity to aspire: Culture and the terms of recognition, in: V. Rao and M. Walton (eds), *Culture and Public Action*. Stanford: Stanford University Press.

Blečić, I., Cecchini, A. B. and Talu, V. (2013). The capability approach in urban quality of life and urban policies: Towards a conceptual framework. *Urban and Landscape Perspectives, 14*: 269–288.

Brenner, N., Marcuse, P. and Mayer, M. (2011). *Cities for People, Not for Profit – Critical Urban Theory and the Right to the City*. London: Routledge.

Boano, C., Hunter, W. and Newton, C. (2013). *Contested Urbanism in Dharavi*. London: The Bartlett Development Planning Unit.

Boudreau, J. (2007). Making new political spaces: Mobilizing spatial imaginaries, instrumentalizing spatial practices and strategically using spatial tools. *Environment and Planning A, 39*: 2593–2611.

Conradie, I. and Robeyns, I. (2013). Aspirations and human development interventions. *Journal of Human Development and Capabilities, 14*(4): 559–580.

Derrida, J. (1997). *Politics of Friendship*. London: Verso.

Dikeç, M. (2009). Justice and the spatial imagination, in: P. Marcuse, J. Connolly, J. Novy, I. Olivo, C. Potter and J. Steil (eds), *Searching for the Just City*. London: Routledge.

Fancello, G. (2011). *A Survey of Applications of the CA on Urban Quality of Life*. Paper presented at the 8th annual conference of the HDCA, 6–8 September 2011, The Hague, The Netherlands.

Fainstein, S. (2010). *The Just City*. London: Cornell University Press.

Forester, J. (1985). Designing: Making sense together in practical conversations. *Journal of Architectural Education*, 38(3): 119–133.

Frediani, A. A. (2007a). Amartya Sen, the World Bank, and the redress of urban poverty: A Brazilian case study. *Journal of Human Development*, 8(1): 133–152.

Frediani, A. A. (2007b). *Housing freedom, Amartya Sen and Urban Development Policies – Squatter Settlement Upgrading in Salvador da Bahia, Brazil*. PhD in Planning. Oxford: Oxford Brookes University.

Frediani, A. A. (2010). Sen's capability approach as a framework to the practice of development. *Development in Practice, 20*(2): 173–187.

Frediani, A. A., French, M. A. and Nunez Ferrera, I. (2011). *Change by Design: Building Communities through Participatory Design*. New Zealand: Urban Culture Press.

Frediani, A. A., De Carli, B., Nunez Ferrera, I. and Shinkins, N. (2014). *Change by Design: New Spatial Imaginations for Los Linos*. Oxford: ASF-UK.

Friedmann, J. (2000). The good city: In defense of utopian thinking. *International Journal of Urban and Regional Research, 24*(2): 460–472.

Harvey, D. (2009). *Social Justice and the City*. Athens, Georgia: The University of Georgia Press.
Jacques, P. B. (2001). *Estetica da Ginga*. Rio de Janeiro: Casa da Palavra.
Lefebvre, H. (1991). *The Production of Space*. Oxford: Blackwell.
Lewis, F. (2012). Auditing the built environment. *Journal of Human Development and Capabilities*, *13*(2): 295–315.
Marcuse, P., Connolly, J., Novy, J., Olivo, I., Potter, C. and Steil, J. (eds) (2009). *Searching for the Just City*. London: Routledge.
Martinez Cure, F. A., Montero Prieto, M. J. and Richardson, A. (2013). Delegated management model: Water kiosk, Manyatta B, in: A. A. Frediani, J. Walker and S. Butcher (eds), *Participatory Informal Settlement Upgrading and Wellbeing in Kisumu, Kenya*. Report of MSc Social Development Practice Field Trip, The Bartlett Development Planning Unit, London.
Miessen, M. (2010). *The Nightmare of Participation*. Berlin: Sternberg.
Nussbaum, M. (2011). *Creating Capabilities: The Human Development Approach*. Cambridge, Mass.: Harvard University Press.
Oosterlaken, I. (2009). Design for development: A capability approach. *Design Issues*, 25(4): 91–102.
Robeyns, I. (2005). The capability approach: A theoretical survey. *Journal of Human Development*, 6(1): 191–215.
Sen, A. (1981). *Poverty and Famines: An Essay on Entitlement and Deprivation*. Oxford: Oxford University Press.
Sen, A. (1999). *Development as Freedom*. Oxford: Oxford University Press.
Soares, M. C. and Epinheira, C. G. D. (2006). Conjuntos habitacionais em Salvador-BA e a transitória inserção social. *Risco*, *3*: 57–65.
Soja, E. (2010). *Seeking Spatial Justice*. Minneapolis: University of Minnesota Press.
Talu V. and Blečić I. (2012). Pedestrian mobility as a fundamental urban right: The possible contribution of children to urban walkability, in: M. Campagna, A. De Montis, F. Isola, S. Lai, C. Pira and C. Zoppi (eds), *Planning Support Tools: Policy Analysis, Implementation and Evaluation*. Proceedings of the seventh international conference on informatics and urban and regional planning INPUT 2012, Franco Angeli.
Teixeira, E. (2002). *Os Alagados da Bahia: Intervenções Públicas e Apropriação Informal do Espaço Urbano*. Salvador: UFBA.
Till, J. (2005). The negotiation of hope, in: P. B. Jones, D. Petrescu and J. Till (eds), *Architecture and Participation*. London: Spon Press, 23–41.
White, S. (2010). Analysing wellbeing: a framework for development practice. *Development in Practice*, *20*(2): 158–172.

4

Constructing Informality and Ordinary Places: A Place-Making Approach to Urban Informal Settlements

Melanie Lombard

Introduction

Since the 1960s, understandings of urban informal settlements have constantly evolved. Almost since this urban phenomenon was first observed – coinciding with patterns of industrialisation and urbanisation in 1950s Latin America – it has been accompanied by debates about the meaning and extent of urban informality, understood as closely linked to urban poverty. Although many advances have been made in terms of theoretical understandings of these places, and the policy responses that ensue, they are still subject to disproportionate levels of marginalisation, including effects ranging from discrimination to eviction and displacement. Some observers suggest that this is reflective of critical gaps in urban theory, deriving from the dominance of particular epistemologies and methodologies within urban studies, which have led to the prevalence of 'apocalyptic and dystopian narratives of the slum'[1] (Roy, 2011: 224). Such accounts reveal the limits of knowledge about urban informality, based as it is on certain privileged circuits of knowledge production which frame urban informal settlements in particular ways. This may lead to 'sanctioned ignorance' (Spivak, 1999 in Roy, 2011: 228), the unseeing of the productive spaces of informality that constitute significant swathes of today's cities; or to stereotyping of particular places and people in terms of their 'illegal', 'illegitimate' status in the urban environment. Both processes contribute to the marginalisation of urban informal settlements.

In response, it has been suggested that urban theorists must seek to understand how knowledge is produced about these marginalised places and their residents. In contrast to technified accounts of urban poverty, which obscure the narratives of those most intimately affected, researchers must uncover and emphasise the perspective of the poor. Exploring the limits of urban theory through a detailed examination of how certain types of understanding about the city are produced and reproduced suggests laying bare processes of knowledge production, and specifically, how they can contribute to marginalisation. This chapter argues that an important element of this is an understanding of how spatial and social processes interact. Following Myers' (2003) suggestion that to understand diverse pressures on urban space[2] in the context of marginalisation, the social meanings of the built environment must be interrogated, this chapter seeks to explore the linkages between social and spatial elements of marginalisation, through a focus on the socio-spatial construction of urban informal settlements as places. Such a focus has the potential to uncover both the processes of knowledge production and the limits to existing knowledge.

More specifically, this chapter presents a framework for foregrounding the spatial dimension of urban informal settlements, using critical social geographic conceptions of 'place' and employing 'place-making' as an analytical lens. Place-making is seen here as the construction of place by a variety of different actors and means, which may be discursive and political, but also small-scale, spatial, social and cultural. As a way of understanding the socio-spatial nature of construction, it captures the messy, dynamic and contextualised processes that construct urban informal settlements, which may include the role of discourses in constructing specific marginalised places. Thus while place-making has the capacity to link individual and collective constructive efforts in place, it also illuminates the relationship between social and spatial marginalisation. In this sense, it highlights gaps in urban theory and the limits of knowledge about these places, relating to particular empirical and theoretical debates.

This chapter focuses on urban informality as a dimension of urban poverty, and looks specifically at shelter informality. It is important to note that while urban informal settlements are frequently associated with poverty, they are not exclusively populated by the urban poor; indeed, urban informality extends beyond the urban poor to encompass the actions of different sectors including middle- and high-income urban residents, the state, and business interests (Roy, 2005; McFarlane, 2012). Conversely, nor do all urban poor live in informal settlements (Bromley,

1978 and see Baud, Chapter 5 of this collection); however, informal settlements may be seen as part of a wider subset of urban poverty experiences, and offer a starting point for describing poverty in terms of the scale of shelter deprivation in cities (UN-Habitat, 2006: 26). Specifically, '[p]oor quality and often insecure, hazardous and overcrowded housing' has been seen as one element of multi-dimensional poverty (Mitlin and Satterthwaite, 2013: 279). However, this chapter argues that rather than reducing informal settlements to a manifestation of urban poverty, and thus downplaying the human agency so fundamental in their construction and constitution, shelter informality offers a way of understanding the spatial dynamics of urban poverty, and gives a more nuanced view of the spatial marginalisation associated with this through a focus on the lived experience of the urban poor.

In particular, this chapter draws on two recent bodies of literature: postcolonial approaches to urban studies which posit the idea of 'ordinary places' in the urban setting, and ethnographic work on urban poverty in informal neighbourhoods. In doing so, it speaks to recent debates about the positionality of theorists writing on urban poverty, informality and the Global South more generally. Responding to the disjuncture between 'works coming out of the South' and 'works about the South' (Rao, 2006: 228), calls for a 'postcolonial comparative urbanism' (Robinson, 2006; McFarlane, 2010) have been taken up and in some cases challenged (e.g., Mabin, 2014: 31). However, the significance of the postcolonial move for urban informal settlements lies in its potential influence on specific technical and professional rationalities, particularly in urban interventions such as planning. Watson (2011: 151) suggests that 'planning perspectives from one part of the globe have shaped a dominant and persistent planning rationality which in turn sets standards of "normality" regarding "proper" living environments in clean, orderly, and "modern" cities'. This chapter urges consideration of the positionality of analyses of poverty and informality, as a means of thinking through and bringing to light specific channels of knowledge production, and the effects that these may have on understandings of and responses to urban poverty.

In support of this, ideas around 'place' from social and cultural geography are proposed as an alternative analytical framework for understanding urban informal settlements. This is undertaken through a brief history of influential theories with discernible effects on policy and practice relating to informal settlements, followed by an examination of theories of place, and a detailed exposition of place-making as an alternative analytical lens for broadening understandings of urban informal settlements. A broad focus on Latin America guides the discussion, although work from other areas is also drawn on where relevant.

Approaches to urban informality

It has been suggested that understandings of the informal city have been dominated by Latin American experiences, originating with the Chicago School's descriptions of massive urbanisation in 'Third World' cities in the 1950s and 1960s (AlSayyad, 2004). In this setting, 'urban informals' were a type of new city migrant condemned to marginal status (Abrams, 1964), often seen as passive members of a 'culture of poverty' (Lewis, 1967), reinforcing the association of informal housing with 'delinquency, breakdown and general social malaise' (Hall, 2002: 272–274). In the 1960s and 1970s, this dominant paradigm of marginality was challenged, again by research carried out in Latin American cities, although often by Western researchers (e.g., Mangin, 1967; Peattie, 1970; Lomnitz, 1977; Lloyd, 1979). Perlman (1976) was particularly influential, arguing that marginality served in Brazil and across Latin America as 'both a myth and a description of social reality' (Perlman, 1976: 242). Contrary to the popular view of the urban poor living in shantytowns characterised by social disorganisation and radical politics, she found that *favela* dwellers were socially well-organised and cohesive, culturally optimistic with aspirations for their children's education and their housing, economically hard working, and politically neither apathetic nor radical: 'In short, *they have the aspirations of the bourgeoisie, the perseverance of pioneers, and the values of patriots*. What they do *not* have is an opportunity to fulfill their aspirations' (Perlman, 1976: 242–243, original emphasis). In fact, the myth of marginality was used for the social control of the poor, who far from being marginal, were integrated into society 'on terms that often caused them to be economically exploited, politically repressed, socially stigmatized and culturally excluded' (Bayat, 2000 in AlSayyad, 2004: 9).

Also during the 1960s and 1970s, the concept of 'self-help' was developed, referring to housing where the owner-occupier constructs some or all of the accommodation, with or without (professional) help. Turner (1968, 1972), working in Peru, was among the first to suggest that dweller control in housing was important. The lack of government will, resources and flexibility to provide the right kind of shelter, combined with a great potential resource in the desire, energy and initiative of families to house themselves, led to his prescription of 'greater user autonomy in the provision of housing' (Turner and Fichter, 1972: xi).

The idea was widely influential in policy terms, with sites-and-services and upgrading policies implemented in many countries during the late 1960s and early 1970s, but it also generated considerable criticism (e.g., Ward, 1982), particularly due to suggestions that 'self-help releases government from its responsibility to provide adequate housing as a basic need for its low-income population' (Moser and Peake, 1987: 5).

The legacy of 'self-help' was arguably a new era of the privatisation of housing supply, championed by the World Bank, which saw large-scale programmes of tenure legalisation (sometimes termed formalisation or regularisation)[3] promoted by international agencies and national governments across the Global South over several decades. In some Latin American countries such as Peru and Mexico, urban land tenure legalisation programmes were instigated in the 1960s and 1970s, in the context of democratisation and poverty reduction measures. More recently, the resurgence of formalisation policies for land and housing has been framed as congruent with 'micro-entrepreneurial solutions to urban poverty', paving the way for further withdrawal of government support (Davis, 2006: 71–72). According to De Soto (2000), whose work is often associated with this approach, provision of legal titles is the solution to informality and poverty: creating property ownership (through titling) and legalisation of assets gives poor people the security of tenure they need to invest in their homes and businesses, and hence invigorate the economy. The prevalence of regularisation programmes in many developing countries, particularly in Latin America, means that evictions and removals have been replaced by relative tolerance of illegal tenure developments. However, such programmes have also been criticised for their oversimplification of complex issues, political usage, and failure to generate expected wealth (Miranda, 2002); ultimately, then, they have not offered a 'solution' to informality.

In fact, some suggest that levels of urban informality are increasing, linked to the liberalisation of cities as one of the consequences of globalisation (AlSayyad, 2004). In this view, urbanisation produces specific spatial structures and forms supporting the (re)creation of social relations necessary for the reproduction of capital, meaning ordinary urban dwellers are marginalised and powerless in the face of mobile capital, part of a new geography of social exclusion 'made up of multiple black holes ... throughout the planet' (Castells, 1998: 164–165). In globalising cities, this has led to low-income shelter crises, due to contradictions between different housing sub-markets (Shatkin, 2004); more broadly, it concurs with influential analyses framing urban informal settlements as a manifestation of urban crisis. For example, Davis (2006: 15–17) locates the cause of urban informal settlements primarily with the imposition of structural adjustment programmes (SAPs) in the 1980s by the World Bank and the International Monetary Fund, which made life unsustainable for millions of rural poor, forcing them to move to cities with resultant explosive urbanisation. In this way, 'cities have become a dumping ground for a surplus population working in unskilled, unprotected and low-wage informal service industries and trade' (UN-Habitat, 2003 in Davis, 2006: 175).

While this account has been contested in some contexts,[4] certainly, in many Latin American countries, observers suggest that structural reforms have perpetuated urbanisation trends originating in the post-war import substitution era, as continued 'massive urban migration attests to a countryside deemed nonviable by neoliberal development models' (Perreault and Martin, 2005: 197). Recent work highlighting the spatial dimension of urban poverty in the region has shown how deindustrialising cities in the context of globalisation have led to the exclusion of large sectors of the urban population, and a concomitant expansion of informal activities; meanwhile, older patterns of informal urbanisation have been accompanied by massive development of state-built social housing and privately constructed elite enclaves on the urban periphery, exacerbating existing inequalities (Cordera et al., 2008; Hernandez et al., 2010; Rodgers et al., 2012; Angotti, 2013). Within Latin American cities, the spatial imprint of neo-liberalism can be seen in urban fragmentation and increasing levels of inequality between rich and poor areas, as gated communities exist side by side with, but entirely segregated from, informal neighbourhoods (Perreault and Martin, 2005; Bayón and Saraví, 2013). A general consensus exists regarding the persistence of the formal/informal divide, although some warn against the simplistic opposition of the *asfalto* (paving) to the *morro* (hill or favela) (Varley, 2013: 13).

Meanwhile, current critical debates on poverty more generally highlight the prevailing dominance of certain views, led by international agencies with an interest in 'the social construction of poverty as the target of international assistance' (Moser, 2009). In this understanding, poverty is 'an entity brought into being through the institutions established to describe, quantify and locate it' (Escobar, 1995 in Moser, 2009: 15). Such conceptualisations as the basis for understanding and acting upon poverty remained dominated by the view of powerful groups rather than the urban poor (Mitlin and Satterthwaite, 2013). Drawing on earlier work by Chambers among others, these critical debates suggest that multi-dimensional understandings of poverty, taking account of elements including shelter and power, are still rarely employed in poverty assessments by national and international agencies, thus masking the structural causes of poverty (Wratten, 1995).

Urban ethnography, poverty and informality

A response to these debates can be found in ethnographic (and often longitudinal) studies by anthropologists and urban theorists in specific communities, which explicitly connect the production of informal settlements to contemporary debates on urban poverty and globalisation. In particular, studies by Moser (2009) and Auyero (1999a; 1999b) from Latin America, and Simone (2004) and Bayat (2004) from Africa, explore how global forces exert pressure on local informal settlements through economic crises, structural adjustment and neo-liberal governance, while simultaneously emphasising the importance of local determinants in shaping particular manifestations of liberalisation in specific cities and their effects on the urban poor. For example, Auyero (1999a: 47) highlights the interaction of rising unemployment, educational exclusion and welfare retrenchment through the lived experience of residents of an informal settlement in Buenos Aires, Argentina, to show how 'these structural processes are perceived and translated into concrete emotions, cognitions and actions by the residents of the slum'. While these processes contribute to increasing marginalisation, they may simultaneously offer opportunities for local urban poor communities to draw on global connections and resources. Cities constitute 'platforms of mediation' through which endogenous groups link to the wider world (Simone, 2004: 18). Thus, in an increasingly globalised setting, the interaction of local and global factors may be the decisive factor in the improvement of living conditions for the urban poor (Auyero, 1999a; Moser, 2009), as the significance of urban informality increases rather than diminishes.

As well as reincorporating local processes into debates about the links between globalisation and urban informality, the detailed empirical research that underpins these studies explicitly challenges stereotypes emerging from essentialist understandings of poverty and informality that still dominate development and urban debates. In response to the 'decontextualisation' and 'technification' of poverty by international agencies (Moser, 2009: 23), ethnographic approaches reveal the heterogeneity of urban poor communities and the informal neighbourhoods they often inhabit, thus highlighting the complexity of measuring, contextualising and responding to urban poverty and informality. Foregrounding the agency of the poor by emphasising the views of urban communities confirms their self-reliance, echoing earlier debates on self-help and highlighting the 'huge creativity, pride and resilience of poor communities' (Moser, 2009: xvii). This is not to romanticise the situation of poor and informal urban communities; in the context of constraints and powerful elite interests, agency may be characterised by 'quiet encroachment', in the sense of 'largely atomized, and prolonged mobilization with episodic collective action', rather than organised resistance (Bayat, 2004: 90). However, by highlighting the struggle and negotiation which poor communities engage in to obtain goods and services, these accounts 'find ways of making visible urban possibilities that have been crowded out or left diffuse or opaque' in debates that often essentialise the identities of informal settlement dwellers (Simone, 2004: 14).

Roy (2011: 224) picks up this thread in her incisive yet sympathetic critique of 'subaltern urbanism', which she locates in accounts of the 'slum' as 'terrain of habitation, livelihood and politics... [which seek] to confer recognition on spaces of poverty and forms of popular agency that often remain invisible and neglected'. While this paradigm offers an important challenge to apocalyptic portrayals of slums, the political agency assigned to urban dwellers risks attributing them with an essentialist 'slum habitus' (Roy, 2011: 228). Rather than attaching a deterministic informal 'identity' to informal settlement residents, Roy argues we must aim to understand the conditions under which knowledge about 'slums' is produced, in order to understand the gaps in history and representations, 'the limits of archival and ethnographic recognition'; in other words, what is left out of urban theory (Roy, 2011: 231).

The dominance of particular paradigms, based on the privileging of certain circuits of knowledge production, is exemplified by dualistic framings of informality. Whether portraying urban informal settlements as crisis or heroism, such framings tend to view formality as fundamentally separate from informality, implying that formalisation is the 'solution' to informality (Roy, 2005). Accounts which portray informality as the opposite of formality tend to negate the reciprocal relationship which often exists between 'informal' and 'formal' sectors. In reality, this relationship is often so messy and tangled as to make the two supposed opposites anything but clearly delineated. This observation is not new (see, for example, Bromley, 1978); yet it is surprising how these problematic assumptions about informality still endure today, despite years of research and policy.

In response, this chapter suggests that it is through detailed empirical research into how informal settlement residents are engaged in constructing cities that understandings of urban informality may be broadened. Precisely, it is through interrogating the relationship between social processes and spatial outcomes that a properly theorised relation between the social and spatial fabric of specific marginalised places can be established. While the above debates emphasise the importance of social relations in the construction of urban informality, usually in a specific place, space as a dimension of informality is frequently present but rarely foregrounded. One exception is Myers' (2003: 8) study of colonialism and space in urban Africa, which suggests drawing on 'cultural geography's rich tradition of studying the built environment for social meaning' to understand the diverse influences which exert pressure on urban space in the context of marginalisation. By linking processes of marginalisation to urban form, space is employed as a means of understanding the impact of urban policies and interventions, but also the constructive efforts of the urban poor majority on the urban environment (Myers, 2003).

Informed by this approach, and more broadly by the long tradition of research highlighting the agency of informal urban dwellers, this chapter suggests a focus on place, and specifically place-making, to explore the spatial and social construction of urban informal settlements. This includes their discursive production through knowledge circuits, in order to reveal the role of place in the reproduction of certain stereotypes, as well as resistance to these. Building on the ethnographic studies mentioned above, it suggests emphasising informal settlement residents' agency through detailed qualitative exploration of their individual and collective place-making activities as a critical driving force for the construction of neighbourhoods and hence cities. This approach allows for an understanding of how specific settlements are discursively constructed from beyond as well as within the neighbourhood; in other words, understanding how dominant discourses at the local and general level construct settlement residents as 'an object to be removed, as an out-of-place population, as the obnoxious and repugnant other, always undeserving and tainted' (Auyero, 1999a: 64). In this way, exploring the discursive construction of specific places in a particular city may reveal both reproduction of and resistance to particular stereotypes relating to urban informality. Linking local discourses to more general understandings of urban informal settlements reveals gaps in existing knowledge and suggests an 'itinerary of recognition' (Roy, 2011: 299) in support of building theory from the ground up. The idea of 'ordinary cities' provides a useful starting point in this sense.

Ordinary cities and the everyday

Robinson (2002: 531–533) has argued for moving away from a developmentalist perspective that views cities of the Global South in terms of what they lack, and towards a view of cities as 'ordinary'; in other words, as 'diverse, creative, modern and distinctive, with the possibility to imagine (within the not inconsiderable constraints of contestations and uneven power relations) their own futures and distinctive forms of city-ness' (Robinson, 2002: 546). Her call for the 'decolonisation' of urban studies, in order to 'produce a cosmopolitan, postcolonial urban studies' (Robinson, 2002: 533) has led others to suggest transcending standardised categories by 'bringing into view and theorising a range of ordinary spaces' in the urban setting (Legg and McFarlane, 2008: 7).

The idea of the 'ordinary' or 'everyday' nature of cities offers a potential alternative for understanding urban informal settlements in terms of the processes which construct them and the agency of actors there. Viewing the city as the site of flows and difference, and seeing 'the constant hum of the everyday and prosaic web of practices that makes the city into such a routinely frenetic place', may open up new possibilities for emancipatory potential through 'numerous forms of ordinary urban sociality' (Amin and Thrift, 2004: 232–234). Gilbert's (1994: 90) description of informal settlement consolidation in Latin American cities echoes this, painting a picture of collective efforts to improve individual dwellings which take place in an atmosphere of gaiety, as 'gradually, what began as a sea of shanties becomes a consolidated settlement'. This resonates with the idea of conviviality, 'autonomous and creative intercourse among persons, and the intercourse of persons with their environment' (Illich, 1980 in Peattie, 1998: 247), suggesting the significance of everyday social contact but also of the context or place in which it occurs and the reciprocal effects that these elements have on each other.

'Ordinary' cities, then, offers a potential alternative for understanding urban informal settlements. Following De Certeau's (1984) suggestion that everyday practices in urban places provide an analytical focus for understanding the city, urban geographers have asserted that 'focusing on the everyday encourages [us] to address the importance of people as more or less autonomous actors who creatively engage with, and shape, their surroundings' (Holloway and Hubbard, 2001: 37). This is all the more important in places commonly categorised as 'disorderly', where a 'peopled approach' may be necessary to disentangle the multiple forces which shape the urban environment and foreground the agency of the marginalised majority (Myers, 2003: xv). Drawing on these ideas, a place-based approach to the investigation of informal settlements allows us to understand how they are constructed spatially and socially: places are 'the stuff of stories, *part of the little histories of the world*' (Friedmann, 2007: 260, original emphasis), and seeing the world in terms of places means seeing its richness and complexity.

Urban informal settlements: ordinary places?

Place is understood broadly as spaces that people are attached to, or 'meaningful location' (Cresswell, 2004: 7). In recent years, human geographers have suggested that 'it has become axiomatic ... that as people construct places, places construct people' (Holloway and Hubbard, 2001: 7). As a socio-spatial construct, 'place' is constituted by location, locale and sense of place (Agnew, 2005). Sense of place, perhaps the most difficult to capture, is described as 'the subjective and emotional attachment people have to place' (Cresswell, 2004: 7), underpinning the social element of place which has preoccupied human geography more recently. This implies a relation with power, opening the possibility for contestation and conflict among different understandings and experiences of places, and about the idea of 'place' itself. Indeed, Cresswell (2004: 12) specifies that '[p]lace, at a basic level, is space invested with meaning in the context of power'. Different groups imbue space and place with different meanings, uses and values (Holloway and Hubbard, 2001). Places do not have single, essential identities; rather, there are multiple identities for any given place, which may be a source of richness but also conflict (Massey, 1991). Cresswell (2004: 51) distinguishes between social constructionist and phenomenological approaches to place, which are particularly relevant in the setting of urban informal settlements, in terms of foregrounding agency and challenging stereotypes. The following sections explore these approaches through a focus on place and lived experience; place and power; and place as process.

Place and lived experience

One of the best-known phenomenological approaches to 'place' is Relph's (1976) *Place and Placelessness*, which sought to respond to abstract discussions of environmental issues that formed the basis of decision-making at that time. As he put it,

> distinctive and diverse places are manifestations of a deeply felt involvement for those places by the people who live in them, and ... for

> many such a profound attachment to place is as necessary and significant as a close relationship with other people (Relph, 1976: i).

Place attachment derives from a deep association with places, constituting a vital source of individual and cultural identity and security. The conditions for an authentic relationship with place are 'a complete awareness and acceptance of responsibility for your own existence' (Relph, 1976: 78) as the basis for a state of 'existential insiderness'.

Relph was heavily influenced by Tuan, who also saw place as the product of and inextricably linked to experience (Tuan, 1977: 201). According to Tuan (1977: 18), experience of a place is through 'all the senses as well as with the active and reflective mind'. Undifferentiated space becomes place when it is thoroughly familiar to us, through kinaesthetic and perceptual experience, as much as formal learning (Tuan, 1977: 72–73). The almost unconscious, repeated, routine activities that we carry out in our everyday lives contribute to a sense of place and the intimacy of place attachment, although '[a]t the time we are not aware of any drama; we do not know that the seeds of lasting sentiment are being planted' (Tuan, 1977: 143). In fact, people's everyday, incremental investment in a place characterises it.

Phenomenological approaches' emphasis on place as the locus of meaning and indeed of human existence offers a human-centred focus and a way of seeing urban informal settlements as sites of complex socio-spatial interaction. Similar to the ethnographic approaches outlined above, the focus on everyday, lived experience emphasises the often-neglected residents' view, and incorporates this into more complex understandings of the city. However, critics suggest that phenomenological approaches are blind to diversity and difference in the experience of place (Cresswell, 2004: 25), exposing their lack of an account of power. Their assumption that everybody has equal claims to place is underpinned by the problematic idea of place as 'essentially a static concept' (Tuan, 1977: 179). In the context of urban informal settlements, place is often anything but static: these places are often conceptualised in the Latin American urban context as places in progress, suggested by the term 'consolidation' ('*consolidación*'), frequently used to describe informal development processes (e.g., Gough and Kellett, 2001). Such neighbourhoods are premised on the idea of change and improvement, captured by the term 'slums of hope' (Lloyd, 1979).

The phenomenological approach outlined above is, then, methodologically useful due to its emphasis on the agentic and experiential elements of human action at the level of specific places, fundamental to constructing informal settlements. However, a critical approach to place in a world of social hierarchies suggests understanding it not simply as an outcome of social processes, but as a tool in the creation, maintenance and transformation of relations of domination, oppression and exploitation (Cresswell, 2004: 29), and ultimately in the production of knowledge about urban informal settlements.

Place and power

Using the concept of place to explore urban informal settlements thus potentially illuminates elements relating to power[5] that may be overlooked in debates on informality and poverty. While multi-dimensional approaches suggest that power is an important dimension of poverty (Mitlin and Satterthwaite, 2013), analyses of informality often refer implicitly to issues of power through a focus on particular forms of power relations, especially between 'the state' and 'the community'. There is still a tendency to take a zero-sum or binary view that sees low-income residents as the 'losers' in power relations, even where resistance is seen as possible. Critical geographic approaches to place offer a response to this: by focusing on the complexities of power in place, it may be possible to better understand the intricate, entangled processes relating to power that occur in urban informal settlements.

Sharp et al. (2000) argue that splitting resistance and domination falls into the orthodox trap of equating 'power' with 'domination'. Instead, these authors argue for a more nuanced understanding of geographies of power, rejecting the binary conception of domination in opposition to resistance, in favour of the messy, spatialised entanglements of 'domination/resistance'. 'Entanglement' suggests the endless circulations of power but also the spatiality of domination/resistance within power, and thus possibilities for change. Here, power is 'conceptualised as an amalgam of *forces, processes, practices* and *relations*, all of which spin out along the precarious threads of society and space' (Sharp et al., 2000: 20, original emphasis). Neither dominating nor resisting power is total, but fragmentary, uneven and inconsistent, hence the use of the Foucauldian dyad 'domination/resistance', which expresses a reciprocal rather than oppositional or binary relation.

Understanding these entanglements of power requires '[a] thorough grounding in the actual urban landscapes and in the biographies of those who helped shape them, paired with those who live in them and give them meaning' (Myers, 2003: 11), to which a place-based approach is well suited. In the context of informal settlements, 'power' may mean, in particular, the power to determine place meaning, expectations of what places are for and what is appropriate behaviour in place. In this sense, it relates to the consolidation of social structures and hierarchies in spatial terms, which may reflect and reproduce processes of marginalisation in support of existing power structures. For example, the 'irregular' nature of many *colonias* in Mexico derives from the sale of *ejidal* land, in the context of an unregulated, private land market sanctioned by the state. This means that residents are dependent on the authorities' decision to legalise their tenure, and thereby regularise their status, affecting which services they can request.

However, residents' activities revealed in research from Mexican urban informal settlements showed how from the point of land acquisition onwards they are involved in the everyday appropriation of space, gradually conferring their own meanings onto the formerly agricultural land on which many settlements are located: tracks become streets, overgrown areas are used as football pitches, meetings are held on vacant lots. Meanwhile, residents may be involved in activities which are illegal or semi-legal (such as connecting the neighbourhood to a 'pirate' water supply), while simultaneously initiating formal processes to obtain official services, thus capitalising on existing supply networks and social relations while strategically aiming to improve their long-term situation through formalisation. These lived experiences of informal places thus reveal both resistance to and compliance with structures through which the state attempts to exert its power to order space.

Place as process

Another strand of critical geographic approaches conceives of place as process, opening up the possibility that the materialities (or structures) of places influence what people do in them, but that these places are in turn influenced by people's activities and agency. Cresswell (2004: 36) uses the example of a square park with bisecting pathways which people bypass in preference of taking a shortcut, walking diagonally across the grass, and eventually creating a mud path. Here, Updike's (1961 in Tuan, 1977: 142) description of '[t]he modest work of human erosion' is called to mind. Pred (1984), in particular, has argued for a disruption of conceptions of place as static, having fixed and measurable attributes. Instead, he emphasises the elements of change and process within place, and sees places as always 'becoming', never 'finished'. Place is 'what takes place ceaselessly, what contributes to history in a specific context through the creation and utilisation of a physical setting' (Pred, 1984: 279). Seeing place as process provides a way of reframing informal settlement dwellers as agents, acting within the constraints of existing structures, but also embodying the possibility of resistance to and even disruption of these structures through incremental change, echoing the suggestion of 'quiet encroachment'.

The idea of place as process, whereby material place is produced by the activities of its users, is extremely pertinent in Global Southern cities, where the proportion of new housing constructed by residents may be as high as 90 per cent (Hardoy and Satterthwaite, 1989: 12). Seeing place as process facilitates increased recognition of the effort that goes into the construction of these places, which remains unrecognised or devalued, despite the long history of debates outlined above. Place as process implies a focus on practice and place as it is performed by the people who use it. It allows a view of urban informal settlements as creative places, the result of social practices. Furthermore, the idea of place as made up of many processes, or as a work in progress, accords with residents' hopes that their neighbourhood will eventually enjoy formal services, proper recognition and full status within the city through 'consolidation'. This does not necessarily imply an end goal of static place – home as place may mean something continually improving, with the ongoing possibility of change.

Taking a procedural view of informality offers a different focus for understanding urban informal settlements: rather than viewing them as physical environments, deficient of basic infrastructure and services, they can be seen 'as complex and changing social processes that play themselves out in intricate spatial arrangements' (Huchzermeyer, 2004: 47). Seeing informal settlements as social processes allows a broader view of these places and the dynamic social and political relations which occur there, as well as more static spatial, technical and legal aspects. Similarly, Roy's (2005: 148) term, 'urban informality', indicates 'an organising logic, a system of norms that governs the process of urban transformation itself'. Here, the standard dichotomy of formal and informal is rejected in favour of the suggestion that 'informality is not a separate sector but rather a series of transactions that connect different economies and spaces to one another' (Roy, 2005: 148).

A place-making approach to urban informal settlements

These strands of geographic approaches to place are synthesised in the analytical lens of 'place-making', used here to emphasise the socio-spatial processes which construct place, and in particular the social and physical construction of places by people. Place-making has been defined by Schneekloth and Shibley (1995: 1) as 'the way in which all of us as human beings transform the places in which we find ourselves into places in which we live'. The objective of exploring urban informal settlements through place-making is to understand the socio-spatial processes of construction in this setting, as a response to the gaps in urban theory and the stereotyping of specific types of place through dominant processes of knowledge production. It also serves to emphasise the creative elements of human action, and interaction – which are fundamental to constructing these places – as locations but also as sites of meaning. Elsewhere, place-making has been defined as 'part of an everyday social process of constructing and reconstructing space', both a communicative process and an individual mental one (Burkner, 2006: 2), highlighting its individual and collective dimensions.

Place-making, then, permits a wide view of the influences and processes brought to bear on a place, and its construction in a physical but also social sense, by emphasising that places result 'from the aggregate of many decisions over time' (Goodman, 1972: 242). Place-making captures the incremental nature of place, in that it includes the activities of the many ordinary citizens who pass through, live in, use, build, visit or avoid a place, and are thus involved, directly or indirectly, in its physical and social construction. The analytical use of place-making here seeks to uncover the everyday activities which construct place, as well as more strategic, one-off events, in the context of exploring the socio-spatial construction of urban informal settlements and revealing assumptions underpinning dominant narratives about these places. It represents an innovative analytical approach in the sense that it brings ideas that have been relatively restricted to Global Northern contexts (e.g., Porter and Barber, 2006; Jones and Evans, 2012), into conversation with debates from the Global South. From within these debates, some discussion of 'place' in the context of informality and poverty can be found (e.g., Stein, 1989; Shatkin, 2004), of which a handful foreground the issue of place meaning (e.g., Higgins, 1990, Hamdi, 2010, Hyrapiet and Greiner, 2012).

As an analytical concept for exploring the social construction of place, then, place-making has the potential to highlight power as a determining factor in socio-spatial relations across different contexts. Place-making may create relationships between people and places, and to each other, in an empowering way, as it is

> a fundamental human activity that is sometimes almost invisible and sometimes dramatic... [which] can be done with the support of others or can be an act of defiance in the face of power. (Schneekloth and Shibley, 1995: 1)

As suggested above, place-making's power dimension incorporates the potential for simultaneous resistance *and* domination; going beyond a simplistic binary conception of domination versus resistance, attention to place-making enables a more nuanced perspective on power relations. In viewing place as the site of complex entanglements of power, place-making offers an analytical focus through which to disentangle some of these complexities. Exploring the intricacies of residents' and other actors' place-making activities allows a view of politics and power relations within the neighbourhood, such as conflicts between neighbours; as well as in the city as a whole, such as adjacent neighbourhoods competing for resources; political relations between different levels of government; or differential interventions in particular places. Below, these issues are explored through the themes of place meaning, and the role of the state.

Place-making and place meaning

In an article by Friedmann, place-making is defined as the process of appropriating space in order to create a 'mirror of self' (Cooper Marcus, 1995 in Friedmann, 2007: 259), for example, by putting up pictures and laying rugs in a new house or room. At neighbourhood level, this occurs by 'appropriating an already existing "place"' (Friedmann, 2007: 259) through learning about the physical place, getting to know local people, and getting involved in local activities. Through making claims on space with activities such as naming, signifying, taking part in social relations and recurrent rituals, such places become lived in, and 'by being lived in, urban spaces become *humanized*' (Friedmann, 2007: 259, original emphasis). This approach, then, offers a response to overwhelmingly negative, technical or quantitative depictions of urban informal settlements and urban poverty more broadly.

The idea of place as a 'mirror of self' implies that identity is generated through place-making. Certainly, as outlined above, phenomenological approaches understand place to be constitutive of human identity. Place identity has been characterised as 'the "glue" of familiarity that binds people to place' (Bruce Hull IV et al., 1994: 110); or 'a cultural value shared by the community, a collective understanding about social identity intertwined with place meaning' (Harner, 2001: 660). These accounts stress the social and cultural dimension of place: imbuing place with meaning leads to the intersubjective construction of place identity and image, on an individual and societal level.

Place meaning as symbolic of individual or collective experience is particularly relevant in the context of urban informal settlements, where incremental building processes which often take place over the course of many years result in houses that are containers of meaning and memory (Kellett, 2002). Much more than just shelter, they express, through their layout, architecture and interior design, ideas about progress, identity and values (Kellett, 2002). To paraphrase Young (1997 in Varley, 2007: 35), place in this setting is important in its representation of effort and ownership, not in terms of private property but 'in the sense of meaningful use and reuse for life'. The physical embodies the social and the cultural, and provides the setting for these aspects of identity. Kellett (2002: 28) remarks that residents' consciousness of their low social position suggests '[t]heir efforts can be interpreted as a striving for dignity and respect'. Thus, place meanings express people's endeavours to transform the places in which they find themselves, on the basis of housing need and economic constraints, into the places in which they live, through everyday social processes of constructing and reconstructing space.

An example from research in Mexico shows how place-making may offer alternatives to dominant discourses, for example, suggesting that housing in *colonias* impedes residents' ability to express their social identity or aesthetic preferences (Walker, 2001). The diverse forms of housing in *colonias populares* reflect the place-making processes that individual households undertake. Whether residents use contractors or do most of the work themselves, their dwellings reflect their own preferences to a certain degree, as the high level of resident participation in house-building means that the design of the house is to the owner's particular tastes. How residents choose to build their homes may depend to a degree on the traditional architecture of the resident's place of origin, as a resident of a *colonia popular* in a central Mexican city explained[6]:

> We're from the south [of Veracruz], and in the south it's hot.... In San Andres, there's lots of vegetation, lots of plants, lots of water, and there are houses with a very high roof, and... a corridor, which here is the entrance hall: the space in front, where you put lots of plants. This was the idea that I had in my house. So I reproduced as far as I could the design of San Andres, the design of the south. (Olga, 5 February 2007)

Architecture adds to the character of these places, as *colonias populares* but also as unique neighbourhoods. As Kellett (2002) suggests, the incremental building process results in houses that are imbued with personal significance: their physical form expresses ideas about progress and tradition, identity and memory, which may in turn express resistance through presenting alternatives to negative or stereotypical discursive constructions of *colonias populares*.

Such accounts stress the social and cultural dimension of place: imbuing place with meaning leads to the intersubjective construction of place identity and image, on an individual and societal level. However, limits on the effects of place-making may be encountered in the regulatory frameworks of the state, reflecting structural constraints more broadly.

Place-making, planning and the state

As an analytical lens, place-making offers a cross-cutting perspective on activities which are often categorised as *either* formal (such as planning by the state) *or* informal (such as land invasion by settlers). In this way, it offers a wide view of influences involved in the spatial and social construction of place, without resorting to standard binary divisions. A place-making lens offers the potential to see all types of activity as equally valid objects of study in the construction of a particular place, in an effort to move beyond normative judgements often entailed by binary conceptions. It allows a perspective which cuts across scale, to include activities in which individuals, families, streets, committees, neighbourhoods, areas, representatives, municipal departments, and so on may all be involved. The benefit of a place-making perspective is that it values these analytical categories equally: therefore, the individual place-making activities of one resident are as important as those of the city council, in analytical (although not necessarily normative) terms. The focus is provided by place, rather than by preordained typologies or hierarchies of activities.

Conversely, place-making views the processes that occur in urban informal settlements as 'ordinary', in that they potentially occur everywhere. Instead of seeing places according to static categorisations, place-making allows a view of the dynamic tensions that interact in a particular place. It thus avoids the homogenisation of urban informal settlements, by emphasising the situated, context-specific elements and processes of a particular place. In particular, place-making is used here to capture the dimension of creativity and productive energy which is invested by the everyday users and producers of a place. If informality is understood as fluid and located in social processes, informal settlements can be conceptualised as work in progress. As described earlier, these places are usually constructed on the basis of their residents' efforts in acquiring land, building houses, obtaining services and setting up networks. Place-making may provide a way of viewing, reassessing and revaluing residents' productive capacity and effort, which continues to be devalued due to the marginalisation of settlements where it occurs.

Part of the problem relating to the recognition of effort in this context may be the state's inability to acknowledge informal processes as place-making. From an official perspective, the construction of urban places is normally associated with 'planning', and 'participation' in planning, which is formally structured, initiated and implemented. The long-standing association of 'planning' with regulatory systems (Campbell, 2002) means that it frequently fails to account for the multitude of other activities involved in the social and physical construction of place. Place-making, then, offers potential to capture activities involved in the construction of place, which overlap with, go beyond, or fall outside formal 'planning' in this sense.

However, while the above discussion suggests potential for urban residents' place-making activities to challenge dominant discourses, and affect urban practices to some extent, Friedmann's (2007: 260) conception of the role of 'the state' in place-making is worth noting here:

> As a collective actor the state can initiate or authorise the erasure of an existing place (e.g. a shanty settlement, a neighborhood slated for clearance) and then turn around to build (or help finance) new housing somewhere else, a project which may eventually evolve into a place that is lived in but until then remains an empty shell. And everywhere, seen or unseen, the state's presence is felt as a constraining influence on everyday life. The physical context for the patterns and rhythms of neighborhood life is controlled by the state.

In this view, 'the state' attempts to regulate everyday life in the city, but this in turn 'lead[s] to resistance, contestations and actions that are often formally illegal' (Friedmann, 2007: 261), under which latter heading much informal settlement is perceived to fall. Friedmann (2007: 261) emphasises the productive nature of this interaction between domination and resistance, asserting that 'some accommodations will be made as a place acquires its specific character, shaped not only from within itself but in response to the demands and decision of... the state'. The undeniable role of the state in establishing and maintaining regulatory structures in the urban context may then be felt through the formulation and upholding of zoning laws; but also in more subtle ways, such as the involvement of residents in formal structures of citizen participation (Lombard, 2013), suggesting the structural limits to place-making.

Conclusion

As outlined in this chapter, place-making offers ground from which to view the multiple, complex relationships that exist between individuals, organisations and institutions involved in the social and spatial construction of place. These relationships fluctuate, meaning that at times, certain actors may be more involved, while at other moments, different actors will dominate. Place-making has the capacity to uncover the complexity of social (and hence power) relations contained within the processes which affect urban informal settlements as places. Building on recent ethnographic approaches to urban informality and the idea of 'ordinary' urban places, which seek to emphasise micro-level activities and the agency of those engaged in constructing them, this paper extends these themes by foregrounding the socio-spatial dimension and thus highlighting how places are produced physically and discursively. In this way, it emphasises the importance of local views and experiences, as well as a global understanding of poverty dynamics.

Different ways of thinking about informality which emphasise dynamic tensions in debates – and the fluidity of concepts according to different contexts, times, places, discourses and so on – suggest potential for seeing urban informality as process, and informal settlements as dynamic, constantly changing places, rather than adhering to static or standardised categorisations. 'Place' offers an alternative analytical lens for understanding urban informal settlements. One objective of exploring urban informal settlements through place-making is to emphasise the creative elements of human action, and interaction – which are fundamental to constructing these places – as locations but also as sites of meaning. A focus on place-making is suggested in order to explore lived experiences of urban informal settlements, to connect social relations with spatial construction, and to see how these places relate to the production of knowledge about them, which may have tangible effects for urban residents.

This is not to suggest that place-making offers a straightforward solution to poverty's structural determinants, but rather to propose it as an alternative mode of understanding. Seeing urban informal settlements as places constructed through the result of multiple influences over time – but especially based on residents' efforts – may reveal them to be as ordinary, and as complex, as anywhere else in the city. In particular, place as a concept foregrounds the link between social and material urban fabric. This allows access to the emotional and psychosocial dimension of the urban environment, often overlooked in urban studies generally, and highlights the territorial dimension of urban informality, particularly relating to stigmatisation (Bayón and Saraví, 2012). In this way, place is a means of exploring knowledge production relating to urban informal settlements, particularly in a discursive sense. It allows for the recognition of collective and individual agency that is central to this project, while also foregrounding how the discursive construction of specific places may permeate at different scales. 'Ordinary places', then, are contextualised within the constraints of power relations; but they also contain the possibility for reinvention, creativity and dynamism. On that basis, this chapter proposes that instead of being seen as the disorderly, illegitimate, 'other' city, informal settlements could be seen as places in their own right, and as places within the wider city. The social, cultural and political processes which influence place-making are inevitably affected by, and reflect, the context where they play out.

Notes

Parts of this chapter are based on Lombard (2014).

1. While the term 'slum' has recently seen a resurgence in urban and development studies (e.g., UN-Habitat, 2003; Davis, 2006), this has been seen as part of a worrying trend towards an over-simplified, negative, universal image of informal settlements (Gilbert, 2007; Varley, 2013). Here, the term 'informal settlement' is favoured over slum, which is only employed in reference to others' work.
2. There is not room to fully consider conceptualisations of urban space here, but after Lefebvre ([1967] 1996), urban space is understood as (potentially) constituted by urban residents, containing the possibility of seeing informality as a form of inhabitance.
3. Despite the conflation of the terms 'legalisation' and 'regularisation' in some Latin American countries such as Mexico, it should be noted that they are referring to separate processes in many contexts – denoting, respectively, titling and socio-spatial integration through upgrading (Fernandes, 2011).
4. Research from East Asian and some Latin American countries shows that economic adjustment has led to changing patterns of rural-urban migration, as reforms which favour rural producers promote demographic shifts away from urban areas (Fallon and Lucas, 2002: 30), while studies from Africa show that return migration offers a strategy to address declining urban prospects (Potts, 2012).
5. According to Foucault ([1982] 2002: 340–341), power is 'a way of acting upon one or more acting subjects by virtue of their acting or being capable of action'; in other words '[a] set of actions upon other actions', which exists only in a relational sense, as exercised by some on others.
6. For a fuller discussion of this aspect of place-making, see Lombard (2014).

References

Abrams, C. (1964). *Man's Struggle for Shelter in an Urbanizing World*. Cambridge, Mass.: MIT Press.

Agnew, J. A. (2005). Space: Place, in: P. Cloke and R. Johnston (eds), *Spaces of Geographical Thought: Deconstructing Human Geography's Binaries*. London: Sage, 81–96.

AlSayyad, N. (2004). Urban informality as a 'new' way of life, in: A. Roy and N. Alsayyad (eds), *Urban Informality: Transnational Perspectives from the Middle East, Latin America and South Asia*. Oxford: Lexington, 7–30.

Amin, A. and Thrift, N. (2004). The 'emancipatory' city?, in: L. Lees (ed.), *The Emancipatory City? Paradoxes and Possibilities*. London: Sage, 231–235.

Angotti, T. (2013). Urban Latin America: Violence, enclaves and struggles for land. *Latin American Perspectives, 40*(2): 5–20.

Auyero, J. (1999a). 'This is a lot like the Bronx, isn't it?' Lived experiences of marginality in an Argentine slum' *International Journal of Urban and Regional Research, 23*(1): 45–69.

Auyero, J. (1999b). 'From the client's point(s) of view': How poor people perceive and evaluate political clientelism. *Theory and Society, 28*(2): 297–334.

Bayat, A. (2004). Globalization and the politics of the informals in the Global South, in: A. Roy and N. Alsayyad (eds), *Urban Informality: Transnational Perspectives from the Middle East, Latin America and South Asia*. Lanham, USA: Lexington Books, 79–102.

Bayón, M. and Saraví, G. (2012). The cultural dimensions of urban fragmentation: Segregation, sociability, and inequality in Mexico City. *Latin American Perspectives, 40*(2): 35–52.

Bromley, R. (1978). The urban informal sector: Why is it worth discussing? *World Development, 6*(9/10): 1033–1039.

Bruce Hull IV, R., Lam, M. and Vigo, G. (1994). Place identity: Symbols of self in the urban fabric. *Landscape and Urban Planning, 28*: 109–120.

Burkner, H. (2006). *Place-making*. PlaceMeg Concept Guidance Paper. Project Workshop on Methods and Concepts, 20–22 February, Institute for Regional Development and Structural Planning.

Campbell, H. (2002). Planning: An idea of value. *Town Planning Review, 73*(3): 271–288.

Castells, M. (1998). *End of Millennium*. Oxford: Blackwell.

Cordera, R., Ramírez Kuri, P. and Ziccardi, A. (eds) (2008). *Pobreza, Desigualdad y Exclusión Social en la Ciudad del Siglo XXI*. Mexico City: Siglo XXI.

Cresswell, T. (2004). *Place: A Short Introduction*. Oxford: Blackwell.

Davis, M. (2006). *Planet of Slums*. London: Verso.

De Certeau, M. (1984). *The Practice of Everyday Life*. London: University of California Press.

De Soto, H. (2000). *The Mystery of Capital: Why Capitalism Triumphs in the West and Fails Everywhere Else*. New York: Basic Books.

Fallon, P. and Lucas, R. (2002). The impact of financial crises on labor markets, household incomes and poverty: A review of evidence. *The World Bank Research Observer, 17*(1): 21–45.

Fernandes, E. (2011). *Regularization of Informal Settlements in Latin America*. Policy Focus Report. Cambridge, Mass.: Lincoln Institute of Land Policy.

Foucault, M. [1982] (2002). The subject and power, in: J. Faubion (ed.), *Michel Foucault: Power*. London: Penguin Books, 326–348.

Friedmann, J. (2007). Reflections on place and place-making in the cities of China. *International Journal of Urban and Regional Research, 31*(2): 257–279.

Gilbert, A. (1994) *The Latin American City*. London: Latin American Bureau.

Gilbert, A. (2007). The return of the slum: Does language matter? *International Journal of Urban and Regional Research, 31*(4): 697–713.

Goodman, R. (1972). *After the Planners*. Harmondsworth: Pelican.

Gough, K. and Kellett, P. (2001). Housing consolidation and home-based income generation: Evidence from self-help settlements in two colombian cities. *Cities, 18*(4): 235–247.

Hall, P. (2002). The city of sweat equity, in: P. Hall, *Cities of Tomorrow*. Oxford: Blackwell, 262–293.

Hamdi, N. (2010). *The Placemaker's Guide to Building Community*. London: Earthscan.

Hardoy, J. and Satterthwaite, D. (1989). *Squatter Citizen*. London: Earthscan.

Harner, J. (2001). Place identity and copper mining in Sonora, Mexico. *Annals of the Association of American Geographers, 91*(4): 660–680.

Hernández, F., Kellett, P. and Allen, L. (2010). *Rethinking the Informal City: Critical Perspectives from Latin America*. Oxford: Berghahn.

Higgins, B. (1990). Geographical revolutions and revolutionary geographies: Nature, space and place in the urban development of Nicaragua. *Trialog, 26*:13–20.

Holloway, L. and Hubbard, P. (2001). *People and Place: The Extraordinary Geographies of Everyday Life*. Harlow: Pearson Education.

Huchzermeyer, M. (2004). *Unlawful Occupation: Informal Settlements and Urban Policy in South Africa and Brazil*. Trenton, NJ: Africa World Press.

Hyrapiet, S. and Greiner, A. (2012). Calcutta's hand-pulled rickshaws: Cultural politics and place-making in a globalizing city. *The Geographical Review, 102*(4): 407–426.

Jones, P. and Evans, J. (2012). Rescue geography: Place-making, affect and regeneration. *Urban Studies, 49*(11): 2315–2330.

Kellett, P. (2002). The construction of home in the informal city. *Journal of Romance Studies, 2*(3): 17–31.

Lefebvre, H. ([1967] 1996). The right to the city, in: E. Kofman and E. Lebas (eds), *Writings on Cities*. Oxford: Blackwell, 63–181.

Legg, S. and McFarlane, C. (2008). Ordinary urban spaces: Between postcolonialism and development. *Environment and Planning A, 40*: 6–14.

Lewis, O. (1967). *La Vida: A Puerto Rican Family in the Culture of Poverty – San Juan and New York*. London: Secker and Warburg.

Lloyd, P. (1979). *Slums of Hope? Shanty Towns of the Third World*. Manchester: Manchester University Press.

Lombard, M. (2013). Citizen participation in urban governance in the context of democratization: Evidence from low-income neighbourhoods in Mexico. *International Journal of Urban and Regional Research, 37*(1): 135–150.

Lombard, M. (2014). Constructing ordinary place: Place-making in urban informal settlements in Mexico. *Progress in Planning, 94*: 1–53.

Lomnitz, L. (1977). *Networks and Marginality: Life in a Mexican Shanty Town*. New York: Academic Press.

Mabin, A. (2014). Grounding Southern city theory in time and place, in: S. Parnell and S. Oldfield (eds), *The Routledge Handbook on Cities of the Global South*. London: Routledge.

Mangin, W. (1967). Latin American squatter settlements: A problem and a solution. *Latin American Studies, 2*: 65–98.

Massey, D. (1991). A global sense of place. *Marxism Today*, June: 24–29.

McFarlane, C. (2010). The comparative city: Knowledge, learning, urbanism. *International Journal of Urban and Regional Research, 34*(4): 725–742.

McFarlane, C. (2012). Rethinking informality: Politics, crisis, and the city. *Planning Theory and Practice, 13*(1): 89–108.

Miranda, L. (2002). A new mystery from de Soto? A review of *The Mystery of Capital*, Hernando de Soto, 2001. *Environment and Urbanization, 14*(1): 263–264

Mitlin, D. and Satterthwaite, D. (2013). *Urban Poverty in the Global South, Scale and Nature*. London: Routledge.

Moser, C. (2009). *Ordinary Families, Extraordinary Lives: Assets and Poverty Reduction in Guayaquil, 1978–2004*. Washington, DC: The Brookings Institution.

Moser, C. and Peake, L. (eds) (1987). *Women, Human Settlements and Housing*. London: Tavistock Publications.

Myers, G. (2003). *Verandahs of Power, Colonialism and Space in Urban Africa*. Syracuse, NY: Syracuse University Press.

Peattie, L. R. (1970). *The View from the Barrio*. Michigan, MI: Ann Arbor/University of Michigan Press.

Peattie, L. (1998). Convivial cities, in: M. Douglass and J. Friedmann (eds), *Cities for Citizens: Planning and the Rise of Civil Society in a Global Age*. Chichester: John Wiley, 247–53.

Perlman, J. (1976). *The Myth of Marginality: Urban Poverty and Politics in Rio de Janeiro*. Berkeley, CA: University of California Press.

Porter, L. and Barber., A. (2006). Closing time: The meaning of place and state-led gentrification in Birmimgham's Eastside. *City, 10*(2): 215–234.

Potts, D. (2012). Challenging the myths of urban dynamics in sub-Saharan Africa: The evidence from Nigeria. *World Development, 40*(7): 1382–1393.

Pred, A. (1984). Place as historically contingent process: Structuration and the time-geography of becoming places. *Annals of the Association of American Geographers, 74*(2): 279–297.

Rao, V. (2006). Slum as theory: The South/Asian city and globalisation. *International Journal of Urban and Regional Research, 30*(1); 225–232.

Relph, E. (1976). *Place and Placelessness*. London: Pion.

Robinson, J. (2002). Global and world cities: A view from off the map. *International Journal of Urban and Regional Research, 26*(3): 531–554.

Robinson, J. (2006). *Ordinary Cities: Between Modernity and Development*. Abingdon: Routledge.

Rodgers, D., Beall, J. and Kanbur, R. (eds) (2012). *Latin American Urban Development into the 21st Century: Towards a Renewed Perspective on the City*. Basingstoke: Palgrave Macmillan.

Roy, A. (2005). Urban informality: Toward an epistemology of planning. *Journal of the American Planning Association, 71*(2): 147–158.

Roy, A. (2011). Slumdog cities: Rethinking subaltern urbanism. *International Journal of Urban and Regional Research, 35*(2): 223–238.

Schneekloth, L. and Shibley, R. (1995). *Place-making: The Art and Practice of Building Communities*. New York: Wiley.
Sharp, J. P., Routledge, P., Philo, C. and Paddison, R. (2000). *Entanglements of Power: Geographies of Domination/Resistance*. London: Routledge.
Shatkin, G. (2004). Planning to forget: Informal settlements as 'forgotten places' in globalising metro Manila. *Urban Studies, 41*(12): 2469–2484.
Simone, A. (2004). *For the City Yet to Come, Changing African Life in Four Cities*. London: Duke University Press.
Stein, A. (1989). The 'tugurios' of San Salvador: A place to live, work and struggle. *Environment and Urbanization, 1*(2): 6–15.
Tuan, Y.-F. (1977). *Space and Place: The Perspective of Experience*. Minneapolis, MN: University of Minnesota.
Turner, J. (1968). Uncontrolled urban settlement: Problems and policies, in: G. Breese (ed.), *The City in Newly Developing Countries: Readings on Urbanism and Urbanisation*. Englewood Cliffs, NJ: Prentice Hall.
Turner, J. (1972). Housing as a verb, in: J. Turner and R. Fichter (eds), *Freedom to Build: Dweller Control of the Housing Process*. New York: Collier-Macmillan, 148–175.
Turner, J. and Fichter, R. (eds) (1972). *Freedom to Build: Dweller Control of the Housing Process*. New York: Collier-Macmillan.
UN-Habitat. (2003). *The Challenge of the Slums: Global Report on Human Settlements*. Nairobi: United Nations Human Settlements Programme.
Varley, A. (2007). *Home and Identity: Housing Narratives from Urban Mexico*. Paper given at postgraduate workshop, 11–13 September, Department of Geography of the Norwegian Institute of Science and Technology, Trondheim.
Varley, A. (2013). Postcolonialising informality? *Environment and Planning D, 31*(1): 4–22.
Walker, A. (2001). *The Social Context of Built Form: The Case of Informal Housing Production in Mexico City*. DPU Working Paper. London: Development Planning Unit, University College London.
Ward, P. (ed.) (1982). *Self-Help Housing: A Critique*. London: Mansell.
Watson, V. (2011). Engaging with citizenship and urban struggle through an informality lens. *Planning Theory and Practice, 12*(1): 150–153.
Wratten, E. (1995). Conceptualizing urban poverty. *Environment and Urbanization, 7*(1): 11–33.

5

Constructing Spatialised Knowledge on Urban Poverty: (Multiple) Dimensions, Mapping Spaces and Claim-Making in Urban Governance

Isa Baud

Introduction

Recently, increasing attention is given to poverty issues in urban areas in the Global South. This follows recognition that population growth is shifting to urban areas, as more than half the world population is found in urban areas, which are expected to grow mainly in South Asia and sub-Saharan Africa in the next 30 years (UN, 2011). What are the implications of this shift? First, governments, academics and advocacy organisations require more insight into the 'dynamics of poverty' (i.e., what deprivations households experience, how they deal with them, and how these processes of engagement change over time). Secondly, what does it imply for urban governance in terms of mandates, power relations and politics? Local governments often have difficulties coping with existing responsibilities and now face rising numbers of households with conflicting agendas – middle-class expectations as well as increasing numbers of poor households experiencing various deprivations (social, economic, infrastructural). Rescaling of government and privatisation processes have reduced their mandates, so that local governments have less leverage to make service provision more inclusive (e.g., Baud and de Wit, 2008). Negotiating with advocacy organisations for urban neighbourhood communities offers ways to tailor provision to local needs and mobilise existing capacities.

These implications suggest that concerned organisations need to deepen their knowledge about the spatial diversity and concentration of urban deprivations and how they are relationally constructed, by their links to the rights and designations of urban areas (illegality or informality), and the ways in which engagements between the state and local communities exacerbate or reduce poverty dynamics. This chapter discusses three major processes in which spatialising dimensions of poverty dynamics, related to local governance, illustrates how such knowledge can be made more pro-poor: 1) how households experience deprivations in 'urban spaces', 2) how city neighbourhoods are relationally constructed and change over time and 3) how urban governments engage with other actors to influence urban spatial development.[1]

Poverty has long been recognised as a multi-dimensional and multi-scalar phenomenon by researchers utilising the assets/vulnerability approach (Moser, 1998; Rakodi and Lloyd-Jones, 2002). The main advantage of such *household-level* approaches is the recognition that not only employment and income but living conditions (environment and infrastructural) and social networks are important factors either supporting or undermining well-being. These approaches also require knowledge of the *neighbourhood-level* physical and social environment in which households live, their time-space use of the city environment both at work and elsewhere, and their *collective engagement* with city-level actors to improve living conditions.

The work done on spatial poverty traps recognises the limitations poor households experience in using the city environment (Grant, 2010; McFarlane, 2012; Chapter 2 of this volume). However, too little is known about the processes by which households 'climb out' of poverty or which undermine their efforts, which are not necessarily the same (Krishna, 2004).[2] Van Heusden's study in Mumbai shows how demolition of informal neighbourhoods destroys both physical and social capital of poor households by destroying their children's access to education when households are suddenly evicted, and how much financial capital it requires to rebuild their house (van Heusden, 2007). Narayan similarly shows how important social networks are for mutual support, and how the lack of dignity accorded poor people undermines their self-respect (Narayan et al., 2000).

Urban spatial diversity has long been recognised by geographers (Massey, 2005; Graham and Marvin, 2001; Coutard, 2008). They have shown how city areas are actively 'constructed' by state initiatives (land, housing), as well as by initiatives of households and civic organisations. State initiatives include generating city areas characterised by informality, with inadequately framed or enforced spaces, leaving the poor vulnerable in dealing with semi-legal actors in these spaces (Roy, 2007; Jaffe, 2012; van Dijk, 2014). Major attention has focused on sub-standard settlements where households attempt to build up their lives, in conditions varying in terms of environmental health hazards, vulnerability from unprotected forms of employment, social diversity, crime and violence, and insecurities arising from variable degrees of recognition from the state (e.g., Dupont, 2011; Sabry, 2009; Nainan, 2008).

What deserves more attention is the impact of new economic growth policies that provincial and national governments have promoted in recent decades in urban areas (cf. Kennedy et al., 2011). Although such policies are usually considered part of globalisation, the process (at least in BRICS countries) is steered equally by opportunities that sub-national governments seize for increasing their city's competitiveness, working with national governments to do so. In Mumbai, the Mumbai 2020 Vision initiative by Bombay First is a prime example of such local initiatives by large companies and state government working together (cf. Nainan, 2012). It is complemented in India by the national urban renewal mission (JNNURM) programme, which provides large-scale funding for upgrading infrastructure (85 per cent) and basic services for the poor (15 per cent) in 63 cities (Sivaramakrishnan, 2011).

Generally, the outcomes of economic growth programmes across countries are negative for poor households, even when improvements in basic services for the poor are included as a goal. Their policies often do not reflect the lived reality of households in obtaining services, building up their housing, or the lack of legality in the claims they make on land and housing ownership (cf. Higgins, Bird and Harris, 2010). As a result, policies to improve competitiveness and quality of life in city neighbourhoods have involved demolitions of sub-standard settlements, resettlement of residents of slum areas to high-rise dwellings in far-off areas, undermining the capacity of households to develop livelihoods and destroying their existing assets (for Mumbai, see Nainan, 2012; Bhide and Dabir, 2010; for Brazil, see Sutherland et al., 2011).

The status of urban neighbourhoods ranges from formally planned and registered areas to completely unacknowledged areas, and all stages in between. One important urban spatial dynamic consists of processes by which sub-standard settlements either try to become more formalised, or alternatively become less recognised and destroyed.[3] Such dynamics are strongly linked with the ways local urban and provincial ruling coalitions promote particular land use and economic growth politics, as well as long-term state policies on slum areas (Nainan, 2008; Hust and

Mann, 2005). It is also the result of collective action of local residents in building up their neighbourhoods, creating urban spaces in which they deal directly with poverty issues (e.g., Hordijk, 2000). The result is a city characterised by a spatial patchwork with differing regulatory frameworks, levels of service provision and legal status, all changing over space and time. Urban local governments have to deal with such patchworks over which they have differing degrees of control, engaging with the political networks representing such areas and their residents. More and spatially disaggregated information on existing urban diversity and change can help determine priorities in decision-making processes (see Chapter 8). At present, such spatialised information is lacking or not used even when available (cf. Baud et al., 2011).

This chapter examines what contributions mapping urban poverty, reflecting the needs of the urban poor, can make to policy discussions on reducing poverty in urban governance. The assumption is that the social construction of knowledge[4] (whose knowledge, what information is included or excluded, and how it is utilised) is embedded in the political processes of urban governance networks (Baud et al., 2011). This chapter focuses on three issues to answer this question.

The first issue concerns the advantage of conceptualising urban poverty as a multi-dimensional concept, reflecting the multi-sited aspects of people's lives and livelihoods. This allows deprivations through social marginalisation, lack of infrastructure and basic services to be incorporated into the analysis of deprivations, questioning whether urban time-space use provides more extensive opportunities than rural areas, or whether spatial segregation limits them (Marques, 2013).

The second concerns spatialising and visualising poverty information into hotspots of deprivation in cities, and analysing the socio-political processes by which urban poverty is maintained there. Such mappings reflect existing uneven provision of services and assets which households can access, and variations in their rights, according to the spatially differentiated regulatory framework across city neighbourhoods.

The third issue concerns how community-based construction of spatialised knowledge increases collective negotiating power of poor households when urban governance networks offer opportunities to link residents' knowledge to intervention programmes (Hoyt et al., 2005). Although such 'negotiating spaces' increase opportunities, the various spatial scales of infrastructural and basic service provision and the political power needed to push through new 'framings' of issues make the investment of time and money for those involved a daunting process.

The main conclusion is that spatialising knowledge on urban poverty provides a better understanding of its multi-dimensional and multi-sited character, and the existing power relations that maintain deprivations. The results also indicate that community-generated spatial knowledge on the 'lived spaces' of poor households can be a resource for claim-making, when state actors in urban governance networks are willing to recognise and engage with such claims (Lefebvre, 1991).

To illustrate the discussion, the chapter uses earlier and ongoing studies carried out in several major cities in India (cf. Baud et al., 2008; Baud et al., 2009; Pfeffer et al., 2011; Martinez et al., 2011).[5] The paper draws on examples from the perspective of households dealing with urban poverty, as well as the perspective of actors in urban governance networks, in the context of Indian cities.

Mapping urban deprivations

Conceptualising urban poverty as a multi-dimensional phenomenon, we recognise that deprivations are linked to the ways households live and work, their (lack of) access to collective and/or state-provided resources and the extent to which poor households can make their needs heard politically or organise collectively (cf. Alkire and Seth, 2008; Mitlin and Satterthwaite, 2004; Rakodi and Lloyd-Jones, 2002). These approaches acknowledge that collective 'structures of constraint' exist, which undermine individual households' efforts to build their assets.[6] Such approaches view households and their members as active actors in their own right. Individuals and their households have differing sets of 'capitals', which they can use to improve their well-being (Rakodi and Lloyd-Jones, 2002). In urban areas, such capitals consist of:

- human capital (health, education and training, employment),
- financial capital (savings and income, household assets (jewelry, other capital goods),
- physical capital (housing and basic services), and
- social capital (extent of collective organisation and social networks).[7]

Although multi-dimensional approaches to urban poverty are substantively great improvements on one-dimensional measures, limitations remain. Early studies were based on localised case studies providing much-needed insights into ways households build up different capitals and the constraints they face but little or no information on the extent to which such deprivations held true across large sections of urban populations (Moser, 1998). Current studies are usually aggregated at national level and cannot provide city-level data (Alkire, keynote speech 2011, York, EADI General Conference[8]). Secondly, the regulatory patchwork within cities leads to fragmented data across various organisations and pertaining to different areas of the city, so that spatial targeting of intervention programmes is almost impossible to coordinate and direct effectively to specific neighbourhoods. This makes it difficult to support organisations (including non-state actors) with targeted information to reduce existing deprivations.[9] Therefore, information on the multiple deprivations faced by poor households disaggregated to the lowest spatial level at which decisions on interventions are made within cities, could support both local communities with information and aid them in influencing others within consultative processes.

Several colleagues and I took up the issue of mapping urban poverty to counter the limitations indicated above (Baud et al., 2008; Baud et al., 2009). For several Indian metro cities we deployed the concept of urban poverty defined as multiple deprivations of the capitals in the livelihoods approach. Based on existing in-depth case studies and our own knowledge of urban poverty in India, fieldwork-based household surveys were carried out in the cities concerned across social groups in selected heterogeneous areas of the city (Baud et al. 2008).[10] These surveys provided insights into people's occupations, housing situations and access to services provision. The results provided indicators for each capital, which characterised most clearly differences between social groups. From these indicators a multiple deprivation index was constructed (see Figure 5.1). Using this index and linking it to the Census of India (2001), we constructed a database for the cities concerned. The Census covered most major aspects of the capitals distinguished, although in some areas proxies had to be used. This applied in the case of 'social capital', which could only be measured by the relative presence of scheduled castes/ scheduled tribes. This is an indicator of lack of social capital, as 'lower' caste status continues to be a major source of discrimination.[11]

The mapping was done to the lowest level of disaggregation for which information was available – the electoral ward level. It represents the lowest level of political representation (ward councillors). In contrast, the executive side of government works with higher levels of aggregation at the administrative ward level (between 10–20 electoral wards comprise one administrative ward). The data had to be requested specially from the Registrar General's office in Delhi and is not available in the public domain in this detail. Local governments or civic organisations usually cannot access such information readily.

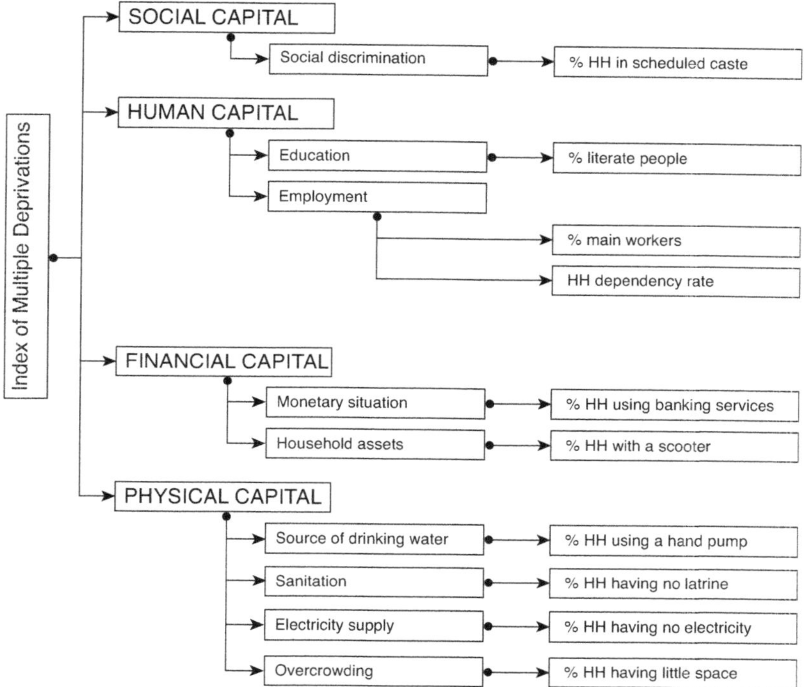

Figure 5.1 Criteria model to map multiple deprivations
Source: Baud et al. (2008).

To map spatial concentrations of poverty at electoral ward level, indicator values (right-hand column in Figure 5.1) were derived from Census tables and matched to the digitised boundaries of the electoral ward zones using the GIS Ilwis Academic 3.3.[12] With the GIS, an attribute map was created for each indicator showing its spatial distribution across electoral wards. To aggregate the indicator maps to the intermediate level of a 'capital' and the final index of multiple deprivation, the attribute maps were standardised to values between 0 and 1 indicating no deprivation (0) and extreme deprivation (1). To compare the wards according to the index of multiple deprivations and the lack of individual capitals, the standardised attribute maps were combined by means of weighted sums, in which each capital (and within one capital each indicator) was considered to have equal weight. In this way the variety of aspects involved in constructing the index of multiple

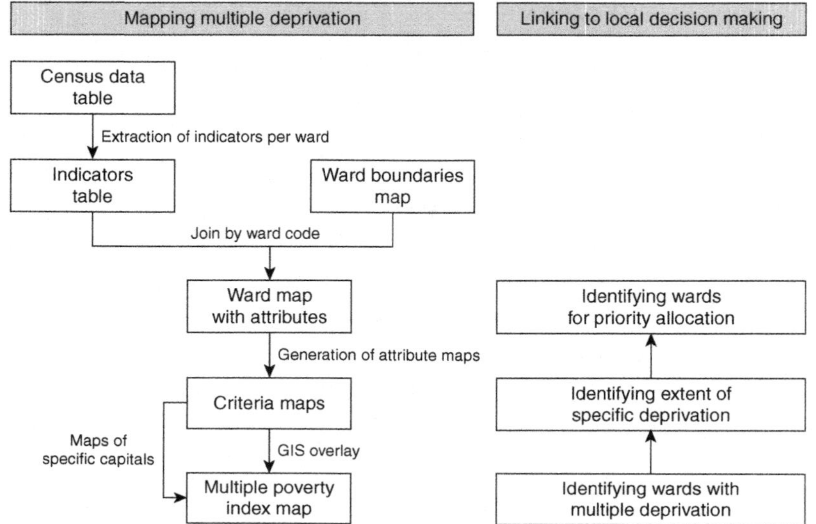

Figure 5.2 Flowchart of the methodology of mapping
Source: Baud et al. (2009).

deprivation was synthesised. The various steps of the operationalisation are illustrated in Figure 5.2.

The results indicate average levels of deprivation in the various 'capitals' experienced by households at the ward level. These were used to compare differences in deprivations across wards in Delhi, Mumbai and Chennai (Baud et al., 2009). Combining attribute maps into a composite index map leads to low performance on one indicator being compensated by high performance on another, resulting in ***average*** deprivation levels across wards. These results were used to compare differences between areas of the city, but they do not allow one to see which types of deprivations actually lead to the resulting 'hotspots' of multiple deprivation (see Figure 5.3). To do that, the final map showing the spatial differences of multiple deprivations was overlaid with the input maps and maps showing the spatial patterns of specific capitals. By means of a lookup table, the loading of each input map (i.e., each indicator) and intermediate map ('capital' level) to the final deprivation index of the ward could be traced back for more specific analysis. This option is particularly important when the link between poverty analysis and governance is made, in which possible interventions need to be matched with specific deprivations occurring in particular areas (see Table 5.1).

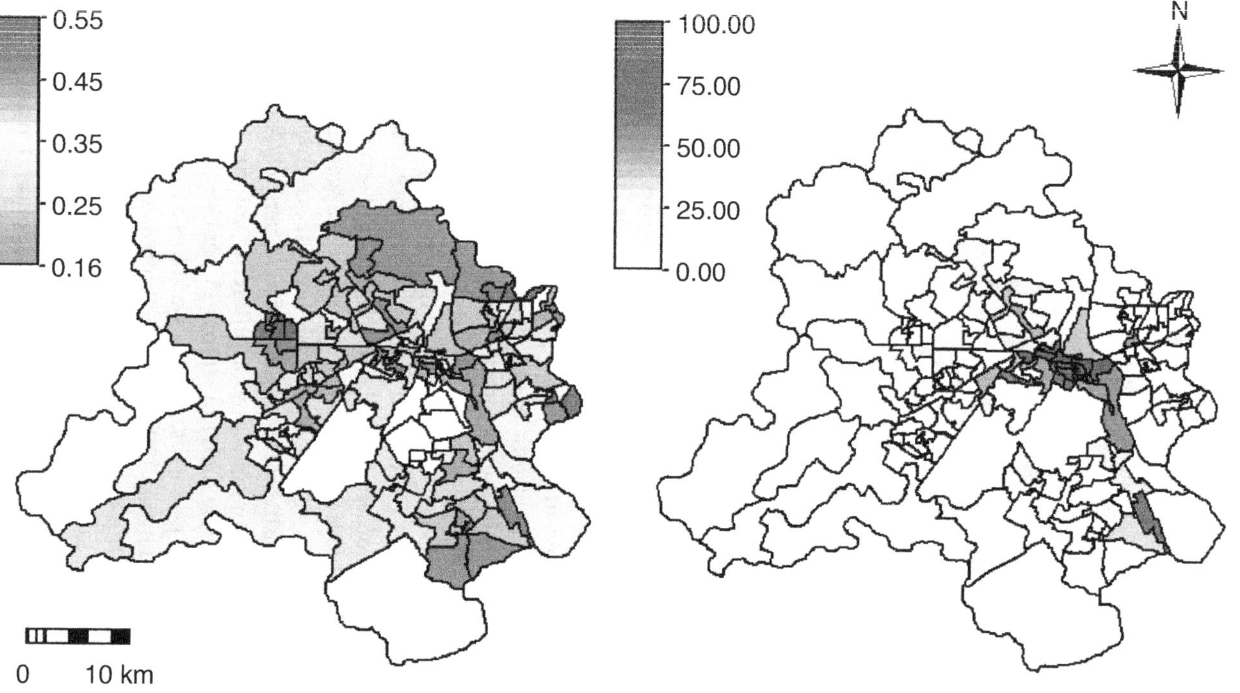

Figure 5.3 Wards with highest poverty levels according to Index of Multiple Deprivations (IMD) (left map) compared with wards with highest % of inhabitants living in slums (right map)[13]

Table 5.1 Summary of deprivations and percentage of slum inhabitants in quintile of Delhi wards with highest levels of IMD

Name	Social capital	Human capital	Financial capital	Physical capital	Multiple deprivation	% Slum inhabitants
Mangolpuri North	0.46	0.55	0.83	0.34	0.55	0.70
Gokul Puri	0.33	0.58	0.81	0.42	0.54	0.00
Kondli	0.44	0.57	0.79	0.38	0.54	23.55
Mangolpuri South	0.44	0.55	0.82	0.32	0.53	2.60
Sultanpur Majra	0.40	0.58	0.81	0.25	0.51	0.00
Mustafabad	0.05	0.67	0.86	0.42	0.50	0.00
Jaffrabad	0.25	0.61	0.80	0.32	0.50	51.77
Harkesh Nagar	0.25	0.52	0.89	0.31	0.50	72.84
Rana Pratap Bagh	0.31	0.53	0.76	0.30	0.48	44.22
Burari	0.26	0.56	0.82	0.26	0.48	0.00
Karawal Nagar	0.17	0.57	0.81	0.37	0.48	0.00
Seema Puri	0.20	0.60	0.77	0.33	0.48	19.93

Source: Baud et al. (2008).

The Delhi maps show the results of deprivation mapping according to the IMD. Hotspots of multiple deprivations are concentrated in several wards in both West Delhi and near the Yamuna River. Site visits to the areas concerned showed that the following two wards consisted largely of resettlement schemes: Mangolpuri North (ward 41) and Mangolpuri South (ward 42) with respective indices of multiple deprivations of 0.55 and 0.53. Although the percentage of inhabitants living in slums is very small in these areas, households in these wards face deprivations across the board. The percentage of households having no latrine is very high (93 per cent and 90 per cent[14]); about 45 per cent of the population is scheduled caste; approximately 36 per cent of the people cannot read and write; just a quarter of all households make use of banking services, and only 10 per cent of households have capital assets, such as a scooter. Population density is also very high, almost 40,000 persons/km^2, contrasting with an average population density in Delhi wards of 7372 persons/ km^2.

The wards on the Yamuna show a different pattern. Kondli has a high percentage of people living in slums (25 per cent), with a population density of 13,571 persons/km^2. This ward has a high percentage of households without latrines (80 per cent), limited access to water services, and almost half the households experience overcrowding. In terms of social capital, it is comparable with Mangolpuri. Kondli has slightly lower levels of deprivations in the use of financial services. Gokulpuri is also located in the east of the city with a population density of 9946 persons/km^2. This ward has no slums according to the Census. However, its IMD is fairly high because of deprivations in physical capital; that is, the high percentage of households using hand-pumps (65 per cent), having no electricity and experiencing overcrowding. In this ward having no latrine is a minor problem. But about 40 per cent of the inhabitants are illiterate and the number of main workers is low. Only 29 per cent of households make use of banking services and only 10 per cent have scooters (Baud et al., 2008).

The wards above were compared with wards in the quintile with the highest IMD in order to trace possible differences (Table 5.1). Other wards in this quintile have similar levels of deprivation in physical, financial and human capital, but show much lower levels of deprivation in social capital (i.e., the percentage of scheduled caste people is much lower). Finally, a major outcome was that the level of deprivations did not correlate with the extent of slums in the Delhi wards (Figure 5.3).

In conclusion, the advantages of the IMD are:

1. Recognition that multiple factors contribute to the level of deprivations within households;
2. Recognition of spatial diversity of deprivations, as different factors contribute to high levels of deprivations by geographical area; and
3. Having a database on existing situations for area-focused policies or interventions.

Some limitations remain. Detailed databases are needed for such analysis within cities. The national sample survey of household consumption carried out every four years in India does not lend itself to this type of analysis because the samples drawn from each city are too small to analyse spatial differences within city populations.[15] Also, administrative boundaries may cut through clustering of deprivations so that cross-boundary concentrations of deprivations are not recognised. Finally, alterations in area boundaries thwart attempts for a trend analysis over time.[16]

The outcomes of the visualisation of Delhi electoral wards (and the subsequent analysis of Mumbai and Chennai – Baud et al., 2009) suggest several conclusions for urban governance. First, deprivations are diverse, so that problem identification needs to be done by area. Second, regulatory frameworks may strongly influence service provision – for instance, older resettlement schemes reveal high levels of deprivations. Finally, the lack of correlation of high levels of deprivations with areas designated as slums needs further examination of the regulatory frameworks steering those areas, as slums are often used as proxy for targeting research and policy (see below).

Visualising concentrations of deprivations and links to city diversity

The results from the visualisation approach discussed above indicate that city diversity is high and is linked to the regulatory framework impinging on the area concerned. This means that the patchwork of regulatory frameworks in Indian cities affects urban poverty in specific areas over time. Grant (2010) has indicated households have difficulties building livelihoods in cities as well as in improving conditions for social reproduction (housing, infrastructure, basic services, and social capital). She suggests that such differences are linked to geographic area, social dynamics and chronic poverty. However, such diversity is also strongly linked to socio-political processes by which deprivations are maintained.

Grant indicates that 'geographic area' makes a difference in poverty. Rather than 'geography', this is the result of the variety of administrative statuses and the (lack of) rights linked to them, found across geographic areas in the city (cf. Holston, 2009; van Dijk, 2014). In India 'standard areas' of the city are provided with infrastructure and basic services as a right. In contrast, areas considered 'encroachments' have no rights to any amenities. In other informal areas, inhabitants have to organise themselves collectively and approach government institutions (Slum Boards) to become a 'recognised slum', after which the process of obtaining certain levels of basic services and infrastructure can begin (cf. Dupont, 2011). 'Slums' can be classified on official criteria, or on the outcome of political lobbying by political representatives (cf. Richter et al., 2011).[17]

Therefore, the urban patchwork of regulatory frameworks needs to be analysed to understand what kinds of administrative and geographic constraints exist for poor households to build up rights. The Indian Census (2001, 2011) provides information on slums in urban areas.[18] However, no database provides information on the status of areas being regularised within cities. Slum boundaries also fluctuate according to the politics of resettling urban residents from sub-standard settlements. In Mumbai, government-introduced, market-based instruments for changing land use patterns included resettling slum residents into new high-rise housing based on commercial incentives to builders (Patel et al., 2002). Such trading development rights, as they are called, have changed large slum areas into neighbourhoods with more standardised housing and services (see also Levy, Chapter 7 of this volume). However, in Mumbai regular settlements also run the risk of being made 'illegal' in order to free them for redevelopment (cf. Bjorkman, 2013). In the new RAY programme slums are also redefined according to the levels of development they have built up in Tamil Nadu.[19]

To understand geographic differentiation within cities, therefore, the links to existing political processes have to be incorporated. Changing patterns of land tenure, rights and administrative status need to be mapped carefully to understand the processes by which 'informality' and slum status is maintained. The implications for levels and types of deprivations faced is well illustrated by comparing Figure 5.3 showing levels of deprivations and slums in Delhi. The highest levels of deprivations are not in wards with high slum concentrations. Although less striking than in Delhi, similar results were obtained in Chennai and Mumbai (Baud et al., 2009).

In understanding spatial differences in poverty we also need to look at the ways different social groups within cities negotiate with street-level government bureaucrats to build degrees of citizenship, particularly in gaining access to infrastructure and services (Gaventa, 2006).[20] Currently, citizenship is defined as consisting of rights, status and identity; here the discussion focuses only on collective rights (cf. Joppke, 2008). Marshall's classic framework of citizenship covers civil, political and social rights (Marshall, 1950). Civil rights guarantee citizens a degree of individual freedom, and political rights underpin political participation. Social rights guarantee a citizen's right to income sufficient to share in the social heritage and life of a civilised being, whether or not his/her value for the labour market is considered (Marshall, quoted in Turner, 2009: 68). Through social rights, the state gives citizens access to a minimum of essential goods and services, or an income sufficient to provide them.

However, the state usually does not consider all citizens to be equal. Gaventa describes several deficits preventing equal citizenship, including unequal entitlements, a lack of *vertical accountability*, where citizens are not able to hold their government and political elite accountable for how they use power; and *weak horizontal accountability*, where bureaucracies manipulate existing checks and balances through patronage, corruption, and by stifling dissent (Gaventa, 2006). Even where states nominally provide all citizens with equal rights, actual allocation can diverge widely (Holston, 2009).

Such inequalities force residents to realise their rights and entitlements through active claim-making on the state. Social groups use different channels for claim-making depending on the 'spaces' available to them (Cornwall and Gaventa, 2001). Spaces are defined as 'opportunities, moments and channels where citizens can act to potentially influence policies, discourses, decisions and relationships, which affect their lives and interests' (Gaventa, 2005: 11). In closed spaces, citizens have no say. In invited spaces, governments offer citizens participation in influencing decision-making processes, ranging from consultations to full participation in designing policies. In claimed spaces, citizens mobilise to create their own opportunities to influence government (Gaventa, 2005). Baud and Nainan (2008) also distinguish negotiated spaces, where citizens negotiate with actors, institutions or organisations, directly or through mediators to influence government.

The question is what effects social inequalities and different regulatory frameworks by geographic area have on the opportunities of social groups to make claims in various types of spaces to influence government. Two recent studies illustrate the effects.

A study in Hubli-Dharwad in North Karnataka illustrates how people with a low socio-economic status and those with middle-class backgrounds both raise different issues about service provision as well as use different channels for negotiation with local government (van Teeffelen and Baud, 2011). Whereas middle-class urban residents hold their local government accountable for operation and maintenance of existing services, lower socio-economic groups make claims primarily about major problems, such as complete lack of service provision. Middle-class residents use new digitised grievance redressal systems through mobile phone networks, whereas poorer groups still work through ward councillors who can negotiate politically with local government or providers. Figure 5.4 shows the differences.

Different regulatory frameworks also influence the opportunities of different social groups to make claims on the government. In Mumbai, local government provided geographically differentiated regulatory frameworks in modernising solid waste management (SWM). In standard areas, it encouraged residents' organisations called ALMs (advanced locality management groups), whereas in slum areas it provided for an alternative system of small enterprises to be run by residents for collecting and handling solid waste under the Slum Adoption Programme. In the former, ALMs monitored SWM collection, removal of building waste from the streets and greening the streets. They also started excluding hawkers and mobilising against slum areas in their neighbourhoods (Baud and Nainan, 2008). ALMs generally worked with the bureaucrats in ward offices and avoided political representatives (councillors). In contrast, in slum areas, councillors were essential negotiators for their constituencies, although they had their own (political and personal) agendas as well (van Dijk, 2011).

The initiatives in Mumbai have impacted both services as well as political rights of different social groups. In middle and elite class areas, service delivery improved through ALMs. Middle-class citizens have

	Invited space	*Negotiated space*	*Claimed space*
Deciding factor in successful use	Human capital and political capabilities	Social capital	Social capital
Citizens use space based on	Rights	Patronage	Community ties
Pitfalls	Awareness Capacity to use effectively Lack of accountability	Clientelism Lack of accountability	Clientelism Lack of power
Use middle class	Space used most by middle-class citizens	Not used by middle-class citizens	Only used by middle-class citizens in exceptional cases
Use LSES	Rarely used by LSES citizens	Councillor is crucial actor for LSES citizens	CBOs and local leaders are crucial actors for LSES citizens

Figure 5.4 'Spaces' for participation and their use in grievance redressal

Note: LSES = lower socio-economic status.

Source: van Teeffelen and Baud (2011).

claimed more rights but are undermining the rights of hawkers and slum residents. ALMs also supported existing political candidates and promoting candidates of their own (since 2007 local elections). In slum areas, SWM service delivery remained the same, or became politically influenced as resources were allocated to the new enterprises.

Coming back to the issues that Grant identifies as necessary to understand how poverty is maintained, I conclude that it is not social dynamics or chronic poverty that explain persistent inequalities, but existing power relationships. These consist of 1) existing inequalities in type and quality of services provided to different social groups, 2) the differing set of rights recognised by the state for specific social groups, and 3) the differing 'spaces' and channels by which different groups negotiate with the state to obtain 'rights' in practice. Differential power relations are linked to geographic areas of the city because of the variety of administrative and regulatory frameworks, ranging from complete 'informality' where people have no rights, to 'standard settlements' where residents enjoy the majority of rights prevailing in the city concerned (Roy, 2007).

Constructing spatialised knowledge in urban governance and claim-making

The third question is how existing power relations can be altered by reframing issues of urban poverty and governance, and whether including community-based construction of spatialised knowledge, can strengthen claim-making processes. Different types of knowledge exist, ranging from scientific-codified knowledge to tacit knowledge, with a variety of contextual-embedded knowledge types in between (van Ewijk and Baud, 2009; Bruckmeijer and Tovey, 2008). Scientific-codified knowledge is linked to accepted expertise derived from professional education and research, which dominates urban planning. Contextual-embedded knowledge includes sectoral knowledge built up from practice, and community-based knowledge linked to spaces, and local political and social situations. This range of knowledge types is rarely acknowledged in urban planning and management, but it plays an essential role in understanding people's priorities in dealing with urban poverty (Massey, 2005; Hoyt et al., 2005; Patel et al., 2002). Spatial knowledge can refer to any type of knowledge together with a geographical location (geo-referenced), that is, to a holistic understanding of facts, interdependencies, connections and dynamics that can be mapped (Pfeffer et al., 2013).

The question is how less recognised forms of knowledge can be made visible and become a resource to gain political power in urban governance networks working to reduce poverty. This requires knowing about opportunities within different socio-political situations to incorporate alternative framings and types of knowledge (cf. Bruckmeier and Tovey, 2008). Knowledge-building processes incorporate the experiences of a range of actors, and outcomes reflect both perceived validity and quality of knowledge, as well as existing power relations (Healey, 2007). Different types of knowledge are used as sources of power, through varying legitimising processes, and have different travelling capacities and transformative power (Healey, 2007: 197; McCann and Ward, 2012). This implies that knowledge of whatever type is inherently socially constructed and situated in its context and time. In analysing the construction of spatialised knowledge in urban governance and claim-making, we need to know which actors participate, their paradigms and different types of knowledge they produce, and how power relations shape the extent to which different types of knowledge and framings are accepted and utilised (e.g., Karpouzouglu and Zimmer, 2012; McCann and Ward, 2012).

The idea of relational knowledge building is vital to 'participatory spatial knowledge building'. It moves away from power in formal political relations, focusing on ways in which social and professional networks can build claim-making and city development strategies, in which trust and exchange of knowledge plays a role (or generates conflicts about goals and strategies). The concept of 'participatory knowledge building' gives primary importance to relational knowledge building, collaborative social learning and re-embedding knowledge in local communities (Healey, 2007; Miranda Sara and Baud, 2014). The major question is to what extent such 'participatory' processes are encouraged in city planning and management.

Applying such ideas to the issue of spatialising knowledge in building up pro-poor urban governance, we can distinguish between dominant models of urban planning and management and how social groups build up and utilise contextual-embedded knowledge. In India, current dominant models are based on the codified knowledge of urban developers and designers at different levels of government. Such models use spatialised knowledge extensively, based on official plans and maps, and government-defined goals (Baud et al., 2011). In Indian cities, development authorities prepare official 'Master Plans' for city development. Recent urban reforms are drawing in other actors and interests; central government is taking a leading role in suggesting tax, land tenure and administrative reforms through the conditionalities and financial incentives of the JNNURM (Sivaramakrishnan, 2011).[21] In the early 1990s, decentralisation measures brought in local political representation through ward councillors, with 30 per cent of such seats reserved for women and scheduled caste/tribe groups (SC/ST), and some limited forms of participatory budgeting (cf. Fung and Wright, 2003).

Most striking is the extent to which private urban developers and companies have become strong partners with local governments in redesigning urban housing growth strategies, through the use of special economic zones (Kennedy et al., 2011) and incentives given to developers in slum rehabilitation programmes. In Mumbai, incentives given to developers for slum rehabilitation in return for trading development rights elsewhere in the city for commercial housing have led to a reconfiguration of city areas, with slum rehabilitation housing becoming concentrated in M-ward, and the up-market housing area of Juhu becoming more densely built up (Nainan, 2012; Patel et al., 2012).

Spatial knowledge production and contestation played a major role in redeveloping sub-standard areas in Mumbai, affecting many people.

First, large areas were brutally demolished in the late 1990s. Secondly, in areas up for rehabilitation, households had to produce official information that they had lived there for certain periods of time (e.g., voting cards, ration cards) in order to be eligible for alternative housing. Owners of houses were eligible for alternative housing, and tenants were not. The government made their own estimates on the numbers of households for whom they would provide housing. These were contested, successfully in some cases. In one resettlement process of households along the railroad tracks, SPARC, a Mumbai-based NGO,[22] produced alternative information on the number of households through their community census, working with local residents (Patel et al., 2012). The results showed a much higher number of households than government estimates, leading to negotiations held to expand the housing to be provided. Similar examples exist for slum settlement mapping in the context of resettlement initiatives in Pune and elsewhere (Joshi et al., 2002). Spatial knowledge on sub-standard urban settlements constructed in cooperation between local community members with strong local NGOs supports their negotiations with government agencies (Special issue E&U, 2012). Such negotiations are strengthened when an international organisation makes community participation mandatory in such processes.

A second example of community-generated knowledge building through a digital GIS, occurred in Delhi, where participatory learning and action (PLA) methods were used by a think tank (NIUA),[23] women residents from the neighbourhood and an NGO to create an alternative database with which to negotiate with the Delhi Jal Board for better water provision (Hoyt et al., 2005). The mapping used leaves, pebbles and chalk, which allowed illiterate residents to participate. The ensuing discussions also brought out issues of power and abuse, and ways of bypassing inequalities to produce more effective and equitable outcomes in the end (Hoyt et al., 2005).

In the examples above, intermediary organisations played key negotiating roles. In contrast, Internet-based social media networks and Google-hosted spatialised interfaces allow individual residents to put up spatialised information without civic organisations being involved – that is, volunteer geographic information (VGI). This is done, for example, by people visiting particular sites, providing their assessments of such sites on the Internet (Poorthuis, 2010). The use of such possibilities is growing explosively through social media; in Latin America, a whole network of urban social movements provides information on making cities just and sustainable.[24] In India, Transparent Chennai, an NGO, is producing a website where groups of young researchers provide information on situations in Chennai (bus routes, beach areas) about local issues (Pfeffer et al., 2013). They utilise such information to negotiate with local government on solving local issues.[25]

Sectoral knowledge on uneven developments within city areas and priority issues is prevalent among government officials and political representatives. Such information can be visualised and spatialised using qualitative participatory GIS methods (cf. Pfeffer et al., 2011; McCall and Dunn, 2012). Such methods can reveal 'multiple realities' and combine codified and tacit information on deprivations and urban poverty. In one research programme in the Mumbai agglomeration, experimental workshops were held with both types of actors around the table.[26] The municipality hosted the workshop and invited officials and political representatives; the researchers provided the contents and processes for the programme. Workshops had four rounds of participatory activities: 1) identifying major issues, 2) ranking issues, 3) mapping areas in need by issue, and 4) discussing outcomes. Major issues were health, water, subsidised food provision and housing.[27] The priority maps, projected on a large screen, generated lively and sometimes acrimonious discussions between councillors and administrators. They reflected tensions on the ways decisions were taken on selecting households in food subsidy programmes and perceived irregularities.[28] Finally, the cumulative spatial concentration of issues found in specific wards led to a discussion of what was driving such uneven development in those areas (see Figure 5.5). The deprivation maps generated through the Census 2001 data were also discussed in the workshop and brought out areas where interventions had occurred since then and situations had changed (Pfeffer et al., 2011).

Conclusions

Three issues were raised in this chapter: first, the multi-dimensional character of urban deprivations, their spatial diversity, and how households deal with deprivations; second, the implications of different spatial regulatory frameworks for urban governance; and third, how detailed spatial knowledge might empower the poor in negotiating a better deal in urban decision-making processes.

The answer to the first question shows the advantages of conceptualising urban poverty as a multi-dimensional construct, reflecting more realistically the aspects of people's daily lives and household livelihoods. This approach allows issues of social marginalisation, lack of infrastructure and basic services to be incorporated into the range of deprivations

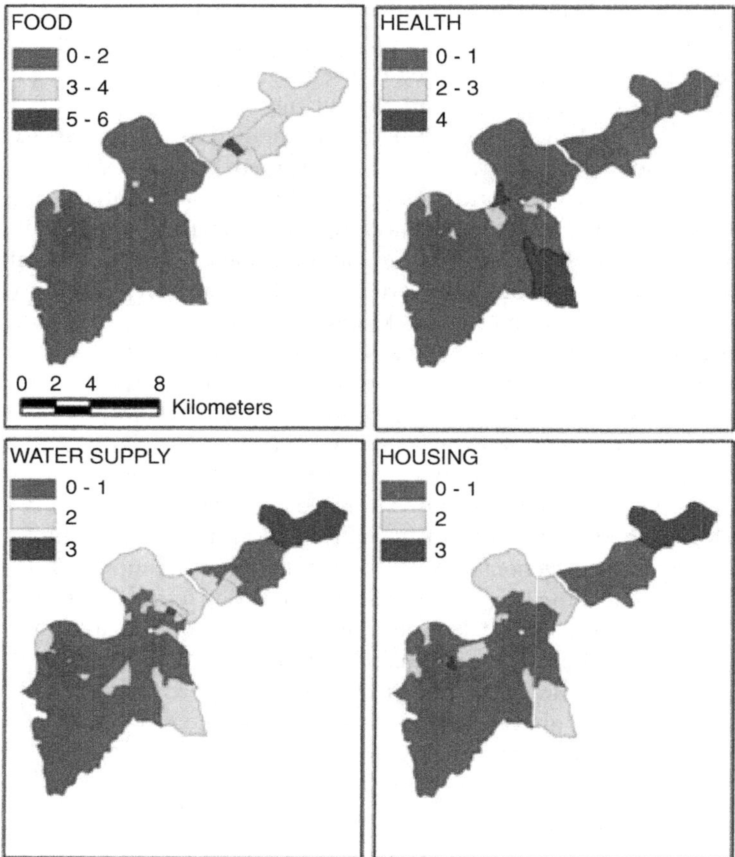

Figure 5.5 Spatial concentration of priority issues by ward in K-D
Source: Participatory mapping workshop K-D (Pfeffer, Martinez et al., 2011).

poor households face. Mapping the multi-dimensional character of urban poverty provides several fresh insights into the (spatial) diversity of urban deprivation patterns, which are not concentrated in defined slums, and which are linked to regulatory frameworks of specific urban areas. Participatory mapping, based on contextual knowledge of social groups in sub-standard settlements provides necessary local knowledge for negotiating changes.

The second issue concerns the potential of visualising hotspots of urban deprivations, and gaining insight into the socio-political processes by which urban poverty is maintained in specific areas. The results reflect democratic deficits, determined by the spatially constructed regulatory framework for city neighbourhoods (with varying levels of rights and entitlements), and the resulting uneven access to and provision and quality of assets and services for households. Combining such knowledge with the knowledge of service providers' priorities, constraints and the channels groups of urban residents use to negotiate better outcomes (based on the [lack of] citizenship), provides insight into the socio-political processes by which poverty is maintained, as such uneven geographies are due partly to the spatial patchwork of regulatory frameworks. It also provides support for NGOs and social movements negotiating with local governments around the structural constraints behind the uneven patterns; obtaining rights for certain city areas deprived of them rather than negotiating with individual politicians.

The third issue concerns the potential of participatory construction of spatialised knowledge to increase the negotiating power of marginalised groups, when urban governance networks offer spaces linking community-based sources of knowledge to urban intervention programmes. Although overlapping spatial scales of infrastructural and service provision as well as the political power needed for the new 'framing' of issues make this a time- and labour-intensive process, advocacy organisations familiar with Internet possibilities and the power to negotiate with local government are crucial in this process. The evidence is clear: alternative spatial knowledge can be utilised as a new resource for claim-making, when urban governance 'spaces' open up, and where intermediary organisations have developed negotiating power and capabilities and are willing and able to represent households in sub-standard settlements.

Our overarching research question is whether mapping urban poverty contributes to urban governance processes dealing with urban poverty, in reflecting the needs of the urban poor. We have argued that the social construction of knowledge and its utilisation is embedded in the political processes of urban governance networks (including [local] government, CSOs and NGOs, and the private sector). We conclude that spatialising and visualising information on urban deprivations, recognising the reasons behind them, improves understanding of the multi-dimensional character of poverty and the diversity of the power relations maintaining poverty. Our results also indicate that alternative spatial knowledge from the 'lived spaces' of poor households can be a strong resource for claim-making when urban governance networks opens up decision-making processes. However, a great deal of committed effort is needed to make and keep such processes effective over time.

Acknowledgements

This paper could not have been written without the many discussions over the past years, which my colleagues and I have had in various research programmes: IDPAD New Forms of Urban Governance, the IP-WOTRO programme on Utilizing Spatial Information Infrastructures in Urban Governance Networks (2007–2012), and the EU-funded and EADI-led Chance2Sustain: City Growth and the Sustainability Challenge network (2010–2014). I gratefully acknowledge their insights and input into the discussion in this paper, reflected in their publications in the reference list. Any errors remain solely my own.

Notes

1. Pro-poor here is defined as those processes and provisions from which the poor benefit absolutely.
2. Krishna's dynamic analysis for rural areas indicated that processes by which households climb out are not comparable with those that throw households into poverty (the former are linked with access to urban labour markets, education, and guaranteed access to water for agriculture, whereas the latter have to do with illness and death of family members).
3. Peru is a case where regularisation processes are legally supported (cf. Hordijk, 2000; Miranda Sara and Hordijk, 1998); Bjorkman (2013) illustrates delegitimation in Mumbai.
4. In this the paper follows Gibbons et al. (1994) mode 2 construction of knowledge as a social process, not a uni-linear process of deduction from theory, experiment, to new conclusions.
5. These studies were carried out under the auspices of the India-Netherlands IDPAD programme New Forms of Urban Governance in India (2005–2008), the NWO-WOTRO funded Integrated Program 'Using Spatial Information Infrastructure in Urban Governance Networks: Reducing Urban Deprivations in Indian Cities', and the currently ongoing EU-funded programme Chance2Sustain: fast-growing cities and the sustainability challenge.
6. For instance, demolitions of housing are a common danger in slums because there is no tenure security. This destroys households' main wealth assets and often destroys an important source of income as well.
7. The last capital – natural capital – is usually considered of less importance in the urban context.
8. The Alkire group is currently working on developing sub-national measures.
9. Governance networks include state actors, private sector actors and civil society organisations (Torfing et al., 2012).
10. Heterogeneous areas were chosen so that differences in locality would be less likely to play a role in the differences between social groups in that area.
11. Health data are also not available from the Census, as the Health Ministry collects such information separately. The two sets of data cannot be compared at such disaggregated levels.

12. ITC (2005) *ILWIS version 3.3.* Enschede, The Netherlands: International Institute for Geo-information Science and Earth Observation.
13. NB: The right picture shows for each ward the percentage of inhabitants living in slums (0–100 per cent), while the left image illustrates the index of multiple deprivation (0–1). The white areas in the centre are New Delhi and Delhi Cantonment, while for the white areas in the outer boundaries no data were available.
14. The Delhi Development Authority constructs rehabilitation colonies with no internal toilets, because the total built-up space per household is limited to 18 square meters per household (pers. com).
15. This problem may have been solved in the latest surveys, according to Mahadevia et al. (2012).
16. If Census enumeration boundaries were made public, this problem would be eliminated.
17. Similar processes of regularisation of 'invasion' areas are found in Lima, Peru, supported by legal frameworks mandating neighbourhood organisations, which take the lead in developing infrastructure, basic services and land tenure rights in negotiations with local government and providers (Hordijk, 2000).
18. Although in the latest Census the extent to which slums have been included in the database seems to vary by state, because the state level determines the definition and the size of slums included.
19. Fieldwork in Chennai has revealed that councillors in the slum areas negotiate with private sector enumerators to decide whether slums should continue to be called slums, or be redefined as non-slum areas.
20. This section draws heavily on the article by van Teeffelen and Baud (2011), and Baud and Nainan (2008).
21. Jawarhalal Nehru National Urban Renewal Mission programme.
22. Society for the Promotion of Area Resource Centres.
23. National Institute of Urban Affairs.
24. Latin American Network of Cities and Territories Just, Democratic and Sustainable, located here: http://redciudades.net/.
25. Personal communication, S. Shekhar, 3 November 2011.
26. The Dutch Science Foundation (NWO-WOTRO) funded the 5-year programme entitled 'Using spatial information infrastructure in urban governance networks: reducing urban deprivations in Indian cities?' led by the UvA (Amsterdam), ITC (Enschede), TISS Mumbai and SPA (Delhi), from 2007–2012.
27. In other cities, similar workshops led to identifying major issues different from those in K-D, a city of slightly more than one million people in Maharashtra.
28. In other cities, the role of private sector consultants in supporting the municipality was challenged, when it became clear that research institutions could provide such information at much lower costs.

References

Alkire, S. and Seth, S. (2008) *Measuring Multidimensional Poverty in India: A New Proposal.* OPHI Working Paper No. 15.

Baud, I.S.A. and Nainan, N. (2008). 'Negotiated spaces' for representation in Mumbai: Ward committees, advanced locality management and the politics of middle-class activism. *Environment and Urbanization, 20*: 483–499.

Baud, I. S. A., Pfeffer, K., Sridharan, N. and Nainan, N. (2009). Matching deprivation mapping to urban governance in three Indian mega-cities. *Habitat International, 33*(4): 365–377.

Baud, I. S. A., Pfeffer, K., Sydenstrycker, J. and Scott, D. (2011). *Developing Participatory Spatial Knowledge Models in Metropolitan Governance Networks for SD*. WP 5 review paper, Chance2Sustain, EADI website, Bonn.

Baud, I. S. A., Sridharan, N. and Pfeffer, K. (2008). Mapping urban poverty for local governance in an Indian megacity: the case of Delhi. *Urban Studies, 45*: 1385–1412.

Baud, I. S. A. and de Wit, J. (2008). *New Forms of Urban governance in India*. New Delhi: Sage.

Bhide, A. and Dabir, N. (2010). *Staking a Claim: Housing Rights of the Poor in Mumbai*, TISS project report. Mumbai: YUVA, Dignity international.

Bruckmeier, K. and Tovey, H. (2008). Knowledge in sustainable rural development: From forms of knowledge to knowledge processes. *Sociologia Ruralis, 48*(3): 313–329.

Cornwall, A. and Gaventa, J. (2001). *From Users and Choosers to Makers and Shapers: Repositioning Participation in Social Policy*. IDS Working Paper No. 127, Institute of Development Studies, Brighton.

Coutard, O. (2008). Placing splintering urbanism: Introduction. *Geoforum, 39*: 1815–1820.

Dupont, V. (2011). The dream of Delhi as a global city. *International Journal of Urban and Regional Research, 35*(3): 533–554.

van Ewijk, E. and Baud, I. S. A. (2009). Partnerships between Dutch municipalities and municipalities in countries of migration to the Netherlands: Knowledge exchange and mutuality. *Habitat International, 33*: 218–226.

Fung, A. and Wright, E. (2003). *Deepening Democracy: Institutional Innovation in Empowered Participatory Governance*. London: Verso.

Gaventa, J. (2005). *Reflections on the Use of the Power Cube Approach*. CFP Evaluation Series No. 4, Institute of Development Studies, Brighton.

Gaventa, J. (2006). *Triumph, Deficit or Contestation? Deepening the 'Deepening Democracy' Debate*. IDS Working Paper No. 264, Institute of Development Studies, Brighton.

Grant, U. (2010). *Spatial Inequality and Urban Poverty Traps*. ODI Working Paper 326, ODI, London.

Graham, S. and Marvin, S. (2001). *Splintering Urbanism: Networked Infrastructures, Technological Mobilities, and the Urban Condition*. New York: Routledge.

Healey, P. (2007). *Urban Complexity and Spatial Strategies*. London and New York: Routledge.

van Heusden, M. (2007). *Ambujwadi: A Slum Reconstruction. Changing Housing Strategies in the Face of Demolitions*. MSc thesis, University of Amsterdam, Amsterdam.

Higgins, K., Bird, K. and Harris, D. (2010). *Policy Responses to the Spatial Dimensions of Poverty*. ODI Working Paper 328, London.

Holston, J. (2009). Insurgent Citizenship in an Era of Global Urban Peripheries. *City & Society, 21*(2): 245–267.

Hordijk, M. A. (2000). *Of Dreams and Deeds: The Role of Local Initiatives for Community Based Environmental Management in Lima, Peru.* PhD Thesis, University of Amsterdam, Amsterdam.

Hoyt, L., Khosla, R. and Canepa, C. (2005). Leaves, Pebbles, and Chalk: Building a Public Participation GIS in New Delhi, India. *Journal of Urban Technology, 12*(1): 1–19.

Hust, E. and Mann, M. (2005). *Urbanization and Governance in India.* New Delhi: Manohar.

Jaffe, R. (2012). Crime and insurgent citizenship: Extra-state rule and belonging in urban Jamaica. *Development, 55*(2): 219–223.

Joppke, C. (2008). Transformation of citizenship: Status, rights, identity, in: E. F. Isin, P. Nyers and B. S. Turner (eds), *Citizenship between Past and Future.* New York: Routledge, 346–348.

Karpouzoglu, T. and Zimmer, A. (2012). Closing the gap between 'expert' and 'lay' knowledge in the governance of wastewater: Lessons and reflections from New Delhi. *IDS Bulletin, 43*(2): 59–68.

Kennedy, L., Robbins, G., Scott, D., Sutherland, C., Denis, E., Andrade, J. and Bon, B. (2011). *The Politics of Large-Scale Economic and Infrastructure Projects in Fast-Growing Cities of the South.* WP 6 review paper, Chance2Sustain, EADI, Bonn.

Krishna, A. (2004). Escaping poverty and becoming poor: Who gains, who loses, and why? *World Development, 32*(1): 121–136.

Lefebvre, H. (1991). *The Production of Space.* London: Blackwell.

Marshall, T. H. (1950). Citizenship and social class, in: J. Manza and M. Sauder (eds), *Inequality and Society.* New York: Norton and Co., 148–154.

Massey, D. (2005). *For Space.* London: Sage Publications Ltd.

Martinez, J., Pfeffer, K. and van Dijk, T. (2011). E-government tools, claimed potentials/unnamed limitations: The case of Kalyan-Dombivli. *Environment and Urbanization ASIA, 2*: 223–224.

McCall, M. and Dunn, C. E. (2012). Geo-information tools for participatory spatial planning: Fulfilling the criteria for 'good' governance? *Geoforum, 43*: 81–94.

McCann, E. and Ward, K. (2012). *Mobile Urbanism.* University of Minnesota Press.

McFarlane, C. (2012). From sanitation inequality to malevolent urbanism: The normalisation of suffering in Mumbai. *Geoforum, 43*: 1287–1290.

Milbert, I. (2008). Law, urban policies and the role of intermediaries in Delhi, in: I. Baud and J. de Wit (eds), *New Forms of Urban Governance in India.* New Delhi: Sage, 177–212.

Miranda Sara, L. and Baud, I. S. A., (2014). Knowledge-building in adaptation management: *concertación* processes in transforming Lima water and climate change governance. *Environment and Urbanization, 26*(2), doi:10.1177/0956247814539231.

Miranda Sara, L. and Hordijk, M.A. (1998). Let us build cities for life: The NationalCampaign of Local Agenda 21s in Peru. *Environment and Urbanization, 10*: 69–102.

Mitlin, D. and Satterthwaite, D. (2004). *Empowering Squatter Citizen: Local Government, Civil Society and Urban Poverty Reduction.* London: Earthscan Publications.

Moser, C. (1998). The asset vulnerability framework: Reassessing urban poverty reduction strategies. *World Development, 26*: 1–19.

Nainan, N. (2012). *Lakshmi Raj: Shaping Spaces in Post-industrial Mumbai – Planning Instruments and Development of Mumbai*. PhD thesis, University of Amsterdam.

Nainan, N. (2008). Building Boomers and Fragmentation of Space in Mumbai. *Economic and Political Weekly*, *43*(21): 29–34.

Narayan, D. et al. (2000). *The Voices of the Poor* (vol. 1–3). Washington, DC: World Bank.

Narayan, D. and Petesch, P. (2007). *Moving Out of Poverty*. Washington, DC: World Bank.

Patel, S., Baptist, C. and D'Cruz, C. (2012). Knowledge is power – Informal communities assert their right to the city through SDI and community-led enumerators. *Environment and Urbanization*, *24*(1): 13–26.

Pfeffer, K., Baud, I., Denis, E., Scott, D. and Sydenstricker-Neto, J. (2013). Participatory spatial knowledge management tools: Empowerment and upscaling or exclusion? *Information, Communication & Society*, *16*(2): 258–285.

Pfeffer, K., Martinez, J., Baud, I. S. A. and Sridharan, N. (2011). Knowledge production in Urban Governance Systems through Qualitative Geographic information systems (GIS). *Environment and Urbanization ASIA*, *2*(2): 235–250.

Rakodi, C. and Lloyd-Jones, T. (2002). *Urban Livelihoods: A People-Centred Approach to Reducing Poverty*. London: EarthScan Publications.

Richter, C., Miscione, G., De, R. and Pfeffer, K. (2011).Enlisting SDI for urban planning in India: Local practices in the case of slum declaration, in: Z. Nedovic-Budic, J. Crompvoets and Y. Georgiadou (eds), *Spatial Data Infrastructures in Context – North and South*. Boac Raon, London, New York: CRC Press, 157–179.

Sabry, S. (2009). *Poverty Lines in Greater Cairo: Underestimating and Misrepresenting Poverty*. London: IIED.

Sharma, K. (2003). *Rediscovering Dharavi*. Camberwell: Penguin Books Australia.

Sivaramakrishnan, K. C. (2011). *Re-visioning Indian Cities: The Urban Renewal Mission*. Delhi: Sage.

Sutherland, C., Braathen, E., Dupont, V., Jordhus-Lier, D., Miranda Sara, L. and Torres, R. (2011). Analysing Policies and Politics to Address Urban Inequality: CSO Networks and Campaigns on Sub-Standard Settlements in Metropolitan Areas. WP3 Review, Chance2Sustain program.

Van Dijk, T.K., (2014). *Subaltern Urbanism in India, Beyond the Mega-city Slum: The Civic Politics of Occupancy and Development in Two Peripheral Cities in the Mumbai Metropolitan Region*. PhD thesis, University of Amsterdam, Amsterdam.

van Dijk, T.K. (2011). Agents of change and obstruction: Municipal councilors and urban development in the Mumbai metropolitan region. *Human Geography*, *4*: 31–47.

Van Teeffelen, J. and Baud, I. S. A. (2011). Exercising Citizenship: Invited and Negotiated Spaces in Grievance Redressal Systems in Hubli-Dharwad. *Environment and Urbanization ASIA*, *2*: 169–185.

Torfing, J., Peters, G., Pierre, J. and Sorensen, E. (2012). *Interactive Governance: Advancing the Paradigm*. Oxford: Oxford University Press.

Turner, B. (2009). Unpacking Urban Inequalities: The Strategic Relational Livelihoods Approach. NAERUS Conference Paper, Rotterdam.

UN. (2011). *World Urbanization Prospects, the 2011 Revision*. New York.

6
Refugees and Urban Poverty: A Historical View from Calcutta

Romola Sanyal

Introduction

Global urbanisation is once again recasting cities as key sites to explore a myriad of issues with uniquely urban characteristics, from politics, to economics, planning and urban social relationships. Urban poverty is increasingly significant in this discussion. A consideration of the history of studying poverty is appropriate which locates the urban squarely within the discourse. Poverty studies have their beginnings in the late nineteenth and early twentieth centuries in urban Britain undertaken by Charles Booth in London and Seebohm Rowntree in York. Rowntree's work, for example, highlighted urban poverty as a new and distinct phenomenon from rural poverty due to the fact that urbanisation and urban living had unique characteristics, from commodification of standards of life to individualisation, and the particularities of the labour market (Mingione, 2008). In the United States, as well, many of the studies on poverty focused not only on urban poverty but on inner city poverty and emphasised questions of race (Beteille, 2003). The concentration of studies on urban poverty in countries in the Global North is partly due to the specific concentrations of poverty and visible poverty in these places, and it can be argued that it is qualitatively different from the poverty in developing countries. In nineteenth and twentieth century Britain, for example, the production of slums and poverty amongst the working classes was largely driven by the Industrial Revolution. In developing countries, urban poverty appears to stem from a number of different issues. Often, studies on poverty have failed to recognise anything specifically urban about poverty or that urban characteristics influence the scale and depth of poverty experienced when it is clear that this is an important factor (Mitlin and Satterthwaite, 2013: 17).

In India, too, the question of poverty has not necessarily focused on urban poverty as an issue in itself as it is seen as part of a larger economic problem stemming from economic backwardness, rather than a sociological phenomenon per se. Hence responses to poverty have been dominated by economists and led by planning commissions who have attempted to use development planning to address these issues (Beteille, 2003).[1] With a more recent 'urban turn' in sociological studies in India (Prakash, 2002), increasing attention has been paid to the experiences of poverty amongst the urban poor, particularly in the large metropolitan cities, including greater focus on the causes and symptoms of urban poverty itself.[2] While standard discussions of poverty in India have been preoccupied with definitions and measurements, more recent academic engagement with urban poverty has turned to the relationship between poverty and urbanisation. For example, in analysing processes of urbanisation such as the production of new towns or global cities, studies have considered how they rely on the existence of a need economy, encouraging eventually, the encroachment of the urban poor on spaces that attempt to exclude them (Bhattacharya and Sanyal, 2011). Urbanisation and poverty therefore go hand in hand. Scholarship has also focused on the lived experiences of poor people including the deprivations they face such as lack of shelter, water and sanitation, adequate living wages, education and so forth. Paralleling this, we also see the rise of commentary on slums as not only visible spaces of poverty unique to the cities in the Global South, but symbolic of the chaotic planning characteristic of the Global South (Rao, 2006; Roy, 2011).

The implicit focus when discussing the struggles of the urban poor in cities of the Global South is often on citizens themselves. This is because the studies of urban citizenship or at least struggles over rights and access to resources in cities engage the cleavages between formal and substantive citizenship rights, between civil and political societies and ways in which populations are governed by the state (Chatterjee, 2004; Holston, 2008; Ghertner, 2011). Such conversations are useful when considering the ways in which politics are reshaped from below and citizenship becomes a process and not just a legal definition. The discussion of poverty, rights and politics of the poor, however, becomes far more complex when engaging with transient populations with ambiguous legal rights who struggle to stake claims to the city despite these obstacles. In this chapter I consider the experiences of urban poverty amongst refugees in Calcutta, particularly those displaced from the partition of India and Pakistan in 1947 using gender, class and caste. I choose to engage with this particular group of people because refugees are often treated as involuntary migrants and victims of violence. Policies towards them are more complicated as a result of the problematic division between them and economic migrants. I argue that refugees from the partition of India have played an important role in the urbanisation process. This is partly because of their peculiar legal and political status as legitimate migrants on the one hand and victims of violence on the other. In Bengal, which bordered East Pakistan (now Bangladesh), this has been even trickier. It has been argued that the migration of refugees along this border has continued till today. The legal status of refugees has also changed repeatedly over the years, leaving many people out of its protection regime. Even for those who legally arrived later, being a refugee was in some ways more a problem than helpful label. One could argue that perhaps the most privileged amongst refugees in India were those that came immediately during and after partition because they were given rights that many others who came afterwards did not have. However, this requires further elaboration as experiences of migration during partition itself was horrific and varied widely based on the identities of refugees.

In 1947, India and Pakistan were partitioned by the departing British colonial government. Partition displaced about 10–15 million people along the western and eastern borders of India, with more refugees arriving in the west from Punjab in the immediate aftermath of partition while continuous migration across the eastern border between Bangladesh and India has led to overall higher numbers in this region. Many of these refugees came to cities such as Delhi and Calcutta and shaped them physically and politically through their presence.[3] A glimpse of the magnitude of the urban crisis is perhaps necessary here. There is disagreement on numbers, but by 1952, approximately 2,517,504 refugees had come in through the eastern border alone, and 73 per cent to West Bengal, making refugees nearly one-tenth of the total population of the state. Three districts accounted for two-thirds of the total refugees – these were the undivided 24 parganas, Calcutta and Nadia, (Das, 2000: 15). At one point, over 3000 people were coming into Calcutta daily (Chakrabarti, 1999: 14) putting significant pressure on already strained resources in the city.

I want to pose two provocations here. One is to consider mass displacements and transient populations such as refugees when thinking about who constitutes the urban poor. The issue of urban refugees is increasingly important as there are already millions of refugees or people in refugee-like situations and more such populations are moving to cities instead of camps when they flee. Generally, in the case of mass displacements which occur largely in developing countries, many do not have significant assets or economic means and hence, they move into informal settlements where they can blend in with the urban poor. Refugees, like other migrants, come to cities in search of economic and social opportunities to rebuild their lives. Like other migrants they, too, place pressure on job markets, housing markets and so forth that may already be overstretched in many cities. But it is their legal condition as involuntary migrants subject to particular protections that makes the relationship of urban poverty and refugees fascinating.[4] While their legal position (where recognised) often protects them from forced removal, host governments can and often do restrict their mobility and access to livelihoods or social goods in order to manage the relationship between refugees and citizens and ameliorate any possibilities of friction between the two. Refugees thus have to either relinquish their protected status and live clandestine lives, or depend on aid agencies to provide them with these services. A parallel system of aid and even rights often develops to address the needs of recognised refugees that has to balance their needs with those of poor urban citizens who may not have much social provision from the state. But this system in many ways also marginalises and impoverishes refugees who are often unable to exercise their rights or access opportunities and yet face the challenges of living in an urban environment.

The experience of partition in India can be considered unique in the discussion of refugees. This is because refugees were given legal recognition and the right to settle (at least for a certain period of time). There were also no international aid agencies present in India supporting refugees.[5] Instead, refugee rehabilitation was largely coordinated between national and state governments who managed matters such as land, housing, food, etc. Nevertheless, I want to suggest that both the issues of migration to the cities and the ways in which government at various scales handled their arrival created conditions of urban poverty amongst refugees. On the one hand, there was the process of migrating into Calcutta from East Bengal/East Pakistan: having lost many assets in the partition process left many with little or nothing when they arrived in India. Added to this were the abysmal and often contradictory policies of the Indian government and friction with the West Bengal government over relief and resettlement efforts that further impoverished refugees. The attempts at trying to rebuild lives with few if any resources provided to them encapsulated the long struggle refugees had with urban poverty in Calcutta. The exceptional moment of partition also created legal and political ambivalence towards refugees. On the one hand, the government wanted to contain their activities, particularly in urban areas where many squatted on public and private land. On the other hand, the lack of substantial relief and general moral dilemmas made it difficult to enforce private property laws and to evict them. This legal and political limbo is encapsulated by the amount of time refugees took to get any rights to their squatted land in Calcutta (approximately 40 years), and to the continuous flip-flopping of the government over the classification of refugees even after the Bangladesh War of Independence in 1971 when more millions of refugees poured into the eastern part of India (Datta, 2012).

My second provocation is to consider the fractures that exist in refugee 'communities'. Rather than consider refugees as a homogenous whole, it is useful to consider the different ways in which displacement is experienced by different refugees. This leads to a richer and more nuanced understanding, and certainly in this study of both partition and the refugee crisis faced by India. What I am calling for here is a careful interrogation of the 'ethnoscapes' (Appadurai, cited in Binder and Tosic, 2005: 608) of refugees, placing greater emphasis on considering how identities may affect the ways in which displacement and its attendant conditions of poverty are experienced. Much like the literature on poverty, it is problematic to consider that the burden of poverty across refugees as an 'imagined community' would be shared uniformly. Rather, the poverty of being a refugee is affected by one's class, caste and gendered position. Being displaced as a refugee is both contingent on such identities and these identities in turn are also affected by the condition of being displaced. For example, while partition did much to change social and gender relations amongst refugees, it is also important to note how resettlement built on already existing relationships of power. It is also important to engage with those voices that are largely left out of narratives of reshaping spaces after displacement. As various feminist historians have pointed out, we need to consider how history is written and by whom and the ways in which history turns particular people such as women and minorities into objects rather than subjects of study. In pressing for more feminist historiographies, authors working on partition have pointed out how women can be agents of change, for example (Menon and Bhasin, 1998; Butalia, 1998). I would like to extend this line of thinking from the history of partition to urbanisation and urban poverty as well. Urbanisation is not a gender-neutral process. As Sapana Doshi (2011) points out in her study of women's participation in neo-liberal urban transformations, various axes of difference including gender, race and class fundamentally shape slum dwellers' political subjectivities and practices as well as their experiences of governance practices. Similarly, what I hope to show in this chapter is that the reshaping of gender, class and caste (the latter two yoked together) among refugees also has implications for the experiences of poverty and the reshaping of urban social relations. This is not an exercise in the mere excavation of subaltern voices, as I recognise that such an exercise is problematic not least because it does not account for the complex ways in which identities are reconfigured and link to larger and varied political and economic agendas and often the consolidation of hegemony.

While much of the literature on refugees and refugee colonies in Calcutta focus on either their victimhood or their entrepreneurial spirit (Sen, 2014), it is obvious that a more nuanced approach is necessary, and one that considers the ways in which refugee communities were in fact divided. Taking gender, class and caste into consideration exposes the hierarchies in the communities, the ways they shifted due to the exigencies of displacement and poverty, and the effects of such divides on the geography of the colonies themselves as this chapter will demonstrate. I draw upon a review of literature on refugees in Calcutta, as well as my own field notes from interviews with refugee women in the colonies in Calcutta, particularly in Bijoygarh, Netaji Nagar and Azadgarh where I conducted fieldwork between 2006 and 2007.[6] I should note here that while I was able to secure interviews with women, I was less successful in doing the same with lower-caste/class members. This is largely due to the snowballing technique that I employed in my fieldwork but also, as this chapter shows, because of the ways in which lower-caste members who came later have been socially and spatially marginalised. I analyse their situation using other primary and secondary data including government reports, biographies and scholarly work.

Women refugees and the urbanisation of refugee-squatter colonies

'Dada, I want to live...' cries Nita, the protagonist of Ritwick Ghatak's *Meghe Dhaka Tara* (*The Cloud Capped Star*) made in 1960. This is a story of a refugee family and their struggles to survive in Calcutta. Here, Nita is the primary breadwinner of her family, compelled to engage in wage labour such that even when her slippers tear on the way to work, she cannot afford to miss work or be late for it. In the movie, Nita contracts tuberculosis as a result of fatigue from overwork and is sent to an asylum for tubercular patients. When her brother comes to visit her at the end of the movie, she cries and tells him that she wants to live. The final images of the movie, in fact, are of the brother who watches another young girl going to work in the morning and tearing her slipper on the way in the same manner as Nita did. She fixes it, smiles at him and leaves. This torn woman's slipper becomes the symbol of sacrifice – of injustice, of female labour and poverty – and the struggle of a people to gain a foothold in a new country. This movie along with others were among a series of films made on refugees and refugee colonies in Calcutta in a period that attempted to bring realism and political consciousness, particularly of living in the city, to Indian cinema (Biswas, 2007). Importantly, also, movies such as *Meghe Dhaka Tara* offer us a glimpse into the complexity of refugee communities in Calcutta after partition. Here, the city enters as a key site that enables relationships among refugees to be reformulated under duress of poverty conditions.

Much has been written on the partition, including its politics (Chatterji, 2007a; Daiya, 2008; Pandey, 2001; Kumar, 1997; Van Schendel, 2005). The question of women has also been central to writings and cinema on partition (Menon and Bhasin, 1998; Butalia, 1998; Daiya, 2008; Weber, 2003). Within the Eastern context, there has been considerable attention paid to refugees in the city of Calcutta as key actors in the expansion and reimagination of the city in the post-partition period of India (Banerjee, 2003; Chatterjee, 1992; Chatterji 2007b; Chaudhuri, 1985; Das, 2000; Ganguly, 1997; Pakrashi, 1971; Ray, 2002; Sanyal, 2007, 2013). Refugees not only expanded the limits of the city and affected its demographics (as noted above), they also played a key role in rethinking rights to the city through their struggles for shelter at a time of crisis and scarcity and general foot-dragging by the government. The lack of support was particularly pronounced for refugees in East India who received far less help from the central government than those from the Punjab. The government was both unable and unwilling to provide many of the thousands of refugees with viable shelter. Although some vacant properties were acquired by the government through a process of *hukumdakhal* (government requisitioned), it was inadequate. Those refugees who were able to stay with relatives did so for sometime while others who were poorer and/or lacked the necessary social networks were compelled to go to camps that were also woefully inadequate and had awful conditions. Those unwilling to go to camps (usually from higher classes) waited for relief on railway platforms, jostling with commuters for a bit of private space on public thoroughfares. In essence, many refugee families were reduced to a state of near destitution despite their class status.

Eventually, under the leadership of a few young men, refugees were organised, and they raided peripheral areas of the city and set up hundreds of *jabardakhal* (forcibly occupied) refugee colonies on public and private land. Here, they built shacks out of bamboo, thatch, tin and tile. They dug their own ponds and roads, set up their own markets, schools and medical care. All this was mostly illegal. The government responded to these land invasions in a mix of tacit approval, attempted eviction (especially at the behest of private landowners), and benign neglect 'enabling' refugees to address their own shelter needs. Refugees, too, addressed their housing needs through self-help and the creation of refugee committees that fought for their rights collectively against government's attempts at trying to evict them (Chakrabarti, 1999; Sanyal, 2009). Refugees attempted to construct themselves as deserving and privileged citizens at the same time by demanding shelter as a right which they believed the government of India owed them (Chatterjee, 1992). After years of struggling through precarious and informal living conditions, eventually many of these refugee squatter colonies became legalised and regularised. Beginning in the 1970s, development efforts funded by the World Bank also resulted in upgraded urban infrastructure including metalled roads, lamp posts and so forth (Ray, 2002: 174). They have evolved into middle-class neighbourhoods today, although they continue to be referred to as refugee colonies.

Two key themes of struggle and perseverance in the face of all odds ran through my fieldwork in Calcutta denoting a kind of heroism in their self-help movement. Refugees came with little or nothing with them (a commonly used phrase to denote the gravity of their situation is to use the metaphor *ek kapor*, literally: *in one cloth*, to suggest that in fact refugees came with little clothing on their backs). While many of those who came in the first waves of displacement to Calcutta were from higher class and caste backgrounds and had social connections, at a fundamental level, they lacked necessary assets to sustain their middle-class lives in the city and were reduced to being part of the urban poor. Interestingly, the discussion of struggle and perseverance also has a rather gendered tone. The victimhood of women has been of particular focus both in popular culture and academic discourse. Some of the popular and other writing from this time has pointed out that refugee women were either compelled or tricked into engaging in prostitution in order to survive in Calcutta (Chakrabarti, Ray Mandal and Ghosal, 2007). This is bitterly ironic given that literature also notes the importance of protecting the honour of women that encouraged many men to leave for India in the first place (Chatterjee, 1992; Bandopadhyay, 1970; Chakrabarti, 1999). The poverty of displacement that refugee squatters faced in the colonies also compelled them to change many of the social and gender relations they may have enjoyed until then. For example, in order to help with household finances, many women were compelled to join the workforce in Calcutta (Weber, 2003) in public and private sectors, from teaching to secretarial work. Thus, the episodic violence of partition functioned in many ways like the structural violence of poverty does in many countries, compelling women to move outside the home to access paid labour. Refugee women often slipped into a role of carrying the triple role of women – of paid work, reproductive labour and often community participation – in order to cope with the fallout of the forced migration (Moser, 1989). I present a few of my interviews to draw on these points.

All my female respondents who had grown up or come to India after partition were educated, had often completed graduate studies and had worked as teachers, office employees and so forth. In other words, they came from very particular class backgrounds that informed the ways in which they framed their narratives. I was introduced to Mrs Sikdar through her brother and we spent many occasions chatting together when I came to visit them in their home in Netaji Nagar. One afternoon, an extensive interview with her highlighted the many ways displacement affected her life. She argued the biggest damage was done to her education. She missed two years of school and when she went back to it, those two years were crammed into one which made it difficult to pick up subjects. From a young age, she was given the responsibility of a number of household duties, such as keeping the household money, taking care of her younger siblings and so forth. When she got older, she wanted to help her father with the household expenditure and she was further urged by her mother to quit her education and begin work and become the second breadwinner for the family after her father. As she had been involved in teaching the neighbourhood children and her own siblings, she felt being a teacher was a natural choice for her. However, after finishing her college degree, she chose to take an office job. First as a typist in a private company and later as an employee in the income tax department, she was able to turn over nearly all her earnings to her family for years till her marriage. She could keep Rs 30 for her personal expenditure which included her tram fare to work. In narrating this story, Ms Sikdar's interview noted the opportunities the city offered to educated women like her for work, despite marginalising her community. It also highlighted the long process of coming out of poverty that many households faced despite their education.

I interviewed Mrs Pal in a separate room after having spoken at length with her husband. She had worked in Calcutta Telephones for many years. She came to Calcutta with every intention of working. It was fortunate for her then that her mother-in-law was on the lookout for a girl from East Bengal with a job. But it was not an easy endeavour. When she first began, she was so unused to the city, she didn't know how to cross the road and would get lost trying to find her way around. Despite contributing with paid labour, she got little or no respite from household work. As the daughter-in-law, she was expected to do all the chores when she came home and felt extremely overworked. Yet, leaving her job was also not an option as there was need for money at home.

Mrs Sinha came to Calcutta with her entire family in 1947 and moved to Netaji Nagar in the early 1950s. She had migrated when she was 16 or 17 years old, interrupting her final year exams and only completing them after they had managed to find a foothold in the city. She made her way through college and further education, and worked in a university. A long discussion about the difficulties of living in an informal settlement shifted slowly over to the discussion of education and work among refugee women. She raised the point that there were two reasons why refugee women worked more than women in Calcutta. One reason she felt was that women in West Bengal were more conservative. They would get educated, but entering the workforce was a different matter as this was a matter of choice. Mrs Sinha suggested that local women travelled differently and better, whilst she and other East Bengali women would have to travel by train or bus. This can be interpreted as a comparison of women who, in her mind, shared similar class backgrounds but no longer shared similar economic positions. The descent into being a refugee meant travel by public transport rather than private means. Another key reason for women's work, she repeatedly emphasised, was that it was done out of necessity. Refugee women had no choice but to enter the workforce because of the conditions of poverty in which they lived, but this in turn freed them and in her mind, set them apart and on a higher footing than their conservative West Bengali counterparts.

This image of the single, young, working refugee woman is portrayed over and over again as a sign of suffering and needs further deconstruction. Rachel Weber, for example, argues that women from East Bengal were not used to crossing over into the outside world and generally observed *purdah* quite strictly (Weber, 2003: 70). However, there is little evidence for this and Weber does not take into account the class, caste positions, rural or urban backgrounds of many of these women. Furthermore, she ignores the complex economic history of Bengal that had, over the past few decades, systematically marginalised women's wage labour (Banerjee, 2006). It can be argued that perhaps it's not that women did not work before in East Bengal, but that many didn't have to, as Mrs Sinha's discussion above suggests. The question of *choice* played an important role in the employment of women. Women's non-participation in wage labour is seen as a marker of respectability and class position. Most refugee families, even in the squatter colonies had lost that privilege after displacement and were compelled to encourage women to work and support the households. This was important because without this additional income, households would not be able to accumulate capital and upgrade their homes, or move up the educational and socio-economic ladders.

Uditi Sen (2011) cautions us against either condemning or celebrating the role of women in political or economic participation in Calcutta. Paralleling the above discussion of choice, she further argues (based on archival analysis) that there is no discernible difference between the participation of non-refugee women in the workforce and that of refugee women or that 'a woman turning to professional work was a trend exclusive to or dominant within refugee families in post-partition West Bengal' (Sen, 2011: 15). Further, she points out the problematic representations of women in writings on partition, particularly in the East. The analysis of the very varied nature of women in refugee colonies and camps in West Bengal and other parts of East India has not been substantial and requires considerably more work to expand our understanding of their position and contribution to post-partition India.[7] For example, partition literature has often focused on the impact government policies have had on refugee women – from forcibly returning them to their conjugal homes, to putting them in permanent liability (PL) camps along with the aged and the infirm.[8] These women, particularly those in the PL camps, or transit/refugee camps in East India are labelled as 'inmates', and then do not enter the discussions of refugee historiography in any meaningful way. Glimpses into their precarious legal condition and crushing poverty are only available occasionally.[9]

A similar caveat is necessary before celebrating or condemning the participation of women in political activities. Women played key roles in the politics of the colonies and resettlement in both confrontational and non-confrontational ways. The image of the refugee woman, bedraggled, exploited, carrying the burden of a gendered displacement on her back is evoked in writings exploring the partition (Chakrabarti, 1999; Bandopadhyay, 1970; Chakravartty, 2005; Chatterjee, 1992; Ray, 2005; Sengupta, 2003). The evocation of the refugee woman standing in as a figure violated by partition traces its history back further to the period of nationalist struggle when the figure of woman as 'Mother India' was evoked to rally people to the cause for the country, be it *swadesh* or *swaraj* (Sarkar, 2001).

Refugee women were used tactically to pressure the government over land and eviction disputes. Commissioner for Refugee Rehabilitation Hiranmoy Bandyopadhyay notes a situation where refugee women repeatedly locked him in over demands for resettlement in better sites than they had been allocated. The women used a number of different tactics over the three episodes they subjected him to in order to plead their case (Bandyopadhyay, 1970). Women were used in the anti-eviction protests between refugees and state authorities such as the police. Often they were placed at the front of the resisting crowd, many with babies in their arms. Such tactics attempted to thwart police action by appealing to normative ideas of social behaviour particular towards women as the weaker sex (Sen, 2011). The presumption being, of course, that the police would not attack women or children and less attention was paid to the danger faced by women in engaging in such activities. Women were also involved in the actual squatting process, often being left to guard the plots of land that had been allocated to families, lest other refugee families came along and squatted on them (Ray, 2002; Chatterjee, 1992: 255). Women also organised committees where colony women would get together and address their needs. In my interview with the widow of Indubaran Ganguly, a key figure in the establishment of Azadgarh, she indicated a long engagement in committee affairs for the colony which included being part of a *mahila samiti* (women's organisation) until internal politics pushed her out. She along with other women engaged in a number of activities for protecting and helping their colony including standing up to the police and thugs when they came to evict the squatters. She also talked about volunteering with other women committee members to take sick people to the hospital, or bring doctors and medical help to the colonies. Middle-class women from outside the colony also appear to have been involved in helping in these committees and being involved in refugee politics. Mrs Ganguly's interview was particularly useful because it provided a unique insight into the political mobilisation of women in the colonies that was often missing in other narratives. Not only did she talk about her own community organising activities, but also about the toll her husband's political activities took on their personal lives (e.g., the effect of his repeated arrests and long spells in jail on their lives together). Her family, who listened through much of our conversation, appeared to be largely unaware of her personal role in colony politics.

While the urbanisation of refugee colonies has a clear class bias, a gendered analysis of the urbanisation of refugee space is useful as it provides a different perspective into the building or refugee life and the effect of urban poverty on women who were displaced. Rather than see them as victims, it is useful to recognise the ways in which refugee women engaged with the city, taking up the opportunities it offered, challenging its laws and authorities to protect their settlements as agents of social and urban change.

Class and caste

Class and caste issues add an additional dimension to the discussion of urban poverty among refugees for a variety of reasons. This is because caste and class played a role in both the migration and the rehabilitation of refugees over the last 60 years. Here, I draw on the discussions of class and caste together. This is because they often feed into each other, and in the case of the colonies of Calcutta, it is useful to consider how partition changed social attitudes towards both. Manas Ray (2002) points out in his piece, 'Growing Up Refugee', that refugees coming to Calcutta were not a homogenous group. Rather, he argues,

> About sixty percent of those who came immediately before or after partition were upper-caste Hindus. A good portion were *Bhadralok*, educated people with varying degrees of exposure to urban life and its different white collar professions. The predominance among the refugees of peasants and various subaltern castes of different trades is a later phenomenon. (Ray, 2002: 151)

Ray also suggests that there was a geographical element to this, as the majority of those who became refugee squatters in Netaji Nagar, the colony where he grew up, were from the middle classes with some urban exposure. 'Those who did not fall in this bracket – fishermen, carpenters, hut-builders, masons, barbers – tended to concentrate in two adjacent wards lying at one end of the locality' (Ray, 2002: 155).

The question of *why* upper-caste Hindus were the first to migrate from East Pakistan is an important issue that is often overlooked. Nilanjana Chatterjee (1992: 57) persuasively argues that upper-caste Hindus in East Bengal dominated the landlord, rent-receiving groups, while Muslims and lower-caste Hindus engaged in cultivation and sharecropping. Even those Muslims who received rents cultivated. Thus she argues that landlordism was linked with upper-caste Hindus, as were notions of exploitation and feudalism. Economic misery in the 1930s and the devastating famine of Bengal in 1943 became the drivers behind the riots of Noakhali and Tippera in 1946, the first incident of partition violence and migration (Chatterjee, 1992: 59). While lower-caste Hindus were also targeted in the rioting, they were generally let off after conversion. Thus they felt less threatened and in fact shared many of the grievances of the Muslims, until later. On the other hand, upper-caste Hindus were compelled to leave, particularly as the decision was made to partition India and Pakistan, with the latter as an Islamic state. Chatterjee argues that upper-caste Hindus, having ridden on the backs of poor Muslims and lower-caste Hindus, were unwilling to give up their positions of power and privilege. Migration was therefore a better option than assimilation with those they considered their social inferiors with whom they were unwilling to share their space or their food. A further elaboration on this point is offered by Joya Chatterji who notes that the migration of different castes took into account a careful calculation of losses and gains both in terms of social status and also economic opportunities, social connections and asset wealth. She notes the paradox that thus emerges in the study of caste migration during partition – that those who had the greatest wealth, the most to lose in terms of worldly goods, migrated early and were also rehabilitated better. On the other hand, those who were the most vulnerable – low castes with little land, or asset wealth, few social connections beyond their nearby areas, and hence the weakest, poorest and most vulnerable stayed back because they had little to gain from the migration. This had implications for their rehabilitation, as well, as they were later driven off through communal violence and in many cases ended up in refugee camps with appalling living and economic conditions (Chatterji, 2007a: 119). Lower-caste migrants who departed later migrated for numerous reasons such as later waves of violence that they faced, discrimination and the loss of livelihoods from their traditional forms of work as that was often tied to patron-client relationships between them and the upper castes who were now gone. They continue to migrate across the border today (Chatterjee, 1992: 59–73; Samaddar, 1999).

The different caste statuses of refugees are potentially important in understanding differences in rehabilitation politics. This is also important for understanding the geography of caste differentiation amongst refugees. Several scholarly articles and government reports allude to the question of caste in the relief and rehabilitation of refugees in the post-partition period. In some cases, it has been argued that the caste differentiation amongst refugees affected their migration as well as their resettlement options in India. Joya Chatterji. for example, argues that lower-caste refugees faced a different rehabilitation scenario than their upper-caste brethren. Because many left with few if any belongings and no prospects or connections in the West, they were subjected to the politics of humanitarian control on the India side (Chatterji, 2007a: 118).

The post-partition situation, in fact, compelled refugees to live together – many of whom were deeply uncomfortable with the situation. Nilanjana Chatterjee (1992: 79) points out that the experience of being a refugee and its attendant destitution ultimately made many turn their backs on caste rules and forgo their 'Bengaliness' as they were forced to live side by side with untouchables, or live in different parts of India. Later migrants who were also made up of predominantly lower castes were affected deeply by shifting rehabilitation politics. In a report written by the Department of Anthropology, Government of India, B.S. Guha also noted the different castes present in Azadgarh colony; namely, Brahmin, Bahhakar or Rishi, Kayastha, Namasudra, Baidya, and Carpenter. The report further noted continuing caste prejudice amongst refugees but the relaxation of orthodoxy. Thus, inter-caste marriage and inter-caste dining while not outright banned were not objected to as vociferously as before (Guha, 1954).

The Indian government responded to the continuous movement of refugees, first by introducing passport systems in 1952, then by creating new classificatory systems for migrants. Those who came between 1947 and 1958 were considered 'old migrants' while those who came between 1964 and 1971 were called 'new migrants' (Dasgupta, 2001). The latter were not even rehabilitated in West Bengal and instead were coerced by the government to relocate to Dandakaranya, a forested area outside the state. Here rehabilitation efforts were piecemeal and poorly executed, leaving refugees struggling to survive in a largely inhospitable environment (Ghosh, 2000). An attempt predominantly by the Namasudras to return to West Bengal and set up a viable self-help community in Morichjhanpi, an island in the Sunderbans, was brutally crushed by the West Bengal government, which was now run by the Communist Party – the same whose electoral victory was indebted to the support it received from previous waves of refugees (Chatterjee, 1992; Jalais, 2005; Chakrabarti, 1999; Ghosh, 2000). There are competing interpretations of this situation with some scholars arguing that the state government could and should have done more to resettle the refugees in West Bengal, while others argued that the state did in fact face scarcity in land while the East Bengali refugees showed tremendous reluctance to resettle outside the state (Chatterjee, 1992; Sen; 2000).

In the city itself, caste and class have played key roles in the resettlement process of refugees. They have determined how upper-caste refugees have dealt with and overcome displacement and placed themselves within the historical and social narratives of the city. East Bengali Hindu middle classes saw themselves as emancipators of the new Indian state and saw the promises doled out by the Indian leadership of protection not as charity or compassion but as obligation (Chatterjee, 1992: 84–87). Moreover, the class and caste position coupled with their educated backgrounds and previous employments placed these individuals as part of the *bhadralok* or genteel society.[10] In Calcutta, although a number of different communities exist, the city is dominated by the Bengali *bhadralok* culture. For Bengalis, in particular, it separates them from the marginals and the informals, or the *chotolok*. It was equally important for middle-class Bengali refugees to be part of the *bhadralok* classes. Indeed, most had belonged to this class already when living in East Bengal, but the partition deprived them of many things including their class positions. Now, however, by virtue of being refugees, and arriving in a country where there was no discernible plan for rehabilitation and in fact there appeared to be an air of hostility, East Bengali refugees found themselves to be part of the 'unwanted'. As a result of their destitution, they faced a descent from *bhadralok* into *sharanatri*, or a charity recipient which was a loss of status (Feldman, 2003: 117). Refugees were not only reduced to becoming urban informals and marginals, but their descent from the *bhadralok* classes now meant that rather than 'speaking for others', they became the classes who were spoken for by others who were once their equals. Self-help and access to white-collar work eventually enabled these refugees to climb out of their condition of poverty and speak for others.

Meanwhile, it is difficult to locate later migrants in the city. In a private interview with a civil servant in charge of refugee affairs in Calcutta, I was told that they do not raise the issue of further refugees coming into the city, though they are aware of the problem. I gained limited interviews with later migrants. In an informal settlement near the middle-class area of Jodhpur Park, I was introduced to an old gentleman who had come in the 1960s. He ran a small tea stall and received no help from the government. He lamented his continued struggle in the city's urban economy. Others eavesdropping on the conversation first piped up to say that they too came recently, but later changed their story and insisted they were from West Bengal. On the periphery of the city, next to the airport, I went to meet a man and his family in their one-bedroom house. He had come in the 1970s to Calcutta and was living a largely clandestine existence. When pressed to ask why he came in the 1970s, he asked why he would have wanted to come earlier. He had no animosity with Muslims and nothing to lose in East Pakistan as he was a poor man anyway. But the Bangladesh War finally compelled him to bring his family over. He pointed across his neighbourhood and told me, most of the people there came after the 1970s, but no one would talk to me because they were too scared of being caught. Refugees have now become infiltrators and the state has silenced their voices. In thinking about the experiences of lower-class and lower-caste members we are compelled to rethink the legacy of partition on the narratives of urban poverty in Calcutta.

Conclusion

It took till 1989 for many of the refugee colonies, particularly around the Jadavpur area to get 99-year leases to their land from the government. It took a further ten years for them to get the right to sell their land (Ray, 2002). The intermediate 40 years saw attempts by refugees to buy their plots of land (often in vain) and the slow regularisation of colony areas and its gradual incorporation from the periphery into the city itself. With the right to sell land also came the rapid gentrification process as real estate developers moved in to buy land and refugee families sold up and moved out. The landscape of the colony changed from being tin and tiled houses to brick-and-mortar multi-storeyed buildings. With the changed demographics also came cultural changes to the colony areas and the sense of being a refugee area began to dissolve. Many refugee families who had struggled with poverty through much of their lives moved into the coveted middle classes partly because of the long, hard struggle to rebuild their lives and build their spaces, and partly because of the gentrification process that took place. These gains were not equally shared by everyone. *Bhadralok* refugees made their way back to their place into the civil society of the city, while later refugees and those who did not have the dispensation to engage in education or white-collar professions have continued to live in poverty. Those who have come later have not only faced the trauma of displacement, but unlike their upper-class/caste counterparts from 1947 they have been treated as illegal immigrants or infiltrators and have been forced to hide their identities while working in the informal economy of the city. We can perhaps argue that refugee poverty continues to be concentrated amongst these latecomers, who are also from lower-class and -caste backgrounds. Calcutta continues to be a refugee city, but these narratives enter the historiography of the city in only partial ways.

As discussed, refugees pose an interesting problem to the understanding of urban poverty in developing countries. Their legal and political status often makes them difficult to place neatly within categories of urban populations, and in turn makes the discussion of their rights and entitlements explosive. However, the need to engage with their presence and their politics is increasingly important as more and more of them move into cities. As this chapter has shown, the urbanisation of refugees is not a new phenomenon. Rather, one can perhaps draw upon the histories of cities such as Calcutta that have been remade through the sweat equity of refugees to consider how, in fact, refugees figure in discussions of poverty and citizenship rights of a city. Raising the politics of urban poverty among refugees also raises the thorny question of differentiating between poor refugees and the vast numbers of impoverished economic migrants who cross international and rural urban divides to remake lives. These largely problematic distinctions between groups of migrants reminds us of the ways in which the state continues to exercise its hegemony over its borders and citizenry, but it also reminds us that urban poverty is an experience that cuts across legal divisions between people. Refugees and their struggles remind us to consider those whose social and political positions may be more transient but who must be brought into thinking about the city.

Acknowledgements

I would like to thank Dr Manas Ray on his helpful comments on an earlier version of this chapter.

Notes

1. Note also that until recently less than a third of India's population was urbanised. Furthermore, issues related to defining what constitutes 'urban' in India have also complicated the collection of specifically urban data. See Sivaramakrisnan, Kundu, and Singh (2005) *Oxford Handbook of Urbanization in India* (2nd ed.).
2. India with the help of UNDP released its first urban poverty report in 2009.
3. Note that large numbers of refugees, particularly from farming and peasant backgrounds, also settled in rural areas. Schemes were created to help them resettle into their former occupations. Others also settled in smaller towns such as Jalpaiguri etc. While this chapter focuses largely on Calcutta, it is also important to note that large numbers of refugees also settled in other parts of the Eastern region, particularly in states such as Tripura and Manipur.
4. Refugees according to the international law on non-refoulement may not be 'refouled' back to their countries of origin until the danger or threat that

caused them to flee has gone. This law is often flouted, however, as countries do deport refugees back to host countries and usually do so by intercepting them midway through their migration. Many of these practices are illegal, but difficult to enforce, as the UN has no system in place to coerce countries to do their humanitarian duties.

5. India is not a signatory to the 1951 Refugee Convention.
6. Names of all my interviewees have been changed to maintain anonymity.
7. Note also that most of the autobiographical work produced on the refugee colonies that forms the basis of much academic research in this area is also predominantly written by men.
8. See, for example, Menon and Bhasin's work on recovering women in the aftermath of partition. Furthermore, reports produced by the Department of Refugee Relief and Rehabilitation, Government of West Bengal, discuss in detail the Permanent Liability Camps that were set up for old, infirm, and single and unattached women.
9. McDougall (2007) 'The Forgotten Refugees who wait for Justice after 60 Years'. Available online http://www.theguardian.com/world/2007/aug/05/india.theobserver, accessed 8 August 2014. For a detailed discussion of women in PL camps, see Ishita Dey (2009) *On the Margins of Citizenship: Principles of Care and Rights of the Residents of the Ranaghat Women's Home, Nadia District*. Refugee Watch, 33. Available online www.mcrg.ac.in/rw%20files/RW33/RW33.pdf, accessed 8 August 2014.
10. Ananya Roy (2003) appropriately describes the formation of the idea of the 'bhadralok' – a Bengali urban intelligentsia forming under colonialism. 'Bhadralok', she argues, has many connotations, but gentlemanly is perhaps the most commonly understood definition of it. 'Bhadralok' classes, she further notes, continue to exert hegemonic control over the culture and voice of the city.

References

Bandopadyay, H. (1970). *Udbastu*. Calcutta: Sahitya Sangsad.

Banerjee, N. (2006). Working women in colonial Bengal: Modernization and marginalization, in: K. Sangari and S. Vaid (eds), *Recasting Women: Essays in Colonial History*. New Delhi: Zubaan, 269–301.

Banerjee, S. (2003). Displacement within displacement: The crisis of old age in the refugee colonies of Calcutta. *Studies in History, 19*(2): 199–220.

Beteille, A. (2003). Poverty and inequality. *Economic and Political Weekly, 38*(42): 4455–4463.

Bhattacharya, R. and Sanyal, K. (2011). Bypassing the squalor: New towns, immaterial labour and exclusion in post-colonial urbanisation. *Economic and Political Weekly, 48*(31): 41–48.

Biswas, M. (2007). *The City and the Real: Chinnamul and the Left Cultural Movement in the 1940s*. Calcutta: Seagull Books, 40–59.

Binder, S. and Tosic, J. (2005). Refugees as a particular form of transnational migrations and social transformations: Socioanthropological and gender aspects. *Current Sociology, 53*(4): 607–624.

Butalia, U. (1998). *The Other Side of Silence: Voices from the Partition of India*. New Delhi: Viking Penguin India.

Chakrabarti, P.K. (1999). *The Marginal Men: The Refugees and the Left Political Syndrome in West Bengal*. Calcutta: Naya Udyog.

Chakrabarti, T., Ray Mondal, N. and Ghosal, P. (2007). *Dhvangso-o-Nirman: Bangiya Udvastu Samajer Svakathita Bibaran*. Calcutta: Sariban, School of Cultural Texts and Records, Jadavpur University.

Chakravartty, G. (2005). *Coming Out of Partition: Refugee Women of Bengal*. New Delhi and Calcutta: Bluejay Books.

Chatterjee, P. (2004). *The Politics of the Governed: Reflections on Popular Politics in Most of the World*. New Delhi: Permanent Black.

Chatterjee, N. (1992). *Midnight's Unwanted Children: East Bengali Refugees and the Politics of Rehabilitation*. PhD dissertation. Brown University.

Chatterji, J. (2007a). *The Spoils of Partition: Bengal and India, 1947–1967*. Cambridge: Cambridge University Press.

Chatterji, J. (2007b). 'Dispersal' and the failure of rehabilitation: Refugee camp-dwellers and squatters in West Bengal. *Modern Asia Studies, 41*(5): 995–1032.

Chaudhuri, P. (1985). *Refugees in West Bengal: A Study of the Growth and Distribution of Refugee Settlements within the CMD*. Occasional Paper No. 55, Calcutta: Centre for Studies in Social Sciences, Calcutta.

Das, S.K. (2000). Refugee crisis: responses of the government of West Bengal, in: S. K. Bose (ed.), *Refugees in West Bengal: Institutional Practices and Contested Identities*. Calcutta: Calcutta Research Group, 7–31.

Dasgupta, A. (2001). The politics of agitation and confession: displaced Bengalis in West Bengal, in: S. K. Roy (ed.), *Refugees and Human Rights: Social and Political Dynamics of Refugee Problem in Eastern and North-eastern India*. New Delhi: Rawat Publications.

Datta, A. (2012). *Refugees and Borders in South Asia: The Great Exodus of 1971*. London: Routledge.

Daiya, K. (2008). *Violent Belongings: Partition, Gender, and National Culture in Postcolonial India*. Philadelphia: Temple University Press.

Doshi, S. (2012). The politics of persuasion: Gendered slum citizenship in neoliberal Mumbai, in: R. Desai and R. Sanyal (eds), *Urbanizing Citizenship: Contested Spaces in Indian Cities*. New Delhi: Sage, 82–108.

Ganguly, I. B. (1997). *Colonysmriti: Prathan Khanda: Udbastu Colony Prothisthar Gorar Kotha (1948–1958)*. Calcutta: Sanjib Printers.

Ghertner, D. A. (2011). Gentrifying the state, gentrifying participation: Elite government programs in Delhi. *International Journal of Urban and Regional Research, 35*(3): 504–532.

Ghosh, A. (2000). Bengali refugees in Dandakaranya: A tragedy of rehabilitation, in: P. K. Bose (ed.), *Refugees in West Bengal: Institutional Practices and Contested Identities*. Calcutta: Calcutta Research Group: 106–129.

Guha, B. S. (1954). *Memoir No. 1: Studies in Social Tensions Among the Refugees from Eastern Pakistan*. Calcutta: Government of India Press.

Holston, J. (2008). *Insurgent Citizenship: Disjunctions of Democracy and Modernity in Brazil*. Princeton: Princeton University Press.

Feldman, S. (2003). Bengali state and nation making: partition and displacement revisited. *International Social Science Journal, 175*: 111–121.

Jalais, A. (2005). Dwelling on Morichjhanpi: When tigers became 'citizens', refugees 'tiger-food'. *Economic and Political Weekly, 40*(17): 1757–1762.

Kumar, R. (1997). The troubled history of partition. *Foreign Affairs, 76*(1) (Jan/Feb): 22–34.

Menon, R. and Bhasin, K. (1998). *Borders and Boundaries*. New Delhi: Kali for Women.

Mingione, E. (2008). *Urban Poverty and the Underclass: A Reader.* Oxford: Blackwell.

Mitlin, D. and Satterthwaite, D. (2013). *Urban Poverty in the Global South: Scale and Nature*. Oxon and New York: Routledge.

Moser, C. O. N. (1989). Gender planning in the Third World: Meeting practical and strategic gender needs. *World Development, 17*(11): 1799–1825.

Pakrashi, K. B. (1971). *The Uprooted: A Sociological Study of the Refugees of West Bengal, India*. Calcutta: S. Ghatack.

Pandey, G. (2001). *Remembering Partition: Violence, Nationalism and History in India*. Cambridge: Cambridge University Press.

Prakash, G. (2002). The urban turn, in: R. Vasudevan, R. Sundaram, J. Bagchi, M. Narula, G. Lovink and S. Sengupta (eds), *Sarai Reader 02: The Cities of Everyday Life*. New Delhi: Sarai CSDS & The Society for Old and New Media, 2–7.

Rao, V. (2006). Slum as theory. *International Journal of Urban and Regional Research, 30*(1): 225–232.

Ray, M. (2002). Growing up refugee. *History Workshop Journal, 53*: 149–179.

Ray, R. (2005). *My Reminisces: Social Development During the Gandhian Era and After*. Calcutta: Stree.

Roy, A. (2003). *City requiem Calcutta: Gender and the politics of poverty.* Minneapolis: University of Minnesota Press.

Roy, A. (2011). Slumdog cities: Rethinking subaltern urbanism. *International Journal of Urban and Regional Research, 35*(2), 223–238.

Samaddar, R. (1999). *The Marginal Nation: Transborder Migration from Bangladesh to West Bengal*. New Delhi: Sage Publications.

Sanyal, R. (2012). Refugee urbanism: Emerging spatial forms and rights in the Global South. *Geography Compass, 6*(11): 633–644.

Sanyal, R. (2009). Contesting refugeehood: Squatting as survival in post-partition Calcutta. *Social Identities, 15*(1): 67–84.

Sarkar, T. (2001). *Hindu Wife, Hindu Nation: Community, Religion and Cultural Nationalism*. Bloomington: Indiana University Press.

Sen, S. (2000). The legal regime for refugee relief and rehabilitation in West Bengal, in: P. K. Bose (ed.), *Refugees in West Bengal: Institutional Practices and Contested Identities*. Calcutta: Calcutta Research Group, 49–64.

Sen, U (2014). The myths refugees live by: Memory and history in the making of Bengali refugee identity. *Modern Asia Studies, 48*(1): 37–76.

Sen, U. (2011). *Spinster, Prostitute or Pioneer? Images of Refugee Women in Post-Partition Calcutta*. Florence: European University Institute Working Paper MWP 2011/34.

Sengupta, D. (ed.) (2003). *Mapmaking: Partition Stories from 2 Bengals*. New Delhi: Srishti Publishers.

Van Schendel, W. (2005). *The Bengal Borderland: Beyond State and Nation in South Asia*. London: Anthem Press.

Weber, R. (2003). Re(creating) the home: Women's role in the development of refugee colonies in South Calcutta, in: J. Bagchi and S. Dasgupta (eds), *The Trauma and the Triumph: Gender and Partition in Eastern India*. Calcutta: Stree, 59–79.

7

Expanding the 'Room for Manoeuvre': Community-Led Finance in Mumbai, India

Caren Levy

Introduction

Urban planning in cities of the Global South does not have a good track record in addressing urban poverty. Infused with colonially inherited planning systems, at best, planning has often been associated with lack of recognition of poor informal areas of the city; at worst, with the eviction of poor households and/or their livelihoods. At the same time, urban planning has often been reticent in challenging powerful actors in the city who are benefiting unequally from its development, creating a system of city management that is neither transparent nor accountable, and contributing to the reproduction of socio-spatial urban inequalities. This tendency is even more pronounced in a neo-liberal age when the aims of planning have been reframed as supporting the market and enhancing the vision of the 'competitive city'.

This chapter explores a case that challenges this kind of urban planning. The Community-Led Infrastructure Finance Facility (CLIFF), which was initially piloted in Mumbai, India, from 2002 to 2008, aimed 'to achieve reductions in urban poverty by increasing poor urban communities' access to commercial and public sector finance for medium to large-scale infrastructure and housing initiatives' (Homeless International, 2002a in Morris, 2006: 111). During this period, CLIFF was a building block in a longer history of community-led initiatives to address urban poverty. What distinguished it is that it sought to achieve its aim 'by developing a sustainable financial facility that can assist organisations of the urban poor to carry out successful community-driven infrastructure, housing and urban services initiatives at city level, in conjunction with municipalities and the private sector...' (Ibid: 111).

The case of CLIFF is positioned within a multi-dimensional view of poverty, in which lack of secure access to decent standards of housing and infrastructure are viewed as a critical aspect of urban poverty (Baud, Chapter 5 of this volume), not just in their own right, but also in the opportunities they open up to meet other rights to the city. It is also positioned in an understanding of urban poverty that prioritises the voices of poor women and men, girls and boys, both in expressing and addressing poverty (Satterthwaite and Mitlin, 2014).

As an experience of organisations of the urban poor at scale, CLIFF demonstrated an alternative to the pressures for eviction of poor households as well as a constructive but critical engagement with powerful forces in the city whose interests did not coincide with the aims of the organised communities. The capacity to assess the 'room for manoeuvre' stands out as fundamental in this experience, both in the conditions that enabled CLIFF to be implemented and in the space to redress urban poverty that CLIFF itself allowed. Through an examination of this case, this chapter seeks to explore the notion of 'room for manoeuvre' to implement purposeful collective action which contributes to socio-spatial justice in the city.

Why 'room for manoeuvre'?

Framing the challenge of planning as tackling urban poverty in the context of addressing socio-spatial justice in the city goes beyond merely the reform of urban planning. It is a call to address urban practices and underlying structural drivers which reproduce urban poverty and socio-spatial inequality, putting in place an alternative trajectory for transformative change for poor women and men, girls and boys, in the city (Levy et al., forthcoming). Based on the deliberations between Young (1990, 1998) and Fraser (1996, 1998a, 1998b) about the definition of social justice, and its translation into a framework for examining notions of socio-environmental justice (Allen and Apsan Frediani, 2013; Levy and Davila, forthcoming) in different urban practices, progress along this trajectory is assessed through three intersecting domains.

The first is *redistribution*, understood in the context of 'deep distribution' – that urban development is 'based on the articulation of power relations in public and private space at the level of the household, community and society that generate structural inequality and dominant relations under which decisions ... are negotiated and made' (Levy, 2003a: 52).[1] This domain focuses on material practices carried out in time and space. In most cases, housing and infrastructure policy and planning has not addressed questions of 'deep distribution'. For example, 'informal settlement upgrading may in some cases perpetuate the spatial arrangements that reproduce social-spatial segregation in cities...and focus on the manifestations of injustices...rather than its causes' (Apsan Frediani, Lipietz and Butcher, forthcoming).

While the entry point for the remaining two domains is institutional, each has material and spatial implications for redistribution. *Inclusive recognition* engages with the 'politics of recognition', prioritising the importance of challenging the discourses of dominant groups, building a platform of equal respect between all groups in the city (Fraser, 1996), whether defined on the basis of class, gender, ethnicity, race, religion or age, and expressed in different spatial geographies in the city. The lack of recognition of informal settlements in urban planning and the resultant labelling of their inhabitants as 'illegal' in many urban contexts, has been one of the most entrenched discursive practices facing more socio-spatially just urban development.

The final domain embraces *parity political participation*, based on an intersection of Young's notion of political participation (Young, 1990) and Fraser's idea of 'parity of participation...[a norm that] requires social arrangements that permit all (adult) members of society to interact with one another as peers' (Ibid: 30). At both informal and formal levels, parity political participation implies participation in relationships of equivalence (Levy, 2007) and can be acted out at different spatial scales – local, neighbourhood, citywide and beyond. While housing policy has a long and contested history of participation (incorporating debates about self-help housing, community participation and the extent of their contribution to empowerment or the maintenance of socio-spatial relations of domination), the planning of urban infrastructure has largely been a top-down process in most cities.

This chapter argues that, since working towards socio-spatial justice defined in this tripartite framework involves challenging powerful interests acting in and on the city, it demands a strategic approach. Such a strategic approach is predicated on a critical assessment of the 'room for manoeuvre' to carry out this kind of transformative planning, at the same time as expanding or opening up the 'room for manoeuvre' for ongoing radical processes and ends.

Defining the 'room for manoeuvre'

The definition of 'room for manoeuvre' explored in this chapter is that proposed by Safier (2002). The following paragraphs seek to contextualise his work in key debates on social change in the social sciences and their application in the planning field. At the heart of any definition of 'room for manoeuvre' is an understanding of power and its articulation in the relationship between 'agency' (in this case, individual and collective urban practices) and 'structure' (in this case, the structural drivers reproducing urban inequality).

Following the rational comprehensive planning ideal, conventional planning is based on an implicit and unproblematised agency-centred view that planners can shape the future. The structuralist critique of this kind of planning provided a formidable spatialised political economy explanation of how this approach more often than not served the interests of powerful groups in cities (for example, writings by Harvey, Scott and Roweiss; Beauregard; Fainstein), but offered little insight into how a more progressive urban planning might be pursued.

Shifting from the materialist to the phenomenological, Healey (1997) grappled with the structure-agency relationship in an 'institutionalist approach', building on the work of Giddens and Habermas, and talked to a notion of 'room for manoeuvre', if not in name. She argues that in transformative strategy making '...there needs to be a "moment of opportunity", a "crack" in the power relations, a situation of contradiction and conflict, which encourages people to recognize that they need to reflect on what they are doing, that they need to work with different people, that they need to evolve different processes' (Ibid: 269–70). While recognising the significance of structure, this is based on her view that '[S]ocial life is an active process of continual "making"' of the web of relations and 'relational cultures' in which we live and which 'will vary in their spatial and temporal span'. She argues that because we have the capacity to be reflective, '...we have choices about what to accept of our structured, social embeddedness, and what to reject' (Ibid: 57). In making these choices, 'structuring power relations are continually re-negotiated and reformed. This creates the possibilities that the "way things are" could be transformed into something different' (Ibid: 58).

Using similar theoretical foundations, Safier (2002) talks directly to the planning imperative of estimating the 'room for manoeuvre'. In addressing the structure-agency paradox, Safier settles on a set of interrelated explanations of social change, based on four theoretical constructs offered by Abrams as 'different theoretical constructs which are regularly used to explain the historical evolution of social change' (Ibid:127). On this basis, Safier (Ibid: 127) derives '...a four dimensional model of the "action space" of practitioners and planning agencies, that estimates the degrees of freedom, or "room for manoeuvre" open to them in promoting progressive interventions in urban affairs'. These four areas are:

- 'Improving technical-professional (in the broadest sense) innovations and individual or group ethics and behaviours;
- extending institutional and inter-organizational reforms – or goals, roles, priorities, procedures and resource allocations;
- expanding social interaction and mobilization – involvement in modes of inclusive, participative and collaborate bargaining and negotiation;
- enlarging the scope of strategic analysis and tactical response to the dynamics of urban development in time and place' (Ibid.: 127–128).

Safier emphasises that '[T]he four dimensions have different but intersecting boundaries which define the likely limits (imposed by various sources of opposition) to action by planners in support of progressive interventions intended to help bring about greater equality, inclusiveness, democratic process and social justice' (Ibid: 128). While the material/spatial forms and institutional/discursive expressions of the intersecting dimensions are context specific, all four dimensions configure the possible action space and need to be considered in developing and assessing progressive strategy.

It is important to emphasise that an estimation of 'room for manoeuvre' is grounded in a critical reflection of urban practices and the structural drivers of urban inequality in which they are embedded, including the positionality of planners and other actors involved in collective action in context-specific urban spaces. This implies an engagement with 'discourse politics' and a critical restatement of the importance of the reflexive practitioner[2] in progressive strategy development.

The following sections explore the performance of Safier's notion of 'room for manoeuvre' in the context of the case of CLIFF, and whether the space for action is expanding or opened up so that the tripartite approach to justice – that is, material redistribution, inclusive recognition and parity political participation – can be addressed in an urban context.

The case of CLIFF

Established in 2002, CLIFF evolved out of the challenges faced by community-driven slum upgrading. Building on a collective formulation, CLIFF was formalised through a research project, 'Bridging the Finance Gap', funded by DfID and carried out by Homeless International (HI) and its partners in different countries. The starting point for the research was that while poor communities and their organisation invest a great deal in improving their living environments, it is difficult and risky for them to scale up this activity because of the gap between 'community or informal financial systems and formal financial markets ...' (McLeod and Mullard, 2006: 9). This gap is a result of a set of barriers related to formal financial criteria and practices, the focus of available – and relatively costly – housing finance on individuals, and difficulties in accessing housing and infrastructure subsidies from the public sector (McLeod, 2001, 2002).

It is this gap that CLIFF was designed to fill – to 'provide loan capital for bridge financing large-scale developments that are prioritized, designed and managed by organisations of the poor' (McLeod and Mullard, 2006: 1), creating the basis for their access to medium- and long-term finance for housing and infrastructure development.

In its final form, CLIFF was managed internationally by HI with local partners in the first pilot country of India (2002), followed by Kenya (2005) and the Philippines (2007). The funding, channelled through the World Bank Cities Alliance Programme, was made up of contributions from DfID (£6.84 million from June 2002–March 2008) and SIDA (£1.6 million from Jan 2003–December 2005 and £1.4 million from Jan 2006–December 2008). Local partners also contributed to CLIFF from their own revolving loan funds. HI also contributed approximately £0.7 million through its Guarantee Fund 'to help secure banking financing when needed...' (CLIFF End of Project Evaluation, 2008: appendix 1).

This chapter will focus on the use of CLIFF in India by the Indian Alliance (2002–2008), HI's long-standing local partner. The Indian Alliance comprises a partnership between

- SPARC (an NGO),
- Mahila Milan (MM) and the National Slum Dwellers Federation (NSDF) (both CBOs) and
- SPARC Samudaya Nirman Sahayak (SSNS) (a legal entity established by SPARC and the NSDF to effect project management and financial services to act as a developer – or 'community developer' for slum rehabilitation).

Project proposals come up from the federations, through SSNS, which administers the CLIFF capital loan funds. The formal and legal responsibility within CLIFF rests with the SSNS and SPARC Boards (which overlapped in the first instance due to the recent creation of SSNS), the HI Board, and the Cities Alliance Consultative Group (left-hand side of Figure 7.1). An operational structure was put in place to serve the Boards at every level (right-hand side of Figure 7.1). A CLIFF India Technical Advisory Group (TAG) was created to review proposals from the communities on the basis of a set of eight criteria derived from the objectives of CLIFF (HI TAG meeting papers, 2002). Once ratified by the SPARC/SSNS Board, the proposals came to the HI TAG who recommended projects to the HI Board.

The analysis of this case study is a 'reflexive practice', based on my involvement in the implementation of CLIFF as a member of the HI Board, but more pertinently, as the Chair of the HI Technical Advisory Group (HI TAG).[3] I was a member of the HI TAG committee established in June 2002 and took over as Chair of TAG from January 2003, in the build-up to initial preparation phase of CLIFF, prior to the official commencement of CLIFF in April 2003.

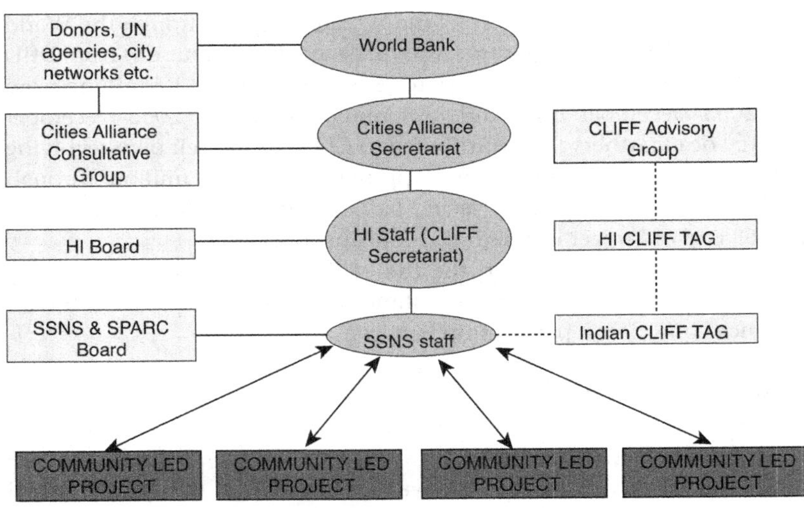

Figure 7.1 Actors and institutional relationships in CLIFF

Source: '"A Discussion of Institutional Roles and Responsibilities within CLIFF'", HI, September 2005.

The following sections explore the particular conditions analysed through Safier's four dimensions of the 'room for manoeuvre', based on the experience of CLIFF India. This analysis does not follow the order in which Safier presented the dimensions but is driven by the particular context of Mumbai and the strategies of the Alliance.

Expanding social interaction and mobilisation

An analysis of the story of CLIFF necessarily – and significantly – starts with an understanding of Safier's third dimension: 'expanding social interaction and mobilisation – involvement in modes of inclusive, participative and collaborate bargaining and negotiation' (Safier: 127–128). This is because CLIFF is an instrument created at a particular moment in a much longer and bigger history in which the mobilisation of slum dwellers to improve their living conditions and to claim their entitlements is central.

The history of this mobilisation and the formation of the Alliance has been documented elsewhere (Patel, 1990, 1996; Patel and Mitlin, 2001, 2004). In brief, the Alliance was established in 1985, as a collective of SPARC, MM and the NSF, with a common commitment to empower the urban poor to articulate their concerns and gain access to resources to upgrade and formalise their settlements. SPARC's establishment as an NGO in 1984 developed an early working relationship with Mahila Milan (MM),[4] women pavement dwellers, 'an organisational form that invested knowledge in women's collectives rather than in male leaders' (Ibid, 2004: 218). The NSDF had been formed in 1974 as a response to forced evictions.

The level of mobilisation and experience of the Alliance was a critical factor in *estimating* the 'room for manoeuvre' for a collective finance project like CLIFF. After years of working with grant funding, the Alliance and its international partner, HI, designed CLIFF to scale up their community-led collective actions to address housing and infrastructure. The success of CLIFF was predicated on the 18-year experience of collective savings and the development of community organisational and management skills. In this sense, there is a threshold of community mobilisation and capacities that need to be in place before a financial facility like CLIFF can be implemented successfully.

The spatial expression of this social organisation is also important, both as a basis for mobilisation and as one of the drivers for the choice of CLIFF projects. The NSDF, incorporating MM, mobilised around specific spatial locations in the city with shared institutional challenges – hence the formation of the Pavement Dwellers Federation, the Railway Slum Dwellers Federation and the Airport Slum Dwellers Federation. While each Federation was formed to address the spatial particularities of a common constellation of state entities (including the land owner on which the slums were located), a system of exchange visits ensured that there was a shared learning building up in the Alliance at intra- and intercity scales.

Did CLIFF strengthen social interaction and mobilisation and the capacity for claim-making, as part of *expanding* the 'room for manoeuvre'? This is a complex question. CLIFF demanded the translation of the energies and capacities of organised communities into a portfolio of projects (see Tables 7.1 and 7.2), which brought with it particular opportunities and challenges. With the arrival of CLIFF, and operating within the framework of the eight agreed criteria, the Alliance prioritised projects for the new financial facility that would build up knowledge and test out strategies to address the different organisational and spatial conditions in which slum dwellers found themselves in the city – with a view to making policies more pro-poor. The availability of land and entitlements built into government policy also had to be factored into the decision. Both the choice of projects and their subsequent development created conditions that often put pressure on both sustaining and extending community organisation itself.

For example, communities that had been mobilised the longest, like the pavement dwellers, had to wait to be re-housed, while other projects where community organisation was more recent went ahead. Organised communities were severely stretched when housing projects were delayed because of regulatory issues (like Rajiv Indira, subject to coastal zone regulations, which the Alliance challenged) (CLIFF, 2008) or because of slow disbursement of public sector subsidies (for example, by the metropolitan corporations in Mumbai and Pune in the citywide sanitation programmes in those cities). The success of the Alliance's community mobilisation capacities was recognised in other citywide government programmes, like the Mumbai Urban Infrastructure Project (MUIP). In this case, in negotiation with the Mumbai Metropolitan Regional Authority (MMRDA), the Alliance was invited to mobilise communities located on the side of roads earmarked for improvement, and to relocate them in the CLIFF-supported project of Oshiwara. These projects shifted the Alliance into a deliverer of government policy, the implications of which will be discussed in the final section.

A major source of these tensions arose from the Alliance's purposeful engagement with the state, which they sought to manage through their in-built routines and strategies, like the routine of daily savings which remained '"the glue" that holds the Federation together' (Patel, 2004: 120), with women playing a key role in this process. Thus the boundaries between expanding social interaction and mobilisation, and the following two dimensions of 'room for manoeuvre' were porous, because of key strategic decisions taken by the Alliance prior to CLIFF.

Extending institutional and inter-organisational reforms

According to Safier's framework, extending institutional and inter-organisational reforms concerns 'goals, roles, priorities, procedures and resource allocations' (Safier: 127). The regulatory frameworks in Mumbai reflected – and reproduced – wide spatial differentials in access to secure housing and infrastructure in different parts of the city, which formed the basis for mobilisation and claim-making in the city (see Baud, Chapter 5 of this volume).

In the years prior to CLIFF, while slum clearance policies remained a key tool of urban and housing development policy in Mumbai, increasingly various slum improvement interventions were also developed. Because of prior successes in collective claim-making and technical innovation (see next section), SPARC and its Alliance associates were recognised as important partners in the development of new policies and procedures to create a more responsive institutional and organisational framework in the city. With the 1995 election,[5] Burra (1999) recounts how the Government of Maharashtra (GOM), based on the recommendations of a study group in which the SPARC Director participated, created the Slum Rehabilitation Authority (SRA) as an independent co-ordinating body. Included in its arsenal of instruments were transferable development rights (TDRs), to compensate public and private sector land owners for giving over their land to slum redevelopment. Thus, the policy context not only recognised a section of slum dwellers and their organisations, but also put in place instruments to leverage land and resources for their use. At the same time, the Alliance's involvement with another citywide project, the World Bank-supported Mumbai Urban Transport Project-II (MUTP-II), through work with the Railway Slum Dwellers Federation and as a member of a 1997 Task Force, resulted in the redrafting of a more progressive Resettlement and Rehabilitation (R&R) policy[6] for MUTP-II and the city. Alongside these evolving slum improvement instruments, there were also subsidies built into state and metropolitan sanitation programmes, but their access by poor communities had been problematic.

This is the policy environment that influenced the design of CLIFF and into which it was introduced. It is no mistake that by 2008, of the 15 projects in the CLIFF portfolio (9 related to housing – 6 in Mumbai; 6 to sanitation – 3 in Greater Mumbai) (see Tables 7.1 and 7.2), six were SRA projects. These projects legitimised community-led projects within the SRA framework, and opened up other relationships with different entities in the private sector. Three of the CLIFF projects resulted in the release of privately owned land for low-income housing development (prior to 2000, no community-managed SRA projects had achieved this).

A partnership of trust was built up between medium-sized contractors drawn into the construction of CLIFF projects and the Alliance, based on the latter's management of the SRA instruments, in particular TDRs. This resulted in the growing confidence of contractors to pre-financing projects, which also reduced the delays associated with other start-up funds.

The CLIFF portfolio was able to attract finance from three different banks (Citibank, ICICI and the National Housing Bank). As Morris (2006) shows, while in June 2002 almost all the financing for the portfolio came from CLIFF or SPARC/SSNS sources, by June 2005 one-third of the financing of the portfolio came from the banks. This happened over time, as the banks gained confidence in the Alliance's capacity to manage private sector financing from one project to the next.

The donors supporting CLIFF were also important actors in the organisational and institutional landscape. In line with their neo-liberal influenced policies, early on in CLIFF they tended to emphasise the involvement of the private banking sector, with less discursive attention given to local government and even the livelihood impacts in the local construction sector. Another interesting impact of CLIFF was the rewriting of World Bank procurement procedures to accommodate the reimbursement of community-based organisation (in this case, MM) in the citywide sanitation programmes.

CLIFF also brought with it organisational reform within the Alliance itself. As noted previously, the Alliance created a purpose-made social enterprise, SPARC Samudaya Nirman Sahayak (SSNS), with the legal powers to develop projects, administer the CLIFF capital loan funds and financial services and project manage the slum rehabilitation. As a newly created entity, SSNS had the steepest learning curve in the Alliance, with the challenge of finding a balance between the formal tools of large-scale developers and the more informal bottom-up routines of the organisations of the poor.

Although CLIFF has contributed to extending institutional and inter-organisational reforms, various threats to sustainability remain: corruption and inefficiency in government; staff turnover in both government and the banking sector; to date, lack of institutionalisation of procedures for community lending in the banking sector; and ambiguous support to urban development in donor agencies (though DfID support for CLIFF has been constant and continues). With delays in the release of subsidies, questions also remain about the commitment of local government to deliver on current entitlements of the poor in Mumbai. The Alliance navigated the high degree of resistance they faced through the '...longstanding nature of the relationships...' (McLeod, 2005: 6) they have developed over the years with individuals in different places, public and private sectors, locally and internationally, and through technical professional innovations.

Improving technical professional innovations

Safier (2002: 127) refers to this dimension as '[I]mproving technical-professional (in the broadest sense) innovations and individual or group ethics and behaviours'. From its inception, the Alliance has recognised the importance of developing its own technical innovations or routines, both as a way to strengthen community mobilisation, capacities and strategies, and also as a way to maintain control over their own processes in their engagement with the state and external 'experts'. They have labelled this as 'precedent setting':

> The idea is that the poor need to be able to claim, capture, refine and define certain ways of doing things in spaces they already control and then use these to show city-officials and external agencies that these are 'precedents' that are worth investing in. This gives legitimacy to the changes that the poor want to bring into a city strategy. (D'Cruz and Satterthwaite, 2004: 37)

The range of community-developed techniques like self-enumeration, mapping, house modelling and exchange visits were all innovations in their time which have become established routines and even officially recognised, planning practices. '[B]ecause they emerge from the existing practices of the poor, they make sense to other grassroots organisations, become widely supported and can easily be scaled up' (Patel and Mitlin, 2004: 233).

CLIFF itself is just such a technical-professional innovation, which was built on the various and established community mobilisation and planning capacities of the Alliance and its partnership with HI and supportive public actors. CLIFF is a demonstration of 'community developers' in action applying a set of technical innovations in combination with more mainstream design, and project and financial management techniques, provided largely by local professionals. In enabling the Alliance to scale up its operations, CLIFF has extended the Alliance capacities for portfolio management, based on a community-formulated and -controlled process of financing housing and infrastructure construction at scale in Mumbai and other parts of India. The financial and technical capacities of portfolio management have also been greatly strengthened in HI.

As an indication of this capacity, as mentioned previously, by 2008, CLIFF was supporting 15 different projects, nine of which related to housing and six to sanitation (Table 7.2). These projects carry different risks, which are balanced within the portfolio, but with each selected to generate different precedents, at least four of which are important here.

The first is to extend technical innovation to address community-led development projects in different spatial and institutional settings. As Table 7.1 shows, six of the housing projects fall within the Slum Rehabilitation Authority (SRA), covering in situ upgrading or the relocation of poor communities to the peri-urban interface (PUI) in Greenfield's development. Despite the spatial differences (for example, Rajiv Indira is on the edge of Dharavi, while Bharat Janata is in the centre of this large informal settlement), they illustrate the application of the SRA framework and procedures, controlled by organisations of the poor, to test developments involving relocation and rehabilitation in the city.

Second, within the construction of these projects, SSNS has also experimented with higher building and design standards for high-rise housing blocks. For example, Rajiv Indira units incorporated a 14-foot back wall, allowing a mezzanine level and increasing floor space, whilst in Bharat Janata and Oshiwara 1, corridors were designed with up to double standard width (Jack, Morris and McLeod, 2005).

The third is to demonstrate options for the different financial blending of resources (including land) from public, private and community sources in which risk is balanced within the Alliance portfolio. Tables 7.1 and 7.2 show the combination of resources put together to finance each project. The SRA projects all include money from TDRs, for land and/or construction costs due at the completion of particular stages of construction (TDRs are unique to Mumbai among the urban areas in which CLIFF operated). Without CLIFF bridging capital and HI

Table 7.1 Summary of CLIFF India housing portfolio

Type	Projected total costs (£)	Buildings and beneficiaries (families)	Financial blending
SRA Housing – Mumbai			
Rajiv Indira In situ upgrading on edge of Dharavi	1,842,000	5 buildings 219 families	Land & infrastructure – government TDR (69%) Loan from Citibank (with HI guarantee) Sale: residential (21%) and commercial units (9%)
Bharat Janata In situ upgrading in middle of Dharavi	1,020,000	5 buildings 147 families	Land and infrastructure – government TDR (37%) Loan from NHB (with HI guarantee) Sale: residential (57%) and commercial units (5%)
Milan Nagar Resettlement of pavement dwellers, greenfield site in PUI	1,338,000	5 buildings 327 families	Land and infrastructure – government TDR (92%) Sale: 30 commercial units (7%) Community contributions (1%)
Oshiwara (Phase 1) In situ upgrading and resettlement of roadside dwellers on greenfield site in PUI	3,139,000	6 buildings 780 families	Private landowner Infrastructure – government TDR (99%) Grant funds (1%) Contractor pre-financing (approx. 30% of construction costs) 38 residential units (handed over MHADA for households with disabled members)

Continued

Table 7.1 Continued

Type	Projected total costs (£)	Buildings and beneficiaries (families)	Financial blending
Oshiwara (Phase 2) Large-scale in situ upgrading and resettlement of roadside dwellers on greenfield site in PUI	11,549,610	19 buildings 2,480 families	Private landowner Infrastructure – government TDR (89%) Contractor pre-financing (approx 30% of construction costs) Loan from ICICI (with USAID guarantee) Sale: residential (5%) and commercial units (5%)
Jollyboard Voluntary resettlement of RSD in greenfield site	374,924	2 buildings 101 families	Private landowner Infrastructure – government TDR (95%) Contractor pre-financing (approx 30% of construction costs) Sale: commercial units (5%)
Other housing			
Solapur bidi, Solarpur Subsidy draw down (test) 1st engagement with unions	805,000	501 tenements 501 families	Private landowner Infrastructure from government (subsidy 31%) Sale: commercial units (57%) Community contributions (12%)
Sunnuduguddu, Bangalore New development	146,000	4 buildings 72 families	Land and infrastructure – government Subsidy from state Sale: commercial units (83%) Community contributions (17%)
Hadaspar (Ph 1 & 2), Pune Combined in situ and greenfield in PUI (test)	651,000	4 buildings 711 families	Land – government Infrastructure – government – VAMBAY subsidy, (68%) Community contributions (29%) Grant funds (3%)

Notes: All projects have benefited from recycled CLIFF funds. All buildings are multi-storied.

Table 7.2 Summary of CLIFF India sanitation portfolio

Type	Project costs	Toilet blocks & beneficiaries	Financial blending
Mumbai & Greater Mumbai			
BSDF (Phase 1) Subsidy draw down test – government	3,928,000	208 toilet blocks 40,000 families	Land – government and private Infrastructure – Municipality (95% contract payments from WB loan to BMC) Grant funds (4%)
Mumbai Sewerage Disposal project (Phase 2)	2, 221,000	150 toilet blocks 30,000 families	Land – government and private Infrastructure (97% contract payments) Loan from UTI bank (with HI guarantee) Grant funding (3%)
Nirmal MMR Abhiyan	19,000,000	1,047 toilet blocks 210,000 families	Land and infrastructure – government (MMRDA) (100%)
Other			
Pune sanitation (Phase 4) Subsidy draw-down test VAMBAY government policy	150,000	23 toilet blocks 2,500 families	Land – government Infrastructure – Municipality (96% contract payments) Grant funds (4%)
Tiruppur sanitation Tamil Nadu First citywide sanitation programme in Tamil Nadu Creating new policy; testing new partnerships	171,000	13 toilet blocks 2,500 families	Land – government Infrastructure – Municipality (96% contract payments) Grant funding (4%)
Pimpri-Chinwad Sanitation Maharashtra	75,000	7 toilet blocks 1,000 families	Land – government Infrastructure – government (94% contract payments) Grant funds (6%)

Notes: Projected costs are rounded and number of beneficiaries is approximate. All projects have used recycled CLIFF funds. *Source*: CLIFF Annual Review 08, Homeless International (2008); for Nirmal MMR, CLIFF End of Project Evaluation (2008).

Guarantees (see Table 7.1), TDRs would not be accessible to the poor, and the banks would not be confident to get involved. The other housing and sanitation projects are largely based on leveraging subsidies form local- and/or state-level government. Although these are subsidies that the Alliance regards as entitlements, since they are enshrined in various national and state policies, their release by government has been fraught with politics and delays.

Finally, with reference to Safier's emphasis on ethics in this dimension, from their inception both the Alliance and HI have placed their technical-professional capacities within a well-articulated framework of ethics. Indeed, their approach interrogates the notion of a 'technical' professional expertise in isolation from socio-economic, political and spatial contextual relations, and which holds itself above community knowledge, procedures and techniques. In this conscious questioning and close interdependence with the dimension of social mobilisation, alongside creating relationships of equivalence with public and private sector organisations and engaging with institutional reform, the Alliance's tremendous orchestration of innovation, including through CLIFF in three of Safier's dimensions, appears to have expanded the 'room for manoeuvre' to address socio-spatial justice in Mumbai. Were these urban practices supported by changes in the structural drivers in the development of Mumbai?

Enlarging the scope of strategic analysis and tactical response

This dimension is set within 'the dynamics of urban development in time and place' (Safier, 2002: 128) and involves, in Healey's terms, 'reading the cracks' and acting to widen the cracks in the spatialised political economy of a particular context.

Mumbai, the site of the highest proportion of the CLIFF portfolio, is the commercial and financial capital of India. It is also a de-industrialising city that is stagnating,[7] leading Mahadevia (2006) to argue that there is a close connection between efforts to stimulate the growth of Mumbai and the future of slum dwellers in the city, given that 54.1 per cent of the MCGM population lives in slums (Census of India 2001 in Mahadevia, 2006). The Vision Plan for the conversion of Mumbai into a 'World Class City' is just such an initiative, led by Bombay First, an organisation of corporate leaders in the city (Bombay First-McKinsey, 2003), and accepted by the Chief Minister's Task Force in 2004. Mahadevia refers to this plan as 'Shanghaing Mumbai'. By playing with the definition of 'citizenship', it has already led to the forced evictions of some 7 per cent of slum dwellers in MCGM. He points to powerful political forces underpinning the evictions, including an influential builder-politician nexus.

In the years prior to CLIFF, there had been significant changes at national level, with the adoption of structural adjustment and liberalisation policies. The liberalisation of the financial sector created more 'welcoming' conditions for CLIFF. In addition, although national policy has shifted from slum clearance to a draft national slum development policy with some progressive features (e.g., secure land tenure), there was resistance to it by central government departments who own slum-encroached land (Burra, 2005). This is of particular relevance in Mumbai, because they own vast tracts of land in the city (related to railways, ports, airports) and, as noted previously, the Alliance set its first successful precedents of relocation at scale with the RSDF on Indian Railways land (Burra, 1999; Patel, D'Cruz and Burra, 2002).

Enlarging the scope of strategic analysis and tactical response, the Alliance has challenged these powerful private and public sector forces both discursively and materially. For example, recognising the importance of upgrading transport infrastructure in the development of the city, they proposed an alternative vision for Mumbai (Ibid, 2002) based on community-led resettlement of the large proportion of slum dwellers living along major transportation routes. CLIFF has contributed to this work by continuing to reinforce a people-centred policy dialogue and to demonstrate the material efficacy of such an alternative vision. Between 2002–2008, 5338 households (4054 in Mumbai) were set to benefit from CLIFF housing projects, while 308,500 households (215,408 in Greater Mumbai) were covered by CLIFF sanitation projects (see Tables 7.1 and 7.2).

CLIFF is one intervention in a history of tactical precedent setting, which seeks to 'widen the cracks' and to strengthen community-led city development in the face of constant challenges by powerful interests in the city. Since 2004, the launch of the Dharavi Redevelopment Plan (DRP) has proved another such encounter. Dharavi, said to be the largest slum in Asia, was always strategically important to the Alliance and was the focus of sanitation and two housing projects in the CLIFF portfolio. Driven by a neo-liberal market approach, the intention of the original plan was to tender out segments of Dharavi to private sector developers for the construction of housing and commercial development, without a commitment to the participation of local residents and without clear rules about who would be eligible for re-housing and resettlement (Patel and Arputham, 2007). From 2007, the Alliance, along with organisations of local residents and other 'concerned citizens' were focused on getting two messages across. The first, was that 'the homes and livelihoods of hundreds of thousands of Mumbai inhabitants are at stake, as is the future of thousands of local businesses in Dharavi that are of considerable importance not only for livelihoods but also for Mumbai's economy' (Patel and Arptham, 2008: 243). The second, was that 'the way in which Dharavi is redeveloped will influence the city's future strategies for dealing with slum dwellers, at a time when real estate development has so much global capital pouring into Mumbai in response to increased demand for high-end housing and commercial space' (Ibid: 244). After a number of difficult challenges, it appears that the collective civil society-led resistance to the DRP has brought about a number of critical changes to the plan, built in part on the credibility and reputation of the Alliance in social mobilisation, technical innovation (at this stage in enumeration) and organisational reform (its experience with the SRA through CLIFF) (Patel Arputham, Burra and Savchuk, 2009). The impact of the global economic crisis on Mumbai has also played its part in slowing down the development process.

Reflections on 'room for manoeuvre'

To what extent did CLIFF expand the 'room for manoeuvre' to contribute to socio-spatial justice in Mumbai? Assessed against the tripartite definition of socio-environmental justice presented earlier in the chapter, a number of observations can be made, keeping in mind that '...CLIFF explores options where state and market driven institutions had failed to produce solutions to the challenges of slum upgrading. In this sense, CLIFF has a path finding function and as such benchmarking performance is fraught with difficulty' (Independent Evaluation of CLIFF, 2006: 3).

With respect to *redistribution*, CLIFF produced secure housing for some 25,500 people (approximately 19,500 in Mumbai) and sanitation for around 1.5 million (336,000 in Mumbai),[8] and on behalf of the communities, SSNS captured land-value surplus through the TDR market. Did it make inroads on the 'deep distribution' processes that continue to make Mumbai a city rife with inequality and spatial separation? While it would be difficult to show that CLIFF had seriously disrupted the reinforcing interaction between the 'spatiality of injustice' and the 'injustice of spatiality' (Dikeç, 2001) at work in the city, it has opened up a credible, alternative up-scaled approach to material distribution in the city.

Did CLIFF contribute to the *inclusive recognition* of the urban poor and their organisations? CLIFF fed into a historically successful process of social mobilisation; contributed to the ongoing development of technical innovations like enumerations, adding portfolio management; and consolidated strong operational relations with the SRA and selected other state agencies. These processes built confidence among women and men in communities, at the same time as bringing increasing recognition to slum dwellers and their capacities to engage positively with re-housing and Resettlement and Rehabilitation in the city. According to Burra (2005), the sanitation projects changed the patron-client relationships that politicians had previously with slum dwellers, treating the provision of toilets as gift giving. '...[N]ow, communities of the poor increasingly perceive it as a right' (Ibid: 84). However, this recognition has come within a neoliberal policy framework of 'entrepreneurial urbanism that foregrounds the 'potential' of the poor as entrepreneurial subjects and the symbolic recasting of poverty as social and economic capital' (McFarlane, 2012: 2797). How does the Alliance address the inevitable conflicts between their engagement as 'deliverers' of such policy, built on their capacities for social mobilisation and technical/organisational innovation, and their long-term struggle for an inclusive recognition and parity political participation of the urban poor as active citizens in the city?

The struggle for the construction of the conditions for *parity political participation* in the city continues, and the Alliance promotes its community-led approach using whatever instruments it can, including CLIFF. In a context where 'slum dwellers have historically had no voice in resettlement processes at all' (Batliwala in Jack, Morris and McLeod, 2005: 41), they now have greater participation in urban planning, both at local and national levels. Yet in a conflictive policy context where forced evictions still take place, parity political participation at scale is yet to be a reality in most aspects of the lives of poor urban citizens.

Nevertheless, as this chapter has sought to show, a civil society-led collective action at scale in Mumbai has laid the foundation for an alternative vision of how planning can address urban poverty in a city-wide, people-centred, accountable manner. Expanding the 'room for manoeuvre' for this vision to seed and take root at scale is an ongoing struggle for the Alliance, particularly as it interacts with other powerful visions for the city. Through the eyes of CLIFF, it has been possible to explore a cumulative set of multi-sited and multi-scalar strategic actions in the four dimensions of 'room for manoeuvre', confronting the complex question of how far it has contributed to a shift in the development trajectory of Mumbai to a more socio-spatially just path.

The Alliance's demand-led approach has driven a particular path through the four dimensions of 'room for manoeuvre', rooted in expanding social mobilisation, with the density of iterative interactions between the dimensions increasing as the complexity and scale of their operation has grown. The CLIFF experience is a key moment in this process. In considering this interaction, Safier (2002: 128) notes that

> (T)he boundary conditions will vary in permeability over time and place, representing the hegemony or vulnerability of specific initial conditions of cultural, political, social and economic constituents of social structures and developmental dynamics.

Indeed, although it has challenged urban planning hegemony in many ways, CLIFF has demonstrated that the process of expanding the 'room for manoeuvre' brings with it a commensurate scale of vulnerabilities, including a high level of risk generated by engagement with the public and private sectors. The delays in disbursing state subsidies, challenging regulations, and acquiring bank lending has been fraught with politics. CLIFF's bridge financing was designed precisely to enable the Alliance to bear such risks. Nevertheless, these delays have direct impacts on the poor women and men who have made decisions related to relocation, budgeting and a host of other everyday activities, which stretch them to the limit. These risks to the survival strategies of so-called 'beneficiaries' are hardly factored into public and private sector discourse and action.

There are also risks of engaging with donors.

> Large-scale projects and the management of a substantial project portfolio have required rapid development of systems and structures for which there is no blueprint. This is particularly difficult when, inevitably, donors and NGOs tend to have more formalised systems and structures which they can impose without realising that they may not be appropriate or helpful to the informal process upon which community capacity is built.(McLeod, 2005: 5)

While, SPARC, SSNS and HI are facilitating intermediaries in this local-international relationship, this role is a challenging one, requiring strong relationships and the joint development of activities in all four dimensions of the 'room for manoeuvre'.

The spirit in which the Alliance approaches collective action is one of constructive engagement. Yet taking the decision of whether and how to engage rests on an assessment of the 'room for manoeuvre' to strengthen their alternative vision for the city. The application of Safier's framework is a useful conceptual framework to highlight the complex decisions and actions taken in each dimension, based on extensive discussion with community leaders and valued allies in different positions in the state, private sector and civil society. Assessing the 'room for manoeuvre' and acting to expand it, is as much about the formulation and implementation of collective actions, as about assessing the risks of failure, co-optation – and the choice not to engage.

Ultimately, as was previously argued, '[T]he capacity for strategic action can be increased by a self-aware agency' (Garikipati and Olsen, 2008: 336). Safier (2002: 128) acknowledges that this is a challenging process: 'Reflective practice and critical analysis can be interchangeably pursued by the same persons, even at the same time, though the demands on personal and professional skills would be very heavy'. Yet it is a central part of estimating the 'room for manoeuvre', and of which the Alliance is acutely aware. For example, more recently in their involvement in Dharavi:

> We are also reflecting on the implications of our involvement in this dialogue. How can we remain accountable to our core organizational mission and constituency while employing a strategy of critical engagement with the state? How can we engage with the government without being co-opted? How can we accommodate the concerns of various strata within Dharavi when solutions will inevitably require compromise? How can we work with professionals, academic institutions and the media in a way that reinforces our primary mission of supporting the poor? (Patel Arputham, Burra and Savchuk, 2009: 250)

In the context of the new challenges in Dharavi, and because of its significance for the city at large and beyond, the Alliance acknowledge the centrality of estimating their 'room for manoeuvre' to formulate and implement collective strategic action to contribute to socio-spatially justice in an increasingly complex environment.

Notes

This chapter draws on a paper entitled 'Defining Strategic Action Planning Led by Civil Society Organisations: The Case of CLIFF, India', presented by the author at the 8th Annual N-AERUS Conference, 6–8 September 2007. It is an output from a wider action research project developed by the author within the MSc Urban Development Planning and the DPU Gender Policy and Planning Programme, sharing a common focus on 'strategic action planning' as transformatory planning practice.

1. While this argument was made in the context of mobility and transport planning, it is applicable to all aspects of urban development.
2. This is a contemporary restatement of Shon's (1983) 'reflective practitioner'.
3. The HI TAG met every quarter to review projects. In the first year, because SSNS was recently established and its Board and local TAG was yet to be established, the HI TAG had a critical role both in the review of projects and in supporting HI and local CLIFF staff in the creation of technical and financial systems. The HI TAG also made two trips to India to review CLIFF progress with the local partners (January 2003 and October 2004). I was also part of a team invited to discuss and propose a monitoring framework for CLIFF. This involved a visit to Mumbai and Delhi in August 2003 and a follow-up visit in July 2004.
4. Translated as 'Women Together'.
5. The new government made election promises 'to provide 8,000,000 free houses for 4 million slum dweller in Mumbai' (Burra, 1999: 72). All slum and pavement dwellers who were on the electoral role on 1 January 1995 were eligible for a free house.
6. In response to widespread criticism of their previous lack of attention to people affected by large-scale projects, the World Bank made R and R a non-negotiable component of MUTP-II. The Government of Maharashtra (GOM) set up a Task Force to formulate a Resettlement and Rehabilitation Policy, which included the Director of SPARC. (Burra, 1999).
7. The city's Net State Domestic Product (NSDP) and Per Capita NSDP growth rates were 2.98 per cent and 4.53 per cent, respectively, during 1999–2000 to 2000–2001. (Mahadevia, 2006: 355).
8. Calculated on basis of 4.8 persons per household (Risbud, 2003).

References

Allen, A. and Apsan Frediani, A. (2013). Farmers, not gardeners: The making of environmentally just spaces in Accra. *City: Analysis of Urban Trends, Culture, Theory, Policy, Action, 17*: 365–381.

Apsan Frediani, A., Lipietz, B. and Butcher, S. (forthcoming). Strategic Upgrading: Lessons from International Critical Practices, in: L. Cirolia, T. Görgens, M. van Donk, W. Smit and S. Drimie (eds), *Pursuing a Partnership Based Approach to Incremental Informal Settlement Upgrading in South Africa.* Cape Town: UCT Press.

Bombay First-McKinsey. (2003). *Vision Mumbai – Transforming Mumbai into a World Class City, A Summary of Recommendations.* Mumbai: Bombay First, and McKinsey and Company.

Burra, S. (2005). Towards a pro-poor framework for slum upgrading in Mumbai, India. *Environment and Urbanization, 17*(1): 67–88.

Burra, S. (1999). Resettlement and Rehabilitation of the Urban Poor: The Story of Kanjur Marg. *DPU Working Paper,* No 99, UCL.

D'Cruz, C. and Satterthwaite, D. (2005). Building Homes, Changing Official Approaches: The Work of Urban Poor Organizations and Their Federations and Their Contributions to Meeting the Millennium Development Goals in Urban Areas. *IIED Working Paper,* No 16, on Poverty Reduction in Urban Areas.

Dikeç, M. (2001). Justice and the spatial imagination. *Environment and Planning A*, *33*: 1785–1805.

Dikeç, M. (2006). *Independent Evaluation of the Community Led Financial Facility (CLIFF)*. Interim Report, Cities Alliance and GHK May/June.

Dikeç, M. (2008). Community Led Infrastructure Finance Facility (CLIFF) End of Project Evaluation, carried out by IPE, HIS and WDP on behalf of Sida and DfID.

Fraser, N. (1998a). From redistribution to recognition? Dilemmas of justice in a 'post-socialist' age, in: C. Willet (ed.), *Theorising Multiculturalism: A Guide to the Current Debate*. Malden and Oxford: Blackwell, 19–49.

Fraser, N. (1998b). A rejoinder to Iris Young, in: C. Willet (ed.), *Theorising Multiculturalism: A Guide to the Current Debate*, Malden and Oxford: Blackwell, 68–72.

Fraser, N. (1996). Social justice in the age of identity politics: Redistribution, recognition, and participation. *The Tanner Lectures on Human Values*. Stanford University 30 April–2 May [http://tannerlectures.utah.edu/lectures/documents/Fraser98.pdf], accessed 30 May 2013.

Garikipati, S. and Olsen, W. (2008). The role of agency in development planning and the development process: Introduction to the Special Issue on agency and development. *IDPR*, *30*(4): 327–338.

Healey, P. (1997). *Collaborative Planning: Shaping Places in Fragmented Societies*. London: Macmillan.

Homeless International, CLIFF Annual Review 08. (2008). Community Led Financial Facility (CLIFF): A Discussion of Institutional Roles and Responsibilities Within CLIFF, HI, September.

Jack, M., Morris, I. and McLeod, R. (2005). Third CLIFF India Monitoring Report, HI.

Levy, C. (2013a). Travel choice reframed: 'Deep distribution' and gender in urban transport. *Environment and Urbanization*, *25*(1): 47–63.

Levy, C. and Dávila, J. D. (2013b). *Planning for Mobility and Socio-Environmental Justice: The Case of Medellín*. Paper presented at workshop on Resilience and Environmental Justice in the Urban Global South, convened the Environmental Justice, Urbanisation and Resilience (EJUR) DPU Research Cluster, 12–13 September.

Levy, C. (2007). *Defining Strategic Action Planning Led by Civil Society Organisations: The Case of CLIFF, India*. Paper presented at the 8th N-AERUS Conference, London, 6–8 September.

Levy, C., Allen, A., Castán Broto, V. and Westman, L. (forthcoming). Unlocking urban trajectories: Planning for environmentally just transitions in the Global South.

Mahadevia, D. (2006). *Shanghaing Mumbai: Visions, Displacements and Politics of A Globalising City*. Paper presented at the IDPAD end symposium Hyderabad (India) 1–3 November.

McFarlane, C. (2012). The entrepreneurial slum: Civil society, mobility and the co-production of urban development. *Urban Studies*, *49*(13): 2795–2816.

McLeod, R. and Mullard, K. (eds) (2006). *Bridging the Finance Gap in Housing and Infrastructure*. Rugby: ITDG.

McLeod, R. (2005). CLIFF – Achievements, learning and issues to be addressed, HI.

McLeod, R. (2002). *Research on Bridging the Finance Gap in Housing and Infrastructure and the Development of CLIFF.* Interim paper prepared as part of Bridging the Finance Gap in Housing and Infrastructure Research Project.

Risbud, N (2003). The case of Mumbai, India, in: *Understanding Slums: Case Studies for the Global Report on Human Settlements.* UN-Habitat.

Patel, S. (2004). Tools and methods for empowerment developed by slum and pavement dwellers' federations in India. *Participatory Learning and Action,* 117–130.

Patel, S., d'Cruz, C. and Burra, S. (2002). Beyond evictions in a global city: People-managed resettlement in Mumbai. *Environment and Urbanization, 14*(1): 159–177.

Patel, S. and Arputham, J. (2008). Plans for Dharavi: Negotiating a reconciliation between a state-driven market redevelopment and residents' aspirations. *Environment and Urbanization, 20*(1): 243–253.

Patel, S. and Arputham, J. (2007). An offer of partnership or a promise of conflict in Dharavi, Mumbai?, *Environment and Urbanization,19*(2): 501–508.

Patel, S., Arputham, J., Burra, S. and Savchuk, K. (2009). Getting the information base for Dharavi's redevelopment. *Environment and Urbanization, 21*(1): 241–251.

Patel, S. and Mitlin, D. (2004). Grassroots-driven development: The Alliance of SPARC, the National Slum Dwellers Federation and Mahila Milan, in: D. Mitlin and D. Satterhwaite (ed.), *Empowering Squatter Citizen.* London: Earthscan, 216–241.

Patel, S. and Mitlin, D. (2001). *The Work of SPARC and Its Partners Mahila Milan and the National Slum Dwellers Federation in India.* IIED Working Paper 5 on Urban Poverty Reduction, London.

Patel, S. and Sharma, K. (1998). One David and three Goliaths: Avoiding anti-poor solutions to Mumbai's transport problems. *Environment and Urbanization, 10*(2): 149–159.

Safier, M. (2002). On Estimating 'room for manoeuvre'. *City, 6*(1): 117–132.

Satterthwaite, D. and Mitlin, D. (2014). *Reducing Urban Poverty in the Global South.* London and New York: Routledge.

Young, I. M. (1998). Unruly categories: A critiques of Nancy Fraser's Dual Systems Theory, in: C. Willet (ed), *Theorising Multiculturalism: A Guide to the Current Debate.* Malden and Oxford: Blackwell, 50–67.

Young, I. M. (1990). *Justice and the Politics of Difference.* Princeton: Princeton University Press.

8
Where the Street Has No Name: Reflections on the Legality and Spatiality of Vending

Amlanjyoti Goswami

> 'What is the name of this street?'
> 'The name of this street is Street.'
> 'How would I ask someone to come and meet me here then?'
> 'Aah, you say come near the *pulia*, or near the cemetery, or the market, and so on.'
>
> (Conversations with a shop owner in Dakshinpuri, Delhi, September 2013)

A couple of months later...

> 'When was this sign put up?'
> 'Oh, a few days ago.'
> 'Why name it Maharshi Valmiki Marg?
> 'Oh, a large number of *Valmikis* live here. It's elections time.'
>
> (Conversation with resident, on seeing a name for the street, finally, a night before Delhi Assembly Elections, December 2013)

Why the street? Why the vendor?

The street is a metaphor for the urban in India (Ahuja, 1997; Edensor, 1998). Understanding the urban is incomplete without understanding the street. The vendor is a ubiquitous presence. In Delhi, where hawkers and vendors ply, the street is a diverse geography of everyday uses. Street life – its bustle and complexity – is manoeuvred by the vendor in a jostle of negotiated interests.

Space matters. Street width often determines decisions of street use. Such use is legitimised at street 'level' and in official fora as 'high' as the Supreme Court, with methods 'strategic' and 'tactical' (De Certeau, 1984) which invoke normative claims. Specific understandings vary, depending on particular location and context.

The vendor, an inevitable, if not indisputable, part of Indian street life, negotiates inches and feet every day, with an appreciation of the local terrain that belies the textbook. The footpath (where there is one), the arena for Jane Jacobs' 'delicate side ballet', is also contested terrain, where the pedestrian finds the street vendor, sometimes a friendly, much-needed presence, sometimes a barrier. Determinations of legitimacy are contingent, local and improvised, while based on open (and vigorously contested) interpretations of what rights are, what informs regulation, where and how.

For street vendors, city living is provisional, tenuous, insecure, fraught with everyday negotiations not only with the state (in its multiple hues) but also with other citizens (pedestrians, car owners, shop owners, residents among others). This delicate side ballet involves more than just the street vendor and becomes a contiguous spatial-temporal narrative of urban life itself, with its everyday insecurities, challenges and meanings.

The vendor, vulnerable but resilient, ekes out a living. Vulnerability manifests in different forms, a fact acknowledged by the state itself. The Government of India's National Urban Livelihood Mission (NULM), in its 'Mission Document', mentions three types of interrelated vulnerabilities: residential (including access to land, shelter, basic services, etc.), social and occupational (NULM, 2013). Vulnerabilities faced by street vendors lie in the interstices of these categories. The National Commission for Enterprises in the Unorganised Sector (NCEUS) highlighted that 'in spite of the fact that the street vendors have a significant role in the daily lives of all individuals in the urban areas, they are considered a hindrance in the urban space by government officials as well as the urban vehicle owners who believe that they clutter the urban space and prevent smooth flow of traffic' (NCEUS, 2007).

Why is the street vendor important to the city? The immediate policy justification is economic. In policy literature on vending, aspects of livelihood and the key role of the informal sector in the economy finds much-needed (if belated) recognition (Chen and Ravindran, 2011; NCEUS, 2007; NULM, 2013). The Mission Document of the NULM highlights how 'street vending provides a source of self-employment and thus acts as a measure of urban poverty alleviation without major

Government intervention' and therefore the NULM ' would aim at facilitating access to suitable spaces, institutional credit, social security and skills to the urban street vendors for accessing emerging market opportunities' (NULM, 2013). The vendor's very enterprise seems to have become part of the state's logic to alleviate poverty, 'without major government intervention'. It is unclear, though, what 'emerging market opportunities' mean and how the state would provide such opportunities.

Estimates vary. About 2.5 per cent of the population in a ward or town in India are perhaps engaged in vending (Parliamentary Standing Committee on Urban Development, 2013; National Policy on Urban Street Vendors, 2009). The Standing Committee quoted the NCEUS figure to be around 1.7–2.5 million. The Master Plan for Delhi (MPD) 2021 quotes a survey conducted by the Directorate of Economics and Statistics that estimated about 200,000 unorganised trading enterprises employing about 318,000 people. Rough figures may lead to about 300,000 street vendors in Delhi (Bhowmick, 2010). For every licensed vendor, there are large numbers of unlicensed vendors not easily enumerated, where licensing itself is fraught with complexities. Unofficial vendors may far exceed official estimates.

However, much is left out of such analysis. Even as space becomes the fulcrum around which meanings of legitimacy get constituted, there is little exploration that connects the dots between the policy justifications on the one hand and the fine grain and texture of 'making do' on the other – those that explore rich interpretive understandings of everyday living with the many circulations between law and space. This absence is one of meaning, palpable on the street if not at the policy discussion table. On the street, space is personal and political, continually reconstituted, contested, shaped by and shaping legality (Massey, 2005). The following sections attempt to fill some gaps, connect some dots and ask new questions. They reflect on where Indian streets might locate themselves in the understanding of India's urban and how street vending contributes to, and departs from, such understandings. It tries to find debates on the legality of street vending in decisions of the Indian Supreme Court and explores spatiality within such understandings. It also seeks to 'sense' how street vending is governed from the eyes of a particular street in Delhi to explore if more nuanced understanding is possible.

Where is the Indian street? Where is the vendor in it?

Arjun Appadurai eulogises the street as the 'guerilla theatre of commerce in contemporary India' where hawkers and vendors 'are the base of street life' and 'streets are many things: thoroughfares, bazaars, theatres, exhibitions, restaurants' (Appadurai, 1987). Sarayu Ahuja finds the 'mood of the street made of not just its tangible elements – the width of the street, the buildings, their architecture, the spaces around, the street monuments', but also in 'something intangible, as though the street was made of several layers, one upon another, so that many elements and activities coexisted'.[1] Jonathon Shapiro Anjaria finds the street 'consisting of an assemblage of technical expertise, law and things, as well as the experiences, practices and imaginaries of its inhabitants' (Anjaria, 2012). Tim Edensor senses that Indian streets 'engender a haptic geography', where 'unforeseen assemblages of diverse static and moving elements provide surprising and unique scenes' (Edensor, 1998).

Yet, regulation of the Indian street (and the discourse governing legality of uses) encounters familiar colonial crossroads. Sudipta Kaviraj critiques colonial 'standardising techniques' which 'through constant intervention' reinforces 'the conceptual distinction between the legal and the illegal, between the reassuring fixity of the shops on the streets and the chaos of the vendors on the pavement' (Kaviraj, 1997). Arvind Rajagopal understands the 'pheriwaala' (literally those who move around) as a 'contested figure in Indian modernity', where 'typically street vendors are seen as offensive, inconvenient and illegitimate', for those attempting 'to impose order on the city', where they become 'a symbol of metropolitan space gone out of control' (Rajagopal, 2001). Lata Mani argues pithily that 'the street is not a road', that 'roads connect points in space, are moving corridors' but 'streets are life worlds'. With a touch of gentle polemic, she adds, 'Street life is in inverse proportion to road width...when roads are not conceived as streets, they trespass' (Mani, 2013). In similar vein, it is curious to find in the policy lexicon, only street vendors, not 'road vendors'.

The National Policy on Urban Street Vendors (NPUSV, 2009), while trying to ameliorate the lot of vendors, is tied to this historical imagining, one in which congestion is pitted with uplift: 'The overarching objective to be achieved through this Policy', it remarks, 'is to provide for and promote a supportive environment for the vast mass of urban street vendors to carry out their vocation *while at the same time ensuring that vending activities do not lead to overcrowding and unsanitary conditions in public spaces and streets*' (NPUSV, 2009, italics added).

Henri Lefebvre criticises 'the form of rigorous planning that suppresses symbols, information and play...a kind of stasis for people passing through because they want to go somewhere else to find something else...the street is more than just a place for movement and circulation...

it contains functions overlooked by Le Corbusier: the informative function, the symbolic function, the ludic function'.[2] The lively, frenetic and difficult encounters on an Indian street are a mix of contestation-negotiation, where an official strategic eye has to confront everyday experience.

At the same time, this negotiation from everyday experience still has to rely on a language of legality. The adversarial encounter is mediated by advocates (in courts or outside) on behalf of vendors. However, understanding around meanings of legitimacy is contingent and ambiguous. At the same time, such ambiguity is part of the assemblage of rules, discourses, ideas and experiences that the Indian street usually is, and where, by circumstance, the vendor finds location.

If the street is understood in urban policy as just a means of getting from here to there – a mobility corridor and no more – the street vendor, by his or her very existence, confounds this understanding. When stationary, the vendor is part of the very street that is supposed to serve the predominant purpose of movement.[3] A mobile vendor is an even more itinerant, regularly irregular presence, who challenges this conception further. He or she goes not just from here to there, or comes back here, but also stops intermittently at various points, and sometimes goes beyond known points, with or without a precise clockwork schedule. Such a presence (or absence) is perhaps in the Deleuzian frame, 'nomadic': one who 'follows customary paths, goes from one point to another, is not ignorant of points' and yet leads 'the life of the intermezzo...in opposition to the law or the polis' (Deleuze and Guattari, 2010). This reality of the vendor makes her or him 'deviant', in relation to the dominant conceptual understanding of the street – a presence that the state tries to 'sanitise' within carved-out vending zones.

Some reflections on legality and spatiality of vending

If the street vendor is a liminal presence constantly redefining limits and boundaries, he or she is within the law and also transgresses it. How does one know where the boundaries are? Who is in a 'position' to decide?

Numerous pronouncements of the Supreme Court have affirmed the vendor's 'Fundamental Right' to livelihood under article 19(1)(g) of the Indian Constitution, while nevertheless subjecting the right to 'reasonable restrictions' that can be imposed by the state.[4] Boundaries are drawn – in time, space and use – as constitutive of the law. No absolute boundaries can be drawn, since the vendor also has the fundamental right to earn honest *roti.* This creates circularity in discourse – the law is premised on meanings of particular space, and the legitimate use of space, in turn, depends on what the law says.

While the Supreme Court is the final arbiter for determinations of legality, such determinations are also read in light of other municipal laws and schemes, traffic regulations, planning strictures as well as sections of respective police enactments. The debate is not just between competing understandings of the street but also competing notions of the law.

The Indian Parliament recently enacted 'The Street Vendors (Protection of Livelihood and Regulation of Street Vending) Act, 2014' (SVL).[5] For the first time, a Central law that specifically governs rights and responsibilities of street vendors is being seen as the legal answer to the interpretive ambiguity.

Such legislation has been considered necessary for three reasons:

First, to address the need articulated by the Supreme Court for a law that clarifies rights and duties of vendors;

Second, in keeping with the historical trajectory of vending rights battles that has used litigation as the primary legal instrument to protect vendors; and

Third, the Executive's imperative to regulate vending, keeping with the livelihood rights affirmed by the Supreme Court while not veering too far away from its own notions of security and order on the street.

The SVL is being seen as a successor to the National Policy for Urban Street Vendors, 2009 (NPUSV) with legal teeth, enforceable in courts. The SVL incorporates representational ideas earlier enunciated in the NPUSV, such as the constitution of a Town Vending Committee (TVC) to oversee issuance of licenses and regulate vendors in particular locations. The SVL is being heralded as a culmination of a long, collective struggle by vending-rights advocates, who aim to protect interests of vendors while demonstrating willingness to engage with the state, whether through collective negotiation methods or litigation.[6] Such a view, nevertheless, does not disagree in principle with the state's overall thrust of legalising, regularising, licensing, identifying and earmarking the 'Other' (here, the vendor), through particular uses of time and space. The SVL is celebrated as the answer to constant harassment that vendors face. Since the law has been ambiguous, the SVL is expected to provide a legal counterpoint to strict municipal codes of street use.

This belief necessitates a peep into legal history

In 1989, a man named Sodan Singh, described as 'a poor hawker making both ends meet by selling readymade garments on an area of 8′ × 24′ near Electric Pole number 12 Janpath Lane, New Delhi', approached the Supreme Court for justice, when the New Delhi Municipal Corporation (NDMC) removed his goods.[7] He argued that he had been paying fees under *'tehbazari'* ('squatting permits') to vend and thereby had a right to vend in that particular place.

Justice Sharma of the Supreme Court affirmed Sodan Singh's fundamental right to livelihood under the Constitution of India, subject to 'reasonable restrictions'. The governing logic was one of pragmatic concern for livelihood. 'If properly regulated', Justice Sharma reflected, 'according to the exigency of the circumstances, the small traders of the sidewalks can considerably add to the comfort and convenience of the general public, by making available ordinary articles of everyday use for a comparatively lesser price'.[8] This tenor of acknowledging rights of poor and itinerant livelihood seekers on the street was refreshingly different from an earlier view articulated by the same Court which had felt that street vendors could cause a 'nuisance' and could 'hold the society to ransom', 'despite herculean efforts' by the municipality 'to clear the streets of these and other obstructions'.[9] Justice Kuldip Singh in a concurring opinion of the Sodan Singh case struck a sympathetic chord, while lamenting that no particular legislation existed on the subject, on the basis of which clearer guidelines could be offered. This paved the ground for the municipal 'Scheme' to serve as guidepost till legislation was enacted.

However, the spatiality of the matter was far from being resolved in Sodan Singh's case. The Supreme Court maintained that the fundamental right to livelihood did not entitle Sodan Singh to vend *at a particular place*. The fundamental right to vend had to be read in light of other uses of the street, where movement of traffic and pedestrians predominated. If vending did not constitute a 'nuisance', it could be allowed, subject to those restrictions.

This position reflected general appreciation of rights, but it left its precise meaning ambiguous. In abstract, the right to livelihood of the street vendor is space-agnostic. However, in its everyday impact, it is entirely space-dependent. This opens wide windows for interpretation, depending on the particular facts and circumstances of a case, which play out in spaces of varying sizes, the width of the street being an important factor.

Since the right to vend did not mean the right to vend at a particular place, what a 'reasonable restriction' is in relation to a particular space would remain a continual legal debate. The everyday existence of Sodan Singh and many others similarly situated would continue to depend on municipal schemes, whose particular requirements had to be adhered to, no matter what rights vendors seemingly possessed. Such requirements would draw from the state's colonial notions of nuisance, congestion and security, existing at the same time with the post-colonial world of Constitutional rights ostensibly guaranteed by the same state to ensure 'justice, liberty, equality and fraternity'.[10] Notions of control, hygiene and order in public places, reinforced in municipal and police legislation, have been used to label street vendors illegal, even in the face of more recent Supreme Court rulings that generally affirm the right of vendors.

Within the right to livelihood, there have been directions by the same Supreme Court in cases that 'put several constraints on the street food shops selling food items in Delhi' (NCEUS, 2007). If the Judiciary mandates strict implementation of planning codes, or reinforces stereotypes of hygiene, order and congestion, or upholds shopkeeper's rights to livelihood against the vendor, this delicate balance begins to unravel. For example, specific sections within police and municipal legislations, which are very spatial in orientation, can be invoked to render vending illegal, in spite of the general reflection of the Supreme Court on the right to livelihood.

Section 83 of the Delhi Police Act states inter alia that 'no person shall cause an *obstruction* in any street or public place by exposing anything for sale or setting out anything for sale in or upon any stall, booth, cask, basket or in any other way whatsoever' (1978, italics added).

Section 322 of the Delhi Municipal Corporation (DMC) Act gives powers to the Commissioner *to remove, without notice,* 'any article whatsoever hawked or exposed for sale *on any public street or in any other place* in contravention of the [Act] and any vehicle, package, box or any other thing in or on which such article is placed' (1957, italics added).

Section 420 of the DMC Act explicitly states that no person, except 'in conformity with the terms of a licence granted by the Commissioner' is allowed to '(a) hawk or expose for sale *in any place* any article whatsoever whether it be for human consumption or not or (b) use in any place his skill in any handicraft or for rendering service to and for the convenience of the public for the purposes of gain *or making a living*' (1957, italics added).

Section 322 of the New Delhi Municipal Council (NDMC) Act prohibits the sale of any article within a distance of *one hundred metres* of any municipal market without the permission of the Chairperson, failing which such person and article 'may be summarily removed' (1994, italics added).

The puissance of 'nuisance'

When the predominant notion is one of obstruction, street vending is rendered vestigial to the street's uses. When there is obstruction, 'nuisance' can be invoked (Mcfarlane, 2008; Valverde, 2012; Ghertner, 2011). The very notion of nuisance (ironically, like beauty) lies in the eye of the beholder. Under the NDMC Act, 'nuisance' is defined broadly enough to incorporate a range of interpretations, from any offence to smell to threats to life. Section 2(28) of the NDMC Act defines 'nuisance' to 'include any act, omission, place, animal or thing which causes *or is likely to cause* injury, danger, annoyance or offence to the *sense of sight, smell* or hearing or disturbance to rest or sleep, or which is or may be dangerous to life, or injuries to health or property' (1994, italics added). This means that nuisance can be invoked even if there is a remote likelihood that such an activity offends or could offend the sense of sight, smell or hearing. The NPUSV did remark that 'public authorities often regard street vendors as a nuisance and as encroachers of sidewalks and pavements and do not appreciate the valuable services that street vendors render to the common man' (Government of India, 2009).

It is not just the invocation of these provisions but the very power *inherent and contained* in these laws that provides sufficient *space* to enable the police and municipality to threaten eviction. Since this power may or may not be actually invoked, the ambiguity also opens the possibility of negotiation. When negotiation fails, litigation is the last resort. Newer cases continue to turn up at the Supreme Court's door, where judges are confronted with the task of resolving particular disputes, with a constitutional language that is space-agnostic, in principle, but dealing with realities deeply spatial. The result is a reliance on contingent directions and orders.

Here are some specific spatial references from Supreme Court cases, drawn mostly from the very municipal schemes prepared to specifically deal with street vendors:

- 'Allotment of sites available is only 2.5 per cent of the total population per Ward based on the census of 2001 ... at some places the width of the footpath is only five feet but the same has been declared to be a squatting area'.[11]

- 'Open space measuring 6′ × 4′for doing non-licensable trades and 4′ × 3′ for the trade of pan, biri, cigarettes will be allowed'.[12]
- 'An area of 1m × 1m on one side of the footpath wherever they exist… we however clarify that aarey/sarita stalls and sugarcane vendors would require and may be permitted an area of more than 1m × 1m but not more than 2m × 1m…there should be *no hawking within hundred meters* from any place of worship, holy shrine, educational institutions and hospitals and within one hundred and fifty meters from any municipal or other markets or from the railway station… there should be no hawking on footbridges and overbridges'.[13]
- 'For example, we see no reason why hawking should not be permitted on J Tata Road or Barrister Rajni Patel Marg in A Ward. Of course hawking cannot be permitted on these roads in the vicinity of Sachivalaya and Vidhan Bhawan…however when BMC sets up a hawking plaza the allotment of 1m × 1m pitches in those hawking plazas must be made on the above terms and conditions…The exclusion of arterial roads, pavements, carriage ways, approaches to railways stations, places of worship and schools as also roads with less than 8.5 meters width, from areas which could be declared as "hawking zones" was approved'.[14]

And so on. Faced with a trenchant legal dispute between street vendors who ask the Court to uphold the constitutionally affirmed right to livelihood and the municipality or the Development Authority which renders such rights obsolete because of particular 'violations' of space, the Judiciary's 'strategic' eye meets the 'tactical', and space becomes political, legal and contingent. There is no permanent space or understanding. Each is open, rending itself to the other, and scathed.

The Supreme Court has admitted that this task is onerous, perhaps even beyond what it can implement. In the Ekta Hawkers case, Justice Singhvi candidly remarked that 'experience has, however shown that it is virtually impossible to monitor day to day implementation of the provisions of different enactments...the problem has aggravated because of the lackadaisical attitude of the administration at various levels...', and that 'street vendors are a harassed lot and are constantly victimized by the officials of the local authorities, the police etc. who regularly target them for extra income and treat them with extreme contempt. The goods and belongings of the street vendors/hawkers are thrown to the ground and destroyed at regular intervals if they are not able to meet the demands of the officials. Perhaps these minions in the administration have not understood the meaning of the term 'dignity' enshrined in the Preamble of the Constitution'.[15] Similar admissions have been made by various government bodies that highlight the deep spatial insecurities faced by vendors in the everyday, and yet fall short of what to do (NCEUS, 2007; NULM, 2013).

Since the state will continue to have powers of Eminent Domain to acquire property, when circumstances change (such as a new redevelopment or a decision to widen the street), it is not impossible to revisit the facts again, in a fresh case. This vagueness within the law, while allowing spaces for negotiation, creates room for rent seeking and harassment (Anjaria, 2006). Law in street vending, as Devlin eloquently wrote, then becomes 'a spectral point of departure' (Devlin, 2011). Vending is a carved out exception – a right, yes – but one that exists in the margins among many rights, similar to the vendor who also stands at the margins of the street.

One way of understanding how the state invokes differential understandings of margins is through the notion of zoning. In street vending, a zonal imagination seems to be the norm, where 'vending and non-vending zones' create demarcated spaces. The NPUSV refers to 'the need for regulation of street vending by way of designated "restriction-free vending", "restricted vending" and "no vending zones" based on certain objective principles' (Government of India, 2009). The litigation battle no longer seems to be about the decision to zone, or in what 'objective principles' such zoning is premised, but rather if a particular space has been 'correctly' zoned or not, or if violations to the municipal or development authority plans have indeed taken place. VIP areas are strictly not for vending since the itinerant nomadic vendor is perceived as a security threat. Attempts at gentrification, reserving specific areas (where available) for vending, or converting ramshackle, makeshift stalls to 'aesthetically pleasing kiosks' (such as those done through a public-private partnership in Bhubaneswar) seem to be touted as examples of the possible (Kumar, 2012). A certain dominant aesthetic seems at work, drawing more from fantasies of order and less from a rooted understanding of the local aesthetic that the vendors themselves use. This view, too, is ocular, less haptic, more eagle-eyed.

Would the new law make it better for street vendors?

The new SVL is a Central legislation, applicable to the entire country. It aims to 'protect the rights of urban street and to regulate street vending activities' (SVL, 2014). The SVL requires vendors to possess licenses (applied to, and distributed by the TVC) upon payment of license fees.

Only licensed vendors would be allowed to vend, subject to terms and conditions provided for in the license.

Section 27 of the SVL states unequivocally that 'notwithstanding anything contained in any other law for the time being in force, no street vendor, who carries on the street vending activities in accordance with the terms and conditions of his certificate of vending *shall be prevented from exercising such rights* by any person or police or any other authority exercising powers under any other law for the time being in force' (SVL, 2014, italics added). This is revelatory, but there is cause to pause. In the same breath, Section 29 states that, 'nothing contained in this Act shall be construed as conferring upon a street vendor *any temporary, permanent or perpetual right* of carrying out vending activities in the vending zones allotted to him or in respect of any place on which he carries on such vending activity' (SVL, 2014, italics added). This reinforces the old dichotomy the Judiciary has been faced with.

In the meantime, the method of survey would identify existing legitimate vendors. This survey would be conducted by the TVC. A rough formula of ensuring vending for 2.5 per cent population in the vending zone would be attempted (subject to a 'holding capacity'). Till the survey is complete, no vendor would be evicted or relocated. This gives vendors time, given the complexities involved in conducting and completing surveys. Since 40 per cent of the TVC's constitution is required to consist of vendors themselves, it is assumed that some representational decision-making would be ensured, especially in decisions to issue licenses, thereby leading to equitable outcomes. Conducting a survey every five years will not be easy. The survey is not just a technical exercise but a political one, especially on matters of inclusion. The survey takes a long time and may be a way to stall evictions.

Four consequences of the SVL seem likely.

First, the SVL, while attempting to regularise vending, would nevertheless create new categories of illegality and legality. There would be a group of vendors deemed legal, with collective bargaining strengths. They would have the license to vend and not ostensibly violate the terms and conditions. But two other categories would also emerge. There would be some vendors who do not have any license to vend, who would be, by definition, illegal. They would not get licenses in a particular space, either because they lack the resources or because the 'holding capacity' has been exceeded. There would be still others who have licenses but are presumed to not comply with the terms and conditions, temporal and spatial. The itinerant vendors would transgress and redefine the very notion of boundaries, and of 'holding capacities'. The efficacy of the SVL in affirming legality would also depend on how many 'legal' and 'illegal' vendors there would be, in each category, which in turn, would depend on where they vend.

Second, the respective municipality and development authority (and the state government in charge of land use) would continue to shape the street in light of its own imagination of what the street should be. It may be difficult to banish the vendor, since the vendor's very insistence on the existence of a specific legislation would continue to serve as a reminder of (her continued) legitimate presence. However, the vendor may still be exiled as a result of municipal strictures, old and new. The municipal scheme for vending would be prepared by the state or Central government in consultation with the municipality, the planning authority and the TVC. The particular irregularities would depend on the fine print of the scheme, and this would again be contested. The unlicensed vendor would continue to be deemed illegal for not conforming to the scheme. In non-vending zones (old and new) or in redeveloped streets, or widened areas (or streets turning into roads) in light of new planning formulations, vending might continue to not be allowed.

Third, 'natural markets' and vending zones could clash with each other. The concept of 'natural markets' has been acknowledged, in the NPUSV 2009 and sparingly in the SVL, as places where vendors have traditionally congregated and where some spatial preference for their continuation may be considered legitimate. Some natural markets existing for more than 50 years could also be deemed heritage spaces, worthy of conservation. If vending works best near intersections, outside hospital gates, places of worship, bus stops, educational institutions, and near traffic lights, and also within 100 metres of licensed markets and similar spaces where people congregate, and if these very areas are rendered non-vending zones in the view of the authorities, the possibility of a clash is imminent. Had 'natural markets' been included in the definition of 'vending zones', doubts would have been allayed. In its absence, there is room for ambiguity. Are 'no vending zones' inimical to 'natural markets' (Bhowmick, 2010)?

Fourth, the SVL would not dispense with the need to approach the Judiciary, since the Supreme Court would continue to be confronted with the impossible task of supervising actual cases of evictions. This fine task would circulate around notions of space, and particular specifics regarding length, width and manner of use of particular public spaces, based on specific legal-spatial formulations such as the municipal scheme, 'holding capacity', vending zone, terms and conditions of the license issued, veracity and efficacy of the survey, 'natural markets' and so on. In other words, without a corresponding amendment of respective municipal or police laws, the Supreme Court would once again be called upon to announce where the SVL stands in relation to such laws. Where concerns of security predominate, it might even be politically naive to expect specific police rules to change because of new street vending legislation.

It is still worth exploring over time what the SVL can do. However, such exploration cannot turn its gaze from the everyday – the various spaces where law finds no ready answer and yet looks for a way of reading.

Ground reflections

An 'ordinary' city street, located in Dakshinpuri, an otherwise marginal neighbourhood in South Delhi, does not invite immediate attention. The history of ordinary streets is difficult to unearth from official records. The fact that the street had no name was intriguing, while the discovery of the name, finally, just before elections, implied political articulation. The larger locality was named 'Ambedkar Nagar' after Dr BR Ambedkar, Chairman of the Drafting Committee of the Constitution itself, a constitutionalist, free thinker, champion of marginalised castes, and enduring political icon. The very act of naming the locality after him was a sign of political mobilisation.

The street had 'place-names' – reference points for the regulars, just like a village. At first glance, it was difficult to tell if it was a road or street. It had vehicles moving back and forth, a large drain behind the vendors, houses and shops. After sunset, a buzz came alive. The vendors would line the edges of the street on one side but not the other. On the other side were shops and the *Jhuggi Jhonpri* (JJ) resettlement colony, recently conferred freehold status by the Delhi government.[16] Did the street remain unnamed for so long because it had to remain under legal radar? Would naming alter the character or mood of the street, by then locating it within planning maps, zoned to such perspicacious detail that autonomous anonymity would be threatened?

Location matters. Vendors converge around and in front of the Delhi Development Authority (DDA) markets. These are 'natural markets' that render obsolete the hundred-metre rule. The vendors are on that side of the street where evening buses stop. The odd passenger would get off and buy a glass of juice. Where people meet, vendors sell more. If the vendor's house is nearby, costs come down. The toilet nearby makes up for lack of facilities. Water can be brought from the house easily. Where rules do not allow cooking on the street, a *biryani* seller can cook at home and still bring the food piping hot.

Territory is not carved fixed for all time, without exception. '*Aage peeche kar lete hain*' ('we move front and back'), a vendor says. Bayat's 'quiet encroachment of the ordinary' (Bayat, 2000) is accompanied by quiet retreats in the same space. On occasions such as Republic Day, Independence Day, and the odd visit by a political leader, it is all 'cleaned up' and vendors are removed for the day. This is considered de rigueur. Then they return. But the night before elections, vending continued brisk, with street lights on. The presence of uniformed policemen was palpable, but they were not there to remove vendors. They had to guard the polling booth and watch out for the odd troublemaker. On election eve, removing vendors from the street would have serious political consequences. Politics creates the space for negotiations, and no event is bigger than elections. Intermediaries among vendors also play a part in canvassing for particular candidates.

On other evenings, though, vendors have to negotiate with the state. 'The police and the "Committee" (a term used for municipal raiding teams in Delhi) would not trouble you if you make your payment and do not create any fuss...we even get informed before the raid begins'. Rent seeking came with reciprocal expectation of 'protection' from the very forces of the state. Another vendor adds a temporal dimension to the raids. 'During the day, if you don't have anyone on your side "inside", it is difficult. The Committee can come and take away your things. It will take me two-three days to get them back from their office. But their office shuts at five. After six, no Committee will raid us. So business after six is fine'. This is an informal, tacit understanding, a fact known to the initiated. This explained the buzz on the street after the sun went down and the odd shop light came up.

'Yes, we cannot set up in front of the shops'. Shop owners wielded influence.

References to the past are indeterminate. 'It was different *before*. Now there are more shops, more cars'. When asked how long he had been on the street, a vendor replies, 'twenty, no twenty-four years'.

'Public and private is one', replied another vendor, who lived on his cot by the side of the street where he sold chicken. 'Others come in the evening, but I live here. Business is all day for me'.

The 'Indian street shopper', Arjun Appadurai remarked, 'typically works in an economy of small differences' (Appadurai, 1987). No two vendors would sell the same product side by side. This is not a territorial earmarking of space to the last chalked detail, but a mutually arrived understanding. The economy of small differences allows enterprise, and leaves gaps. 'The big shops can sell the same things next to each other', a vendor remarked, 'but not small folks like us'.

There is also a sense of local aesthetic, though governed by pragmatic considerations. 'It should look good', says the juice vendor, who places the big juicy *mausambis* in front. Others arrange utensils, knives, paper plates and spoons where hands can reach, and not far from the eye. If the Lefebvrian right to the city is also a right to oeuvre, some attention could dwell on the aesthetic vendors already draw from – what the vendor's 'style' already is – instead of just focusing on 'design-friendly' carts.

It all hovers around interpretation. Meanings of law, space, power, are particular and contingent, and there are spaces within the margins for negotiation. Meanings are fragmentary. This precarious and tenuous relationship with the law, the everyday insecurity, is accompanied by a prescient informal understanding of one's presence amidst the transience, and this appreciation creates a permanent state of temporariness. The vendor, 24 years in the same location, lives a day at a time, without promise or guarantee. Municipal and police officials are transferred, new lists made of 'who is where', customers change preferences ('momos sell more now'), but things remain continually provisional. It is the very provisionality that seems to breed improvisionality.

There is room for give and take, more or less, here or there, so long as payments are made and 'things' are kept in good humour. A Damocles sword – the threat of eviction hangs over – but this did not seem imminent or permanent. As long as one 'plays by the rules' of the street (which include the law), collective bargaining and negotiation would ensure continuity. Law is neither absent nor a persistent presence. It exists, in degrees, and the greys and cracks in-between are as significant as what is officially determined. This is not self-regulation. Vending is not entirely self-governed, but rather part of a grey terrain where the law is invoked (or can be invoked) as deemed necessary. 'If there are fights here, of course the police will interfere more', a vendor added. The honesty, dignity and enterprise of the vendor confound easy binaries of legal and illegal. The law is not binary – legal or illegal – but can become so, with alarming consequence – when the authorities think necessary.

Why law marks space?

Every vendor possesses a keen awareness of the various uses and users of the street. The vendor depends on the bus traveler, the pedestrian, the office goer, the lounger. The shifting back and forth in space manifests appreciation of the street's multiple uses. Street vending policies, which exist in the margins of urban policy, show awareness of such multiple uses. However, it is difficult to find similar awareness of space in transport and infrastructure policies, which pass the vendor by.

Why is this so?

Deleuze and Guattari distinguish between 'smooth spaces' ('vectorial, projective, topological...space is occupied without being counted') and 'striated spaces' ('metric...space is counted in order to be occupied'), where 'one of the fundamental tasks of the State is to striate the space over which it reigns, or to utilise smooth spaces as means of communication in the service of striated space. It is a vital concern of every State not only to vanquish nomadism but to control migrations, and more generally establish a zone of rights over an entire 'exterior' over all the flows traversing the ecumenon'.[17] In such a frame, the 'nomad space' which is a 'tactile space or rather "haptic" a sonorous much more than a visual space', is constantly striated through 'management of the public ways'.

Street vending may be a smooth space, mobile, itinerant, irregular. It may be easier for the state to striate that space, if vendors represent a marginal political constituency, only eventually reliant on a distant Judiciary. Boundary marking is the tool law uses to regulate space. If street vending is perceived as smooth space, tactile and haptic, the state striates the space with its rules. At the same time, transformation of that smooth space into striated space is never complete. The state uses legality to regulate vending through various instruments (judicial rulings, laws, licensing, police and municipal demarcations of territory), while vending, being 'nomadic' in orientation, would continue to negotiate around spaces in between. These spaces would be grey areas in the laws; between vending and non-vending zones; interpretations regarding 'natural markets'; periods before and between licenses; spaces where a temporal restriction is fulfilled if not a spatial one; changing, visible and invisible boundaries; the mobile vendor weaving in and out of zones and meanings around similar navigations.

The state envisages hawking plazas, licensed vendors, even capacity building, in a more sanitised street. For example, the Master Plan for Delhi 2021 does incorporate vending in its understanding of 'informal units', whose location would be considered 'on a case to case basis' within hawking zones, earmarked areas (in consultation with middle-class Resident Welfare Associations) and with spatial restrictions (for example, no informal unit would be allowed within a distance equivalent to half the width of the road from an intersection). Every act of earmarking is an act of limiting – space, time and land – use. There are specific planning norms which could allow informal shops/units to be located within larger spaces (such as retail trade, commercial centres, hospitals, bus terminals, schools, parks, residential and industrial areas and railway termini). The implementation of such planning norms would, however, lie in the hands of the municipality, which would rely on its scheme.

Where does space go? The road to regularised spaces is being paved with intention. The NULM notes that 'under NULM, states and cities will conduct a periodic socio economic survey of street vendors, register street vendors and issue identity cards for street vendors. A data base of street vendors will be developed and maintained at each city. This will enable states/urban local bodies to prepare pro vending urban planning and provide space to street vending' (Government of India, 2013). The link to spatial insecurity is left to surveys and databases, for the state to allow particular spatial locations to be earmarked for vending.

Will the street not change when everything is striated, earmarked, enclosed?

Deleuze and Guattari find that 'assemblages are passional, they are compositions of desire...the rationality, the efficiency of an assemblage does not exist without the passions the assemblage brings into play, without the desires that constitute it as much as it constitutes them' (Deleuze and Guattari, 2010). The street itself is an expression of a haptic encounter, constantly dealing with, and working around, notions of order and legality.

What then is being regulated here? Is it the street and its uses, the street vendor or the haptic encounter? Is it vending or the notion of what a street must look like? Who will be legitimised in demarcated vending spaces, hawking plazas and new gentrified street corners? What of the urban is inevitably going to be lost?

A preoccupation with certain fantasies of the well-ordered urban life is, one that is 'convenient', dependent on vehicles, and uncomfortable with visible disorder, finds an easy target in the street vendor. In the name of removing disorder from the street, the vendor is removed. This is a view of the street from above, one which does not locate order within the fine textures of detail within a street, in the nooks and crannies, in the traces of presence and absence that such multiple uses of the street represents. The ubiquity of the law does not mean it is applied uniformly for all people at all places. Much of the shaping, interpretation and application of law are predicated not only on a set of relationships among actors but also where such actors are situated. In its geographical complexity, law may also be seen as a 'space' where determinations are revisited and find new grounds of meaning. This is why the debate on legality goes to the heart of what a street is, who it is for and for what competing uses.

In a study on 'street criers and the urban refrain', Kreuzfeldt quotes Emily Thomson's study 'The Soundscape of Modernity' where 'disciplinary acts of silencing in early 20th century North America cleared the way for another kind of noise: "ironically by silencing peddlers and removing them from the streets altogether, city officials only cleared the way for more powerful noises of motorised traffic"' (Thomson, 2004). This perhaps explains why cars are not deemed to 'encroach the street', even when parked in it all night long, but vendors seem to. If the argument is that street vendors provide valuable services, especially to pedestrians, bus commuters and bicyclists, it is worth asking what future policy imaginations for the street holds, not just for the vendor but also for those who avail of these services. If it is accepted that safe streets are also the result of vendors plying their trade, rather than empty, lonely stretches for automobiles to zip past, it is curious that street vending does not find adequate mention in urban policy making, especially in areas such as transport and infrastructure (Tewari, 2000). Street vending then becomes a metaphor not just for vendors alone but also begins to speak silently about the nature of the urban imagination.

In the regulation of the haptic encounter, and its subsequent exile and removal, the street vendor is rendered redundant. Similar to the street criers, some types of vending may well become endangered if not extinct – and along with it, certain imaginations of the organic urban. Indian streets do have something enduring about them. The vendor is the one persistent presence, who reminds us what street life and commerce has been and would continue to be. Vending reaffirms an organic character of Indian streets. What is contested is not just that it is legal, or why certain uses become less legal than others, but that it is also this organic character.

If the street is conceived only as a place for ceaseless movement, the rush to and fro of vehicles – largely private automobiles – then the multiple uses of the street – as a place for encounter, for desire, for conversation and livelihoods – will slowly lose out to the super highway of an artificially imposed modernity. Reducing congestion might then be an excuse for widening streets and reducing life worlds. This is why the legal debate on vending appears specious at times, and leads one to explore the little known streets with no name.

Acknowledgements

The author thanks Kaye Lushington for research assistance, Colin Marx for the opportunity, and street vendors in Dakshinpuri, Delhi, for conversations and sharing experiences. For reasons of protecting their identity, they remain unnamed.

Notes

1. Ahuja, 1997, *Where the Streets Lead*, pp. 50–51.
2. Lefebvre, H. (2013). *The Urban Revolution*, translated by R. Bononno. Minneapolis: University of Minnesota Press: 18–19, 98.
3. For example, Justice Sharma in Sodan Singh etc. vs New Delhi Municipal Committee & Anr, 1989 AIR 1988 stated 'proper regulation is however a necessary condition as otherwise the very object of laying out roads – to facilitate traffic – may be defeated'.
4. Sodan Singh Etc. vs New Delhi Municipal Committee & Anr, 1989 AIR 1988; Bombay Hawkers' Union and Ors vs Bombay Municipal Corporation and Ors, 1985 AIR 1206; Gainda Ram and Ors v MCD and Ors, (2010)10SCC715; Maharashtra Ekta Hawkers Union and Anr. vs Municipal Corporation, Greater Mumbai and Ors 2013(11)SCALE329; Sudhir Madan and Ors v Municipal Corporation of Delhi and Ors, [2007]8SCR1.
5. Such a legislation to be enacted requires passing by both Houses of India's Parliament: the Lok Sabha and Rajya Sabha.
6. See the work of the National Association of Street Vendors of India (NASVI).
7. Sodan Singh Etc. vs New Delhi Municipal Committee & Anr, 1989 AIR 1988.
8. Sodan Singh Etc. vs New Delhi Municipal Committee & Anr, 1989 AIR 1988.
9. Bombay Hawkers' Union and Ors vs Bombay Municipal Corporation and Ors, 1985 AIR 1206.
10. Preamble, Constitution of India.
11. Sudhir Madan and Ors v Municipal Corporation of Delhi and Ors, [2007]8SCR1.
12. Gainda Ram and Ors v MCD and Ors, (2010)10SCC715, taking note of the court's observations in Saudan Singh etc v NDMC etc. (1992) 2 SCC 458.
13. Maharashtra Ekta Hawkers Union and Anr v Municipal Corporation, Greater Mumbai and Ors, AIR2004SC416; see also Bombay Hawkers' Union and Ors vs Bombay Municipal Corporation and Ors, 1985 AIR 1206.
14. Maharashtra Ekta Hawkers Union and Anr v Municipal Corporation, Greater Mumbai and Ors, AIR2004SC416.

15. Maharashtra Ekta Hawkers Union and Anr. vs Municipal Corporation, Greater Mumbai and Ors 2013(11)SCALE329.
16. Notification dated 20 June 2013, Department of Urban Development, Government of NCT of Delhi.
17. Deleuz and Guattari, 2010. *Nomadology: The War Machine.*

References

Ahuja, S. (1997). *Where the Streets Lead.* New York: Penguin Books.

Anjaria, J. S. (2006). Street hawkers and public space in Mumbai. *Economic and Political Weekly, XLI*(21): 2140–2146.

Anjaria, J. S. (2012). Is There a Culture of the Indian Street? Streetscapes: A Symposium on the Future of the Street, Seminar #636.

Appadurai, A. (1987). Street culture. *India Magazine, 8*(1): 12–22.

Asher Ghertner, D. (2011). The nuisance of slums: Environmental law and the production of slum illegality in India, in: J. Shapiro Anjaria and C. Mcfarlane (eds), *Urban Navigations: Politics, Space and the City in South Asia.* Routledge: 23–49.

Baviskar, A. (2003). Between violence and desire: Space, power, and identity in the making of metropolitan Delhi. *International Social Science Journal, 55*(175): 89–98.

Bayat, A. (2000). From dangerous classes to quiet rebels: Politics of the urban subaltern in the Global South. *International Sociology, 15*: 533–557.

Bhowmick, S. (2010). Legal protection for street vendors. *Economic and Political Weekly, XLV*(51): 12–15.

Bombay Hawkers' Union and Ors vs Bombay Municipal Corporation and Ors, 1985 AIR 1206.

Chen, M. and Raveendran, G. (2011). *Urban Employment in India: Recent Trends and Patterns.* WIEGO Working Paper No. 7.

De Certeau, M. (1984). *The Practice of Everyday Life.* Berkeley, CA: University of California Press.

Deleuze, G. and Guattari, F. (2010). *Nomadology: The War Machine.* Seattle, WA: Wormwood Distribution, 18–19, 43–44, 50–51, 70–71.

Delhi Development Authority. (2010 reprint). Master Plan for Delhi 2021.

Delhi Municipal Corporation Act. (1957).

Delhi Police Act (1978).

Devlin, R. T. (2011). An area that governs itself: Informality, uncertainty and the management of street vending in New York City. *Planning Theory, 10*(1): 53–65.

Edensor, T. (1998). The culture of the Indian street, in: N. R. Fyfe (ed.), Images of the Indian Street: Planning, Identity and Control in Public Space. London: Routledge, 212.

Gainda Ram and Ors v MCD and Ors. (2010). 10SCC715.

Government of India. (2007). National Commission for Enterprises in the Unorganised Sectors.

Government of India. (2009). National Policy for Urban Street Vendors.

Government of India (2012). The Street Vendors (Protection of Livelihoods and Regulation of Street Vending) Bill, 2012 (report). Standing Committee on Urban Development, 15th Lok Sabha.

Government of India. (2013). National Urban Livelihood Mission.
Jacobs, J. (1961). *The Death and Life of Great American Cities.* New York: Random House.
Kaviraj, S. (1997). Filth and the public sphere: Concepts and practices about space in Calcutta. *Public Culture, 10*(1): 83–113.
Kreutzfeldt, J. (2012). Street cries and the urban refrain, *SoundEffects, 2*(1): 62–80.
Kumar, R. (2012). *The Regularisation of Street Vending in Bhubaneswar, India: A Policy Model.* WIEGO Policy Brief (Urban Policies) No. 7.
Lal, V. (ed.) (2013). *Oxford Anthology of the Modern Indian City: Volume I: The City in its Plenitude.* India: Oxford University Press.Lefebvre, H. (2013). *The Urban Revolution.* Trans. by R. Bononno. Minneapolis, MN: University of Minnesota Press, 8–19, 98.
Maharashtra Ekta Hawkers Union and Anr. vs Municipal Corporation, Greater Mumbai and Ors, 2013 (11)SCALE329.
Maharashtra Ekta Hawkers Union and Anr vs Municipal Corporation, Greater Mumbai and Ors, AIR2004SC416.
Mani, L. (2013). The Integral Nature of Things: Critical Reflections on the Present. London: Routledge: 35–36.
Manushi Sangathan vs Delhi Development Authority and Ors, 159(2009)DLT82.
Massey, D. (2005). *For Space.* Sage: 9–11.
Mcfarlane, C. (2008). Governing the contaminated city: Infrastructure and sanitation in colonial and post-colonial Bombay. *International Journal of Urban and Regional Research, 32*(2): 415–435.
New Delhi Municipal Council Act. (1994).
Olga Tellis and Ors vs Bombay Municipal Council, [1985] 2 Supp SCR 51.
Pallasmaa, J. (2013). *The Eyes of the Skin: Architecture and the Senses.* Hoboken, NJ: John Wiley and Sons.
Paterson, M. (2009). Haptic geographies: Ethnographies, haptic knowledges and sensuous dispositions. *Progress in Human Geography, 33*(6): 766–788.
Rajagopal, A. (2001). 'The Violence of Commodity Aesthetics: Hawkers, Demolition Raids, and a new Regime of Consumption', Social Text 68, Vol. 19, No. 3, Duke University Press: 67
Robinson, J. (2006). *Ordinary Cities: Between Modernity and Development.* London: Routledge.
Scott, J. C. (1998). Seeing Like a State: How Certain Schemes to Improve the Human Condition Have Failed. New Haven, CT: Yale University Press.
Sodan Singh etc. vs New Delhi Municipal Committee & Anr, 1989 AIR 1988.
Street Vendors (Protection of Livelihood and Regulation of Street Vending) Act. (2014).
Sudhir Madan and others v Municipal Corporation of Delhi and others, [2007]8SCR1
Thomson, E. (2004). *The Soundscape of Modernity: Architectural Acoustics and the Culture of Listening in America 1900–1933.* London and Cambridge: MIT.
Tiwari, G. (2000). Encroachers or Service Providers? Street Vendors: A symposium on reconciling peoples livelihood and urban governance, Seminar, No. 491.
Valverde, M. (2012). *Everyday Law on the Street: City Governance in an Age of Diversity.* Chicago: University of Chicago Press.

9

Gangs, Guns and the City: Urban Policy in Dangerous Places

Gareth A. Jones and Dennis Rodgers

Introduction

Over the past decade, a host of publications have examined the relationship between (under)development, security and violence (e.g., Buur et al., 2007; DFID, 2007; Keen, 2008; World Bank, 2010, 2011). International development agencies in particular have become concerned by 'the challenge of repeated cycles of violence' and evidence indicating that new forms of conflict are emerging with the potential to become linked to each other in ways that are very difficult to control, especially in 'fragile' contexts (World Bank, 2011: 276, 2). A basic premise of many such studies is that poverty, as well as unemployment, income shocks, rapid urbanisation and weak institutions, enhances the risks of violence. Violence, in turn, makes development more difficult, suggesting to one influential figure that we need to understand conflict as 'development in reverse' (Collier et al., 2003: 13) and 'accept the links between security and development outcomes' (World Bank, 2011: 31). On this last point there seems to be a broad consensus, leading some to claim that addressing poverty is impossible without first creating the conditions to control conflict (Collier, 2010; World Bank, 2011).

A great many of the ideas that form part of the 'security-development' debate are both original and audacious. Nevertheless, a notable but underreported feature of most of these studies is that they either pay no attention to urbanisation and cities, or conceptualise cities as sites of particular forms of violence but without providing a detailed examination of how urban space and violence are related. The 2011 *World Development Report* (hereafter, WDR), for example, refers rather loosely to 'urban' as a seemingly generic locale inhabited by 'over 1.5 billion people', yet characterises the equally vague 'rapid urbanisation' as undermining 'social cohesion'.[1] Differently, and despite adopting the definition of violence as 'political violence' common to political science and development studies, Collier (2010) ignores cities in his analysis of the relationship between violence and democracy, despite the proven historical correlation between cities and democratisation (Borja and Castells, 1997; Dyson, 2001).[2] One consequence of ignoring or treating cities in particular ways is underplaying the social dimensions of violence which often come to the fore in cities.[3]

In the first part of this chapter, therefore, we explore how violence and cities have been understood, including in ways that consider violence to be related to urbanisation or urban form. In exploring this relationship we aim to complement the call made by Parnell (Chapter 1 of this volume) to emphasise the materiality of the built form and the structural role of 'the city'. We echo Parnell's claim that we need to 'bring "the city" back into urban poverty studies' by suggesting that we need to resituate the city into studies of violence as conceived by development policy institutions. In so doing, policy might also be more effective at understanding and addressing urban poverty, as it should come as little surprise that violence disproportionately affects the poorest and makes the places where they live, work and relax more difficult to intervene in.

In the second part of the chapter, however, we question the association between security and development. Drawing from an example of what we call 'security governance' – the *Unidade de Policía Pacíficadora* programme (UPP) in Rio de Janeiro – we argue for greater attention to how security is to be achieved in complex urban environments and what form and for whom development is said to take place and at whose expense. Finally, we discuss the problematic nature of contemporary policy studies that do not adequately understand the specific relationship between cities and violence, and even more importantly, the form that this leads violence to take. We demonstrate this through a consideration of research on a paradigmatic form of urban violence – gangs – in order to show how the phenomenon is generally predicated on specific conditions that pertain to social, political and economic conditions within cities, which furthermore manifest themselves along particular spatial urban configurations. A final section offers some tentative conclusions.

Urbanisation and violence

In contrast to the aspatial approach of much work concerned with 'security and development', there exists a long-standing concern in the social sciences that urbanisation amplifies the salience of violence (Wirth, 1938). More recently, there is a sense in which cities are increasingly understood as key sites of violence, as well as of the failure of development and/or political processes, in the contemporary world (Beall, 2006; Beall et al., 2013; Brennan-Galvin, 2002; Davis, 2006; Goldstone, 2002; Rodgers, 2009). The fact that much recent conflict, terrorism and civil disorder has occurred in cities such as Beirut, Baghdad, Mumbai and Nairobi, or that the world's highest homicide rates afflict cities in Colombia, Central America, South Africa or, most recently, Mexico, has become ever more noted, and has clearly added to the ubiquitous notion that cities and violence are intimately related. Nevertheless, many studies are vague, and often quite contradictory, on how urbanisation and violence combine, and how causation might be understood. The relationship between urbanisation, social cohesion and violence is a case in point.

The 2011 WDR notes that social cohesion is generally lower where urbanisation is most rapid, claiming that this was the case in Latin America in the past, and Asia and Africa today. Cohesion is deemed to be broken down by structural inequality, unemployment, and access to drugs and firearms, which makes people vulnerable to gangs and criminal groups (World Bank, 2011: 7), all of which are issues that can intuitively be related to the specificities of urban contexts. The claim that social cohesion is affected by urbanisation prompts support for civil society-state partnerships and 'community policing' initiatives as responses to violence (World Bank, 2010).[4] Yet, a range of studies have dismissed the idea that the incidence or severity of disorder and violence are simply related to the magnitude or pace of urbanisation per se (Buhaug and Urdal, 2013; Fox and Hoelscher, 2012). According to Buhaug and Urdal (2013), the 'urbanisation bomb' might be a 'dud'.[5] Indeed, there has long been a case that 'rapid urbanisation', properly managed, might make a positive contribution to 'security' and safety. Indeed, Samuel Huntington famously argued in the aftermath of the Tet offensive in Vietnam that an 'American-sponsored urban revolution' presented a critical opportunity for 'winning the war' by weakening the Viet Cong's rural support base (1968: 650, 652). In other words, rather than instability and conflict being about the pace of urbanisation, concentrating people in cities not only made them easier to control, but also potentially undermined revolution as aspirations for modernisation were met.

The contrast between today's fear of urbanisation and the optimism for modernisation of the past could not be starker. An emerging strand of research has focused on the relation between urbanisation and economic conditions, and more specifically the fact that while living standards may be greater in cities and governance is generally better, in states with low capacity and/or faltering economic growth, the demand for violence may increase as aspirations go unmet and material conditions are put at risk where large numbers of people reside in a bounded environment (e.g., Beall et al., 2013; Cole and Gramajo, 2009; Goldstone, 2002; Urdal, 2012; World Bank, 2010). Three interrelated issues can broadly be said to have focused most attention in this respect: namely, poverty and inequality, the 'youth bulge', and the strength of political institutions.

A prominent claim is the direct connection between violence and urban poverty, often made in relation to the global increase in slums, which a 2007 report by the United Nations Office for West Africa, for example, portrayed as hotspots of crime and violence (UNOWA, 2007). Associated with these spaces especially, is the fear that a demographic 'bulge' of young men with few opportunities to attain worthwhile jobs, despite educational attainment, and disenchanted with conventional outlets to vent their frustration, will be susceptible to 'fundamentalism, terrorism, insurgency and migration' (Huntington, 1996: 103; Fearon, 2011; but see Urdal, 2006). Pointing to rising material inequalities, frustration provoked by media images of consumer goods that prove unattainable and the retreat of states, Rapley (2006: 95) argues that contemporary cities herald a 'new medievalism' in which slums and ghettoes provide 'variegated informal and quasi-informal state-like activities'. This free-flow of cause-effect relies on a putative urban ecology that determines violence with particular spaces and therefore resident archetypes, rather than unpacking the relationship of violence to issues of power within cities.

And the dystopian associations extend even further. Marking a shift of concern with fragile or failed states to failed cities, Richard Norton (2003: 97) has famously suggested the imminent possibility of future cities as 'feral' spaces, 'sprawling urban environments [that are] now a vast collection of blighted buildings, an immense petri dish of both ancient and new diseases, a territory where the rule of law has long been replaced by near anarchy in which the only security available is that which is attained through brutal power'. In this diagnosis, portions of a city are controlled by 'criminals, armed resistance groups, clans, tribes, or neighbourhood associations' with, again, the suggestion that slums are an especially auspicious space for such takeover (Norton, 2003: 98; see also Rapley, 2006). A feral city would be a 'magnet' for terrorist organisations interested in exploiting the protection afforded by the absence of policing and the possible connections to illegal international trade and communication. Grading cities according to their likelihood for 'ferality' from Green (Healthy) to Yellow (Marginal) to Red (Going Feral), the suggestion is that the future violence will be urban-based but beyond the control of states at that level.

This association of cities with violence, much of it perpetrated by non-state actors, at possibly increasing rates and in 'irregular' forms, have promoted a sense of cities as actually or quasi-militarised spaces, 'urban terrains' and 'battlespaces' (Graham, 2010). Within this space 'policing' has given way to 'security', characterised by the greater involvement of private security agencies, and also underpinning grand claims about 'national security' which justify the greater direct involvement of military agencies in city life (Abrahamsen and Williams, 2011; Samara, 2011). This 'security governance' marks a shift from more classic forms of urban governance predicated on being about broader societal development; instead it is now about the achievement of 'security'. Thought of as a spectrum of practices, security governance in cities involves discreet projects of urban design for crime prevention that may complement measures to privatise access to public space and use of surveillance, through to community policing, zero-tolerance and the deployment of forces trained in counter-insurgency (see Graham, 2010). While cities such as New York, Los Angeles and Paris perhaps led the way with such urban 'security' innovations in the past, it is now cities of the Global South that are considered the laboratories for such measures, including, for example, the infamous *Mano Dura* anti-gang measures in Central America, or the 'security partnerships' in South Africa (Bénit-Gbaffou et al., 2008; Felbab-Brown, 2011; Jütersonke et al., 2009).

Cities, security and pacification

One of the best-known contemporary examples of urban crime and violence prevention is Rio de Janeiro's Urban Pacification Programme. The programme has been praised by the World Bank – explicitly so in the 2011 WDR – and UN-Habitat, which has featured it prominently on its webpage and appears to have supported it financially.[6] Begun in 2008 with the deployment of specially trained Police Pacification Units (*Unidade de Policía Pacíficadora,* UPP) in the city's *favelas* (slums) the UPP appeared to be different from the previous practices of the military police and condoned actions of *milicia* (militia) mostly formed of serving or former police and military to 'clean up' areas controlled by gangs known as 'commando', criminal organisations and political opponents. Drawing some inspiration from measures taken in Medellin and methods deployed by US forces in Iraq, as well as the experience from previous policing projects in Rio, the programme has used army units and special military police – the *Batalhão de Operações Policiais Especiais*, or BOPE – to occupy a *favela* (intervention phase), before introducing UPP officers (stabilisation phase), and finally establishing state and private infrastructure and social projects (consolidation phase). The UPP claims legitimacy as a break with past policing practice and ideology, and the explicit aim to deliver security and development initiatives (Jones and Rodgers, 2011). It is argued that unlike previous attempts to 'integrate Rio' or 'normalise' the *favela* through upgrading projects the UPP makes *favela* residents (*favelados*) into full citizens and 'reclaims' state sovereignty over the 'ungoverned' spaces of the city (Muggah and Souza Mulli, 2012). Following Huntington (1968) and Scott (1998), one might argue that pacification renders the *favela* a 'legible' space – one in which the state and private sector can therefore act.

We do not deny that the UPP has had considerable support from residents of Rio (*cariocas*) and especially, at least in its earliest years, from *favelados* (see Cano, 2012; Costa Vargas, 2013). Observers have commended the unusual degree of coordination between state agencies and the tripartisan support from national, state and municipal officials. The extension of the programme from an initial three *favelas* in 2008–2009 to 12 by 2010, and 36 by the end of 2013, has also been welcomed as a sign of state commitment beyond the immediacy of electoral cycles. The extension also served to deflect criticism that UPP was intended to 'lock down' only those *favela* closest to middle- and high-income neighbourhoods, possibly only for the duration of the FIFA World Cup and Olympics, by which time 100 UPP interventions were promised (see Jones and Rodgers, 2011: 989–991). There was also considerable surprise that the intervention phases were carried out without significant bloodshed; faced with overwhelming force the commandos tended to withdraw. Moreover, in the aftermath of the intervention and stabilisation phases the homicide rates appeared to fall and general perceptions of safety improved (Cano, 2012; Muggah and Souza Mulli, 2012).[7] Finally, there was evidence in the first phase of new policing practices being undertaken by specially recruited and trained officers, which contrasted strongly with the generally brutal tactics of the past. UPP officers were seen patrolling *favela* streets and a clever public relations campaign represented them taking time to talk with *favelados*, engage with community groups, and participate in *baile funk* parties, cultural events and festivals.[8]

Nevertheless, the experience of UPP also illustrates the difficulties of delivering 'security and development' in the complex social, political and economic context of cities. A first problem relates to the institutional capacity of the state. The fast-paced rollout of the programme has put a strain on the quality of training, undermining the important perception that policing during stabilisation and consolidation would be qualitatively different from the old regime (Teixeira, 2011). The commitment to pay UPP more than regular officers has put the policing budget under pressure and raised questions about the sustainability of the commitment to officer-intensive community policing (Freeman, 2012). It was clear during field visits to Complexo do Alemão and Rocinha, 'pacified' in 2010 and 2011, respectively, that the UPP-marked cars contained regular military police and the territory of the much-praised foot patrols was restricted to areas of major infrastructure, new public housing in Rocinha and the cable car stations in Alemão. These 'community' patrols were highly armed units that seemed more like 'security' intent on governing key spaces and actors, rather than working with residents and the often delicate balance of interests that mark *favela* economies, politics and social lives (Cano, 2012).[9]

Second, a rationale of the UPP has been to establish state presence in 'secured' *favelas* as a means to enhance economic integration and development. But the nature of this integration and its benefits to residents is in much doubt. As Freeman (2012) has recorded, the intervention of the BOPE in some *favela* has been followed in as little as 24 hours by teams removing illegal utility hook-ups, and then a day or so later by representatives from banks and credit providers, chain stores, telephone, entertainment and utility companies encouraging people to sign up to new services (also Costa Vargas, 2013). These practices expose a contested interface between the claims to community policing on the one hand, and a strategy to open a space for intervention by private capital on the other. This tension surfaced long before the demonstrations of 2013 and 2014, as the state initiated large-scale infrastructural projects in a number of pacified *favelas*. The most famous intervention is the US$250 million *teleférico*, a cable car system that connects five hilltops in the Complexo do Alemão, and which have been followed by other projects in Mangueira and Providencia.[10] In Alemão, the cable car delivers some benefits to the local population but offers a weak match-up with pedestrian patterns, links with shops and schools, and closes early in the evening. The officially promoted 12,000 journeys each day for a *favela* complex with an estimated 100,000-plus population also suggests a modest 'revealed demand', and an inappropriate service priority for an area that, at the time, was without a major health facility and adequate school provision.[11]

Although investment in *favelas* represent a significant allocation of public funds – upwards of US$550 million between 2008–2012 – against the sums devoted to other projects, the poorest areas of Rio receive less than 20 per cent of the infrastructure budget, excluding the sum allocated to new and remodelled stadia (Felbab-Brown, 2011). However, it is the nature and alleged purpose of these investments that has prompted controversy and conflict. In Providencia, the teleférico addresses – without having seemingly consulted with – a long-standing community complaint about the quality of the steps leading from the base of the hill to the top. But, the teleférico has been part of a project of large-scale demolition both to construct pylons and open spaces for the installation of private and public facilities: upwards of 800 houses have been identified for demolition (Freeman, 2012). The remodelling of the *favela* overall is an attempt to connect Providencia to Puerto Maravilla, the largest investment project in the city that has involved the massive transfer of public land to private developers, sunk large sums of public money and involved mass displacement (Limas Carlos, 2010). In a number of *favelas* there is evidence of rapidly rising real estate prices and rents, displacement of residents – some by force – and claims that 'development' has led to gentrification (Freeman, 2012; Muggah and Souza Mulli, 2012).

Third, a more subtle difficulty with the pacification approach relates to how it considers the social, economic and political relations between the state, *favela* residents and gangs. In common with many security initiatives, the UPP regards these various institutions as distinct from one another, as broadly having different agendas, and being competitors for legitimacy and resources. Pacification entails the state, through the police, replacing gangs and other agents as the legitimate organisations for the distribution of public services (Souza Mulli, cited in Jones and Rodgers, 2011: 989). This strategy depends on the BOPE and then UPP disrupting local networks of power, including the ability of the gangs to provide stability to residents and promise of social mobility to members (see Carvalho and Soares, 2013; Misse, 2007). However, while the representation of police action against the commandos, assisted by careful media use, relies on a lawless *favela* being 'retaken' by a professional, strategic, and public security initiative, the reality is far more complex (Costa Vargas, 2013; Robb Larkins, 2013). Police informants warn commandos of upcoming actions, residents often fear police as much as gangs, violence often increases after police takeover, and captured gang members may be 'hostaged' by police to rivals (see Arias, 2013). As Penglase (2009) puts it, conditions of insecurity are co-produced. Considered in terms of certainty, reliability, and 'reasonableness' against prevailing norms, legitimate justice is consequently not necessarily the preserve of the police and state, even if people's actual 'security' under commandos relies as much on myth and fear as on fair dealing in practice (Arias and Rodrigues, 2006; Penglase, 2009).

The unfolding experience of the *favela* 'pacification' poses a number of dilemmas for how we might better understand violence and the city. It suggests that the objectives of 'security governance' are not unambiguously about exerting state sovereignty, extending the rule of law, and making the city secure for all. Not only is security governance through the UPP partial and uneven over space, but its effects, including its benefits, are not evenly felt. Costa Vargas (2013) suggests that UPP has continued the long-standing practice of conflating blackness with danger and violence, and therefore targeted spaces occupied by mostly black, and poorer, people. Indeed, Rio might be seen as part of a larger process whereby neo-liberal forms of governance conceive of 'inclusion' as a set of managed 'exclusions' (Samara, 2011). In rendering the *favela* secure, legible and a space for 'development', the UPP also involves significant uncertainty about what types of change are envisaged, their sustainability, and who will gain from the process. Security governance is predicated on simple arrangements of legitimate and illegitimate forms of violence, and violent actors, and relations with residents and local institutions. Yet, on the ground, common sense, clear-cut distinctions between state–slum, police–gang, and security–violence are not so evident. Arrangements are blurred, people's social relations and economic interests complicate simple analytic binaries and policy prescriptions (Arias, 2013; Penglase, 2009).

Unpacking violence and the city: the gang considered

It is striking that in most discussions about the UPP not only is the city as a particular type of space never reflected upon directly, but moreover, there is little specific consideration of the violence that the UPP is actually tasked with reducing; namely, gang violence. This is all the more surprising considering that gangs emerge as major bugbears in the studies of development agencies, to the extent that they are repeatedly invoked in an almost talismanic manner, as a shorthand means of describing the threatening 'other'. In the case of the WDR, gangs are even lumped together with other very different violent actors such as drug cartels, terrorists, or rebel groups.[12] While young people's motivations for joining gangs or rebel groups may hold some conceptual similarities, presenting things in this manner clearly reinforces the notion that two very different types of violence are analogous, and concomitantly that they should be dealt with in similar ways.

Although, as John Hagedorn (2008: xxv) has pointed out, 'today's youth gang might become a drug posse tomorrow, even transform into an ethnic militia or a vigilante group the next day', this is by no means inevitable, and moreover these groups have fundamentally different logics and dynamics (see also Jones and Rodgers, 2009; Hazen and Rodgers, 2014). To this extent, lumping them all under the same category is clearly potentially dangerous. Even if the WDR only associates gangs and rebel groups on the basis of their origins, it is only a small step to connect them in terms of their motives and objectives, and while rebel groups may or may not be political organisations, they generally have – at least at a rhetorical level – the objective of overthrowing a government and seizing state power, something which can rarely – if ever – be associated with gangs.[13] More importantly, such an approach to gangs also clearly constructs them in a de-contextualised manner. As a long-standing and venerable social scientific literature has explored in detail, however, if we are truly to get to grips with gangs, it is critical to understand the context within which they emerge. Certainly, research has consistently offered two major insights into the nature of gangs. On the one hand, they are fundamentally epiphenomenal social formations, and on the other, they are inherently urban in nature. Both of these aspects of gangs are more often than not ignored in policy circles which prefers to offer gangs as a universal narrative trope, ubiquitously emergent actors that highlight the necessity of linking development with security.

In his pioneering study of the phenomenon, however, Chicago School sociologist Frederic Thrasher (1927: 487) paradigmatically suggested that 'the gang and its problems constitute ...one of many symptoms of the more or less general disorganisation incident to ...the rapid growth of cities and all the internal process of kaleidoscopic movement and rearrangement which this growth has entailed'. Indeed, Thrasher (1927: 26, 37–38) argued that 'the beginnings of the gang can best be studied in the slums of the city where an inordinately large number of children are crowded into a limited area. ...Such a crowded environment is full of opportunities for conflict', which 'coupled with deterioration in housing, sanitation, and other conditions of life in the slum, give the impression of general disorganisation and decay'. In a manner clearly reminiscent of Louis Wirth's (1938) famous analysis of 'urbanism as a way of life', Thrasher contended that such conditions provoked social breakdown and anomie that in turn led to the emergence of 'an inevitable repertoire of predatory activities and a universe of discourse reflecting the disorganised social environment', most obviously manifest in the existence of gangs (1927: 257).

Thrasher's research is by no means the only study inherently linking urban contexts and violent phenomena such as gangs. Second-generation Chicago School gang researchers such as Clifford Shaw and Henry McKay (1942) or William Foote Whyte (1943), for example, also identified this relationship as key in their studies of gangs, and the same is true of many subsequent gang researchers who are not associated with the Chicago School. Invoking just a few examples, Claude Fischer (1975: 1328) pointed out that there needed to be a 'critical mass' of youth within any given population for a viable delinquent gang culture to emerge, and that this could only come about through population concentration in cities. Albert Cohen (1955), on the other hand, contended that gangs were subcultural, institutional arrangements that reflected the cultural isolation and alienation of urban lower-class youth from mainstream society. Martin Sánchez Jankowski (1991) for his part depicts gangs as institutional vehicles for economic enterprise that result from the intense competition over scarce resources in low-income urban areas.

Much of this gang research, however, arguably simultaneously undermines the notion that there exists an inherent relationship between urban contexts and violence. Many of the gangs that Thrasher studied were ethnic in nature, which contradicts the idea that violence emerges as a result of the superficiality and anonymity of urban social relations, insofar as it suggests that gangs can be based on elementary forms of social connection. Thrasher (1927: 30) attempts to explain this paradox by suggesting that the actions of social agents cannot go beyond their individual experiences, and that gangs therefore had to have their 'beginning[s] in acquaintanceship and intimate relations which have already developed on the basis of some common interest'. In addition to ethnicity, he thus also lists kinship and feelings of local neighbourhood belonging as basic vectors for gang formation, all of which have also been highlighted by other gang researchers in a range of locations around the world (see Hazen and Rodgers, 2014, for an overview).

In many ways this is not surprising, however. Anthropologists have provided us with a plethora of studies of neighbourhoods, *favelas*, *barrios*, or *quartiers* in cities around the world that describe how urbanites effectively reproduce small-scale community forms of living within urban contexts by interacting repeatedly with relatively small numbers of individuals, moreover within a normally localised territory. As Oscar Lewis (1965: 497) put it, 'social life is not a mass phenomenon' but 'occurs for the most part in small groups', and therefore 'any generalisations about the nature of social life in the city must be based on careful studies of these smaller universes rather than on a priori statements about the city as a whole'. While this makes eminent sense, it also suggests that it is important to examine the underlying nature of gang violence more closely in order to truly understand the way that the phenomenon articulates with urban life in general, and the city in particular.

Understanding the political economy of violence in the city: the gang reconsidered

Thrasher (1927: 22–23) justifies focusing on slums by arguing that they constitute 'geographically ...interstitial area[s] in the city', and that just as 'in nature foreign matter tends to collect and cake in every crack, crevice, and cranny', so '*life*, rough and untamed' materialises in the interstitial areas that constitute 'fissures and breaks in the structure of social organisation'. Gangs, from this perspective, are 'rich in elemental social processes significant to the student of society and human nature' (Thrasher, 1927: 3), because they represent an unmediated form of life, a primordial reflection of the violence that inherently bubbles under the surface of things and inevitably erupts at points where the social fabric is weak. Such a perception of violence manifesting itself when social order breaks down clearly constitutes the phenomenon as something that exists outside of the social order. Although this kind of thinking is part of a long tradition, which perhaps finds its most obvious expression in Thomas Hobbes' (1996 [1651]) classic argument that violence is an incipient facet of being human in a state of nature that is held in check by the establishment of an encompassing social order, it is a viewpoint that also naturalises violence by projecting it as an autonomously pre-existing phenomenon that comes to the fore organically and automatically as a result of the existence or absence of certain objective conditions. For Hobbes, this was the absence of the Leviathan, but in relation to Thrasher's framework, it was the existence of cities, or at least of the particular social relations that he associated with the spatial characteristics of cities as anomic, disorganised social spaces.

When seen from this perspective, it can be argued that urban space is not necessarily violent per se, but rather constitutes a particular type of territorial space with intrinsic characteristics that naturally unleash the violence inherent to being human. As David Harvey (1973) points out in his classic work on *Social Justice and the City*, however, the notion of space is not only concerned with the territorial environment but is also fundamentally about social relations. The gang literature once again provides us with an interesting window onto this, including Philippe Bourgois' (1995) ethnographic study of drug-dealing gangs in East Harlem, for example. This presents a nuanced analysis of the gang phenomenon that balances economic motivations and individual choices with structural constraints, showing how the Puerto Rican gangs that he studied could be understood in terms of a mixture of local resource distribution, cultural identity, and implicit political resistance. Bourgois describes in great detail how gang violence was an instrumental means to protect markets, enforce contracts, and ensure that the local drug economy ran smoothly in order to provide for neighbourhood inhabitants in a context of limited resources, and how it built on local cultural norms and networks. But he also ultimately links the emergence of gangs to the way in which the wider urban labour market effectively condemned the inhabitants of poor neighbourhoods to dead-end jobs, which made joining drug-dealing gangs a logical aspiration, particularly for youth rejecting the low-grade options on offer to them. In doing so, Bourgois highlights how gangs in East Harlem emerged not just as instrumental adaptations to a context of limited resources, but also very much as responses to a broader context of limited *access* to resources within a broader city context characterised by extreme socio-economic marginalisation.

Bourgois thereby suggests that gangs are not a natural ecological feature of a city's spatial form, but rather epiphenomena of a very specific broader order, which he labels a context of 'urban apartheid'. In doing so, he draws attention to an active and purposeful process of segregation occurring between the inner city and the rest of New York. At the same time, however, he also comments how if inner city neighbourhoods such as East Harlem represent 'the United States' greatest domestic failing, hanging like a Damocles sword over the larger society', 'ironically, the only force preventing this suspended sword from falling is that drug dealers, addicts, and street criminals internalise their rage and desperation', and 'direct their brutality against themselves and their immediate community rather than against their structural oppressors'. The reasons for this are a complex 'mesh of political-economic structural forces, historical legacies, cultural imperatives, and individual actions' (Bourgois, 1995: 318), but in the final analysis reflect the fact that gangs are desperate forms of social mobilisation, whether viewed from a micro or a macro perspective. Locally, the fact that they are limited institutions means that they can only benefit a minority within the ghetto, while at the macro level they simply do not have the strength to challenge the citywide system of oppression, which is backed by an extensive apparatus of power and control. Seen from this perspective, it can be argued that it is this latter form of structural subjugation that is ultimately the most devastating type of urban violence that can afflict cities.

This is something that Steffen Jensen (2008, 2014) similarly explores in the context of the Cape Flats in South Africa. Drawing also on the work of Pinnock (1984), he first traces the origins of the contemporary Cape Town gang phenomenon to the destruction of traditional neighbourhood ties due to the forcible relocation of centrally located coloured communities to the Cape Flats during the Apartheid era. He then goes on to point out that a major difference between past and present gangs is that the former had previously roamed throughout the (inner) city, while the latter now find themselves spatially isolated within the Flats, and notes how this changed patterns of gang violence, including in particular leading to more brutal forms of gang warfare. This, Jensen argues, has permitted a more repressive form of policing, through a dual process of stigmatisation of particular urban figures such as the '*skollie*' as well as more targeted forms of both public and private security. Deborah Levenson (2013: 75, 104) makes a similar point in her study of Guatemalan gangs, tracing how the country's conflict to post-conflict transition led to a continuation of the 30-year civil war by other means, including a securitisation of urban life that transformed gangs from social constitutive institutions that were 'rich in life, ambiguities, creativities, and contradictions... [that] had the possibility of developing in different directions, for better or worse' to 'victim[s] of a system of dispositions that reproduced war without the war ...a target'.

In some cases, the very urban fabric of the city itself can become the means for repression, as Dennis Rodgers (2004, 2009, 2012) highlights in his work on urban violence in post-revolutionary Nicaragua. More specifically, he shows how the urban development of Managua over the past two decades has been largely linked to securitisation concerns, with particular forms of road-building actively constituting a form of 'infrastructural violence' that aims at isolating poor neighbourhoods in order to contain crime – and more specifically gang violence – within them, and has led to a concomitant intensification of violence within these areas, as well as a shift in the underlying nature of gangs, which has shifted from being solidaristic with their local neighbourhoods to predatory. Rodgers (2008, 2012) further traces how this elite-oriented process is underpinned by a particular oligarchic political economy that is fundamentally reflected in the city's morphology, thereby highlighting how urban violence is ultimately always a function of broader socio-political structures rather than a 'natural' phenomenon.

This is a phenomena that emerges very clearly from a historical perspective, with gangs frequently emerging as major indices of regimes of injustice, which often become especially apparent in urban contexts where process of power, inequality and oppression are both more intense and can become more visible. This is something that is apparent in Andrew Davies' (2013: 393–394) recent study of Glasgow gangs in the 1920s and 1930s – significantly called *City of Gangs* – where he notes that

> the history of Glasgow's gangs ...reminds us that crime does not exist on the margins of urban life ...It is ...no coincidence that gangs were embedded in districts characterised by high levels of economic and social deprivation. It is no coincidence, either, that gangs formed deeper roots in Glasgow than in other British cities during the 1920s and 1930s. Deindustrialisation was more acute, and more sudden, in Glasgow than elsewhere, while the city's enduring sectarian antagonisms provided recurrent incendiary sparks.

Davies goes on to contend that 'it is also no coincidence that the most optimistic stories to emerge from Glasgow ...stemmed from attempts to work with – rather than against – young people in the city's poorest districts', and as such, he reminds us that in the final analysis it is not so much that development is a function of security, but rather that security is a function of development.

Conclusion

Despite the empirical and theoretical evidence in favour of approaches that take questions of political economy into account, the vision that violence is an inherent feature of urban contexts continues to be extremely persistent. The World Bank's 2011 WDR is in many ways a paradigmatic exemplification of this kind of conceptualisation, which it achieves by actively not considering the relationship between the city and violence in anything other than a vague and impressionistic manner, relying on sensationalistic narrative tropes about gangs rather than empirical-based analysis to press the point that cities are violent spaces. One possible reason for this is that a framework projecting violence as a naturalised feature of cities effectively obscures and shifts the blame away from the pernicious socio-political urban regimes that are often at the root of violence in cities.

As this chapter has sought to demonstrate, urban violence is generally predicated on quite specific conditions pertaining to the particular social, political and economic processes that manifest themselves within cities. Their variable articulation gives rise to a range of different spatial morphologies and urban governance regimes that can have a range of different outcomes. This is particularly visible in relation to gangs, which wax and wane according to urban morphology, thereby fundamentally challenging universalising assumptions about cities and violence. Yet gangs tend not to be recognised as intimately linked to particular urban political economies but are rather seen as naturalistic epiphenomena of cities, which are simply considered to be violent spatial locales. Moving away from such a vision of things is all the more important in view of the fact that cities have become key sites for contemporary innovations in 'security governance' by both public and private agencies, with the UPP in Rio de Janeiro a paradigmatic example.

Such initiatives have arguably fuelled a conflation of security and development, insofar as urban violence is implicitly associated with criminality spurred on by poverty, and security governance emerges as a solution. Certainly, debates concerning the association of violence with development within the context of initiatives such as UPP have focused on the way that the former undermines possibilities for the latter, emphasising that security brings necessary certainty to private and public investment decisions, reduces the scope for further criminal activity, and reasserts the authority of the state. From this perspective, security interventions are seen as developmental because they transform cities from spaces of violence (associated with underdevelopment) to spaces of peace (necessary for development). This approach overlooks two major factors. The first – well highlighted by Robert Bates (2001) in his book *Prosperity and Violence*, significantly subtitled *The Political Economy of Development* – is that development is an inherently conflictual process, to the extent that historically, development has frequently been extremely violent. The second is that cities are complex spaces that contribute and mould particular formations of violent actors and forms of violence.

Certainly, there has been too little critical attention to how the state engages with violence in cities; as the analysis of UPP in Rio de Janeiro starkly illustrates, 'development' is not a natural consequence of the state removing the 'bad guys'. At the same time, however, it is striking how the motivations underlying the implementation of such policies frequently have more to do with securing urban space for capital than ensuring public safety for all, to the extent that they can be quite perniciously perverse. In general terms, such policies are more often than not based on processes of segregation, extreme violence and the disregard of certain populations (read: the poor). To this extent, when seen from the street-level perspective of many developing world cities, the notion of urban spaces being 'insecure' often has less to do with any putatively natural urban violence, and more because of the policies that aim to 'secure the city'. As such, far from being inherently violent, cities emerge starkly as sites of social antagonism, and urban violence as an indicator of the existence of profoundly unequal processes of under- and unfair development.

Notes

1. A table summarising causative and correlated factors that explain violence simply categorises 'rapid urbanisation' as an 'Economic and Internal Stress', along with severe corruption, youth unemployment, natural resource wealth, and the low opportunity costs of rebellion (World Bank, 2011: 7).
2. In earlier work Collier did note that urbanisation is associated with fewer deaths by armed conflict, although his analysis is limited to organised civil war (Collier and Hoeffler, 2004).
3. Robert Bates (2001: 50) makes the far more nuanced point that violence signals a contested political settlement, while peace or circumscribed violence means that conflict is being successfully managed or at least partially channelled. Bates, however, considers conflict to be organised 'within society' rather than as some aberration of social and political practice.
4. When the focus does move to the city and violence, the World Bank (2010) adopts a much broader conceptualisation of violence, including criminal and domestic violence, and puts less emphasis on state-threat and conflict.
5. They do find that conflict in cities is a result of weak political institutions, economic shocks and – with faint tautology – civil conflicts. The findings are based on a more nuanced appreciation of 'political violence' measured as riots, disturbances and lethal conflicts, although they ignore what is for most people the main 'problem' with violence, that is to say, robbery, mugging and homicide.
6. The Bank seems to like the UPP because it is partially financed by the private sector including leading entrepreneurs such as Eike Batista (Muggah and Souza Mulli, 2012). In fact, the UPP depends on the federal government's $250 billion Programme for Accelerated Growth (PAC) for its budget.
7. In fact the homicide rate had been falling before UPP was introduced possibly due to a truce between the major commando factions as control of the drug economy stabilised after a period of turf competition and/or an agreement between security forces, politicians and commando in the run-up to selection of Rio for the FIFA World Cup and Olympics.

8. The PR campaign has presented the police as strategic, uncorrupt and sensitive to community needs. An iconic figure in the campaign has been Major Pricilla Azevedo, commander of the UPP in the first pacified favela (Dona Marta) and later in charge of Rocinha.
9. There is widespread belief that pacification has focused on favelas controlled by commandos but ignored those controlled by milicia or even prepared some favela for milicia takeover. Similarly, there have been reports that pacification has simply displaced commandos rather than eliminated them, and that violence has been moved to other favelas. See http://www.abril.com.br/noticias/brasil/milicias-ja-dominam-41–5-favelas-cariocas-aponta-estudo-511295.shtml.
10. During a visit to Providencia in 2009, before UPP had occurred, one of us – Jones – met with a municipal official and an engineer busy setting out the potential route of the cable car.
11. The PAC has *subsequently* funded the construction of a health centre, education facilities and housing in Alemão.
12. For example, in figure 1.1 on page 53 of the WDR, a graphic comparison is made between the media coverage concerning gangs, terrorism, civil war, and trafficking, highlighting that this has followed very similar trends for all of them, particularly since 9/11. Similarly, at a national level, figure 3 on page 113 discusses insecurity in Colombia in a manner that merges the violence of urban crime, gangs, FARC and ELN rebel groups, implicitly suggesting they are equivalent forms of violence (conspicuously, paramilitary violence is not discussed).
13. Having said this, where gangs can sometimes be compared to rebel groups is in terms of their potential position within a broader structural context. As has been described in relation to Central America and South Africa, gangs in both contexts, while not explicitly revolutionary in nature, can be analysed as emergent vanguard social forms. Perhaps not revolutionary for themselves, but certainly in themselves, even if their rage is generally little more than a spontaneous and anarchic cry against situations of inequality, exclusion and injustice (Jensen and Rodgers, 2008; Rodgers, 2009).

References

Abrahamsen, R. and Williams, M. C. (2011). *Security beyond the State: Private Security in International Politics*. Cambridge: Cambridge University Press.

Arias, E. D. (2013).The impacts of differential armed dominance of politics in Rio de Janeiro, Brazil. *Studies in Comparative International Development*, *48*(3): 263–284.

Arias, E. D. and Rodgrigues, C. D. (2006). The myth of personal security: Criminal gangs, dispute resolution, and identity in Rio de Janeiro's favelas. *Latin American Politics and Society*, *48*(4): 53–81.

Bates, R. H. (2001). *Prosperity and Violence: The Political Economy of Development*. New York: W. W. Norton & Co.

Beall, J. (2006). Cities, terrorism and development. *Journal of International Development*, *18*(1): 105–120.

Beall, J., Guha-Khasnobis, B. and Kanbur, R. (eds) (2010).*Urbanization and Development: Multidisciplinary Perspectives*. Oxford: Oxford University Press.

Beall, J., Goodfellow, T. and Rodgers, D. (2013). Cities and conflict in fragile states in the developing world. *Urban Studies, 50*(15): 3065–3083.

Bénit-Gbaffou, C., Didier, S. and Morange, M. (2008). Communities, the private sector, and the state contested forms of security governance in Cape Town and Johannesburg. *Urban Affairs Review, 43*(5): 691–717.

Borja, J. and Castells, M. (1997). *Local and Global: The Management of Cities in the Information Age*. London: Earthscan.

Bourgois, P. (1995). *In Search of Respect: Selling Crack in El Barrio*. Cambridge: Cambridge University Press.

Brennan-Galvin, E. (2002). Crime and violence in an urbanizing world. *Journal of International Affairs, 56*(1): 123–145.

Buhaug, H. and Urdal, H. (2013). An urbanization bomb? Population growth and social disorder in cities. *Global Environmental Change, 23*(1): 1–10.

Buur, L., Jensen, S. and Stepputat, F. (eds) (2007). *The Security-Development Nexus: Expressions of Sovereignty and Securitization in Southern Africa*. Cape Town: HSRC.

Cano, I. (2012). *Os Donnos do Morro: Uma Avaliação Exploratória do Impacto das Unidades de Polícia Pacificadora (UPPs) no Rio de Janeiro*. Rio de Janeiro: Fórum Brasileiro de Segurança Pública.

Carvalho, L. and Soares, R. R. (2013). *Living on the Edge: Youth Entry, Career and Exit in Drug-Selling Gangs*. Paper presented to the 5th Annual Meeting on the Economics of Risky Behaviors (AMERB), Zurich, Switzerland, 5–7 April 2013, available online at: http://www.iza.org/conference_files/riskonomics2013/soares_r1995.pdf.

Cohen, A. K. (1955). *Delinquent Boys: The Culture of the Gang*. Glencoe: Free Press.

Cole, J. H. and Gramajo, A. M. (2009). Homicide rates in a cross-section of countries: Evidence and interpretations. *Population and Development Review, 35*(4): 749–776.

Collier, P. (2010). *Wars, Guns and Votes: Democracy in Dangerous Places*. London: Vintage.

Collier, P. and Hoeffler, A. (2004). Greed and Grievance in Civil War. *Oxford Economic Papers, 56*: 563–595.

Collier, P., Elliott, V. L., Hegre, H., Hoeffler, A., Reynal-Querol, M. and Sambanis, N. (2003). *Breaking the Conflict Trap: Civil War and Development Policy*. Washington, DC: The World Bank.

Costa Vargas, J. H. (2013). Taking back the land: Police operations and sport megaevents in Rio de Janeiro. *Souls: A Critical Journal of Black Politics, Culture, and Society, 15*(4): 275–303.

Davies, A. (2013). *City of Gangs: Glasgow and the Rise of the British Gangster*. London: Hodder & Stoughton.

Davis, M. (2006).*Planet of Slums*. London: Verso.

DFID (Department for International Development). (2007).*Preventing Violent Conflict*. London: DFID, available online at: http://reliefweb.int/sites/reliefweb.int/files/resources/94F326327650B3D3C12572DD004BD0CF-dfid-conflictprevention-may07.pdf.

Dyson, T. (2001). A partial theory of world development: The neglected role of the demographic transition in the shaping of modern society. *International Journal of Population Geography, 7*(2): 67–90.

Fearon, J. D. (2011). *Governance and Civil War Onset.* World Development Report 2011 Background Paper, Washington DC: World Bank. Available online at: http://siteresources.worldbank.org/EXTWDR2011/Resources/6406082–1283882418764/WDR_Background_Paper_Fearon.pdf.

Felbab-Brown, V. (2011). *Bringing the State to the Slum: Confronting Organized Crime and Urban Violence in Latin America: Lessons for Law Enforcement and Policymakers.* Washington, DC: Brookings Institution, available online at: http://www.brookings.edu/~/media/research/files/papers/2011/12/05%20latin%20america%20slums%20felbabbrown/1205_latin_america_slums_felbabbrown.pdf.

Fischer, C. S. (1975). Toward a subcultural theory of urbanism. *American Journal of Sociology, 80*(6): 1319–1341.

Fox, S. and Hoelscher, K. (2012). Political order, development and social violence. *Journal of Peace Research, 49*(3): 431–444.

Freeman, J. (2012). Neoliberal accumulation strategies and the visible hand of police pacification in Rio de Janeiro. *Revista de Estudos Universitários, 38*(1): 95–126.

Goldstone, J. A. (2002). Population and security: How demographic change can lead to violent conflict. *Journal of International Affairs, 56*(1): 3–21.

Graham, S. (2010). *Cities under Siege: The New Military Urbanism.* London: Verso.

Hagedorn, J. (2008). *A World of Gangs: Armed Young Men and Gangsta Culture.* Minneapolis: University of Minnesota Press.

Harvey, D. (1973). *Social Justice and the City.* London: Edward Arnold.

Hazen, J. M. and Rodgers, D. (eds) (2014). *Global Gangs: Street Violence across the World.* Minneapolis: University of Minnesota Press.

Hobbes, T. (1996 [1651]). *Leviathan,* edited by R. Tuck. Cambridge: Cambridge University Press.

Huntington, S. (1968). The bases of accommodation. *Foreign Affairs, 46*(4): 642–656.

Huntington, S. (1996). *The Clash of Civilizations and the Remaking of World Order.* New York: Simon & Schuster.

Jensen, S. (2008). *Gangs, Politics and Dignity in Cape Town.* Oxford and Chicago: James Currey and Chicago University Press.

Jensen, S. (2014). Intimate connections: Gangs and the political economy of urbanization in South Africa, in: J. M. Hazen and D. Rodgers (eds), *Global Gangs: Street Violence across the World.* Minneapolis: University of Minnesota Press.

Jensen, S. and Rodgers, D. (2008). Revolutionaries, barbarians, or war machines? Gangs in Nicaragua and South Africa, in: C. Leys and L. Panitch (eds), *Socialist Register 2009: Violence Today – Actually Existing Barbarism.* London: Merlin Press.

Jones, G. A. and Rodgers, D. (eds) (2009). *Youth Violence in Latin America: Gangs and Juvenile Justice in Perspective.* New York: Palgrave Macmillan.

Jones, G. A. and Rodgers, D. (2011). The World Bank's World Development Report 2011 on Conflict, Security, and Development: A critique through five vignettes. *Journal of International Development, 23*(7): 980–995.

Jütersonke, O., Muggah, R. and Rodgers, D. (2009). Gangs, urban violence, and security interventions in Central America. *Security Dialogue, 40*(4–5): 373–397.

Keen, D. (2008). *Complex Emergencies.* Cambridge: Polity.

Levenson, D. (2013). *Adiós niño: The Gangs of Guatemala City and the Politics of Death.* Durham: Duke University Press.

Lewis, O. (1965). Further observation on the folk-urban continuum and urbanization with special reference to Mexico City, in: P. H. Hauser and L. Schnore (eds), *The Study of Urbanization*. New York: Wiley.

Limas Carlos, C. A. (2010). Una mirada crítica a la zona portuaria de Río de Janeiro. *Bitácora Urbano\Territorial*, *17*(2): 23–54.

Misse, M. (2007). Mercados ilegais, redes de proteção e organização local do crime no Rio de Janeiro. *Estudos Avancados*, *21*(61): 139–157.

Muggah, R. and Souza Mulli, A. (2012). Rio tries counterinsurgency. *Current History*, *111*(742): 62–66.

Norton, R. J. (2003). Feral cities. *Naval War College Review*, *LVI*(4): 97–106.

Penglase, B. (2009). States of insecurity: Everyday emergencies, public secrets and drug trafficker power in a Brazilian favela. *PoLAR: Political and Legal Anthropology Review*, *32*(1): 407–423.

Pinnock, D. (1984). *The Brotherhoods: Street Gangs and State Control in Cape Town*. Cape Town: David Philip.

Rapley, J. (2006). The new Middle Ages. *Foreign Affairs*, *85*(3): 95–103.

Robb Larkins, E. (2013). Performances of police legitimacy in Rio's hyper favela. *Law and Social Inquiry*, *38*(3): 553–575.

Rodgers, D. (2004). Disembedding the city: Crime, insecurity, and spatial organisation in Managua, Nicaragua. *Environment and Urbanization*, *16*(2): 113–124.

Rodgers, D. (2008). A symptom called Managua. *New Left Review*, *49*(Jan-Feb): 103–120.

Rodgers, D. (2009). Slum wars of the 21st century: Gangs, *Mano Dura*, and the new urban geography of conflict in Central America. *Development and Change*, *40*(5): 949–976.

Rodgers, D. (2012). Haussmannization in the tropics: Abject urbanism and infrastructural violence in Nicaragua. *Ethnography*, *13*(4): 411–436.

Samara, T. R. (2011). *Cape Town after Apartheid: Crime and Governance in the Divided City*. Minneapolis: University of Minnesota Press.

Sánchez Jankowski, M. (1991). *Islands in the Street: Gangs and American Urban Society*. Berkeley, CA: University of California Press.

Scott, J. C. (1998). *Seeing Like a State: How Certain Schemes to Improve the Human Condition Have Failed*. New Haven: Yale University Press.

Shaw, C. and McKay, H. (1942). *Juvenile Delinquency in Urban Areas*. Chicago: University of Chicago Press.

Teixeira, E. T. (2011). Brésil – La pacification des favelas de Rio de Janeiro: Une 'contre-insurrection préventive'. *DIAL (Diffusion de l'Information sur l'Amérique Latine)*, 3150, 9 May, available online at: http://www.alterinfos.org/spip.php?article4919.

Thrasher, F. M. (1927). *The Gang: A Study of 1,313 Gangs in Chicago*. Chicago: University of Chicago Press.

UNOWA (United Nations Office for West Africa). (2007). *Urbanization and Insecurity in West Africa: Population Movement, Mega Cities and Regional Stability*. Issue Paper, October, Dakar: UNOWA.

Urdal, H. (2006). A clash of generations? Youth bulges and political violence. *International Studies Quarterly*, *50*(3): 607–629.

Urdal, H. (2012). Demography and armed conflict: Assessing the role of population, in: G. Brown and A. Langer (eds), *Elgar Companion to Civil War and Fragile States*. London: Edward Elgar.

Whyte, W. F. (1943). *Street Corner Society: The Social Structure of an Italian Slum.* Chicago: University of Chicago Press.
Wirth, L. (1938). Urbanism as a Way of Life: The City and Contemporary Civilization. *American Journal of Sociology, 44*(1): 1–24.
World Bank. (2010). *Violence in the City: Understanding and Supporting Community Responses to Urban Violence.* Washington, DC: World Bank.
World Bank. (2011). *Word Development Report 2011: Conflict, Security, and Development.* Washington, DC: World Bank.

Conclusion

Colin Marx and Charlotte Lemanski

In their contributions to this volume, the authors have responded to and extended our view that the spaces of urban poverty matter. Rather than simply interpreting urban poverty as poverty happening *in* cities and towns, they have explored the multiple ways in which spaces matter to the constitution of urban poverty. The ways in which this approach to understanding urban poverty as *of* the city (i.e., urban poverty is *in* the city, and the city is *in* urban poverty) are utilised vary significantly according to each chapters' theoretical, empirical and sectoral context, as detailed below.

Susan Parnell takes aim at a broad failure amongst both scholarly and policy approaches to focus on what 'the urban' means in the contemporary Global South. She suggests that the ways in which poverty and the city interact has been overlooked in recent years as the focus has fallen on personalised experiences of poverty *in* the city. In her view, it is clear that in order to understand and respond to urban poverty it is necessary to engage with the infrastructural and material spaces of the city as well as individual experiences. She draws on earlier feminist work to renew the focus on how the ways in which the city is built, serviced, managed and experienced clearly play a role in the processes and dynamics that make urban poverty such an intractable social issue. From her chapter it is evident that there are structural elements in the institutional functioning of 'the city' as a spatial form that translates into poverty.

Sylvia Chant and *Kerwin Datu*'s chapter also acknowledges its debt to the spatial insights of feminist work, by locating urban poverty within explicit gender dimensions that highlight its multi-dimensionality and multi-sitedness. That urban poverty has these two features means that Chant and Datu are extremely wary of claims that women and girls can benefit from the prosperity often associated with cities. Their conclusion is that interaction between different intra-urban spaces does not necessarily mean that women benefit from urbanisation. Instead, women and girls continue to confront disadvantages at a number of different scales, a finding easily highlighted by a multi-sited approach to urban poverty.

While the first two chapters explicitly trace their insights to feminist scholarship, *Alexandre Apsan Frediani* acknowledges a different heritage in poverty studies. Drawing on Amartya Sen and Martha Nussbaum's profoundly important analyses of poverty as related to capabilities, entitlements, endowments, and claims, Frediani extends work in this vein by considering how insights from critical urban studies help clarify the interactions between urban space and poverty. Working with a multi-dimensional account of urban poverty, he shows how the spatial production of the built environment in upgrading informal settlements can create new obstacles and reproduce cycles of marginalisation for poor women and men. Then, using an example of a city-level institutional feature that Parnell calls for, he looks at how processes related to water management structure spaces. Through the municipal delegated management model of water delivery in Kisumu, Kenya, he demonstrates how the commodification of urban services can use spatiality to entrench inequalities in abilities to transform urban environments (and ultimately to overcome urban poverty).

Melanie Lombard also draws on informal settlements and sets off a new theme in the book in relation to how knowledge is produced about urban poverty. She examines the knowledge production processes in relation to informal settlements as one locus of urban poverty. She uses 'place-making' as a knowledge production tool to disrupt the dominant view of informal settlements as 'other' spaces by seeing them as ordinary. In this way, her 'place-making' approach identifies new forms of (spatialised) power that are overlooked in debates on informality and poverty.

Isa Baud also addresses the theme of the production of knowledge to consider how the knowledge that underpins 'mapping' can assist in generating new options. Shifting the lens from Latin America to India, Baud illustrates how embracing new sources of knowledge about spatial diversity and the concentrations of deprivation uncovers the highly relational ways in which deprivations are constructed. Enriched by the type of multi-sited spatial analysis that Chant and Datu argue for, Baud's approach demonstrates how knowledge produced at household, neighbourhood and city levels reveals the ways in which poverty dynamics are embedded in political processes.

Romola Sanyal also develops the critique identified by Parnell, namely that the focus of urban poverty analysis is typically on the poor citizens themselves. While Parnell advocates for the importance of the institutional features of the city, Sanyal uses the marginal spatial figure of the refugee to consider how their historically overlooked urban spaces of poverty served to disrupt existing, and create new, forms of impoverishment in Calcutta. Sanyal's perspective is important in adding a historical approach that confirms the long-standing importance of urban spatiality in the midst of an argument that is typically over-focused on the consequences of very contemporary processes of urbanisation.

In recognition of the multi-sited nature of urban poverty, *Caren Levy* considers the specific entry point of 'top-down' approaches of urban planning. In common with Goswami's chapter which focuses on another instrument of intervention – the law – Levy's chapter considers how urban planning can effectively address urban poverty using the example of a bridging finance mechanism in different cities in India. Her argument is clear: in order for planning to address poverty it is not sufficient to reform the way it intervenes in space. Instead it is necessary to change the framework in which planning operates in order to create spaces that provide 'room for manoeuvre' in securing material redistribution, inclusive recognition and participatory processes.

Remaining in India, *Amlanjyoti Goswami* poetically tracks back and forth between the space of the street, its metaphorical representation as urban life in the legal courts and the figure of the (poor) street vendor. In many ways, providing a timely example of the ways in which it is possible, and necessary, to work with both individual experiences of urban poverty and the impoverishing and/or enabling institutions of city functionings. In this example, space is the fulcrum around which the life of poor street vendors is negotiated, and their ability to use space to escape poverty is caught up in a never-ending circularity where laws are defined by space, but space requires laws.

Finally, *Gareth Jones* and *Dennis Rodgers* take us into the complex space woven between problematic representations of poverty, violence and the city – where all three create a nexus of universalising assumptions of poor people's experiences in cities. Drawing on different experiences of responding to (undifferentiated) accounts of violence in Latin American cities, they show instead how a careful reading of spatial configurations is required if interactions between poverty, violence and cities are to be addressed in ways that benefit poor people. Their focus on the importance of spatiality in better understanding the relationship between urban violence and urban poverty echoes and confirms our arguments about the dynamic (rather than static) role played by urban space in urban poverty construction and perpetuation.

Taken together, these contributions raise three themes that reflect the arguments of the authors, and demonstrate the value of the particular perspective adopted in this volume. We discuss these themes in the final section.

Themes

This book has aimed to extend, and make more explicit, the spatiality of urban poverty. Within an overall framework that 'space matters', we are extremely concerned that while the spatiality of urban poverty remains unexamined, it is likely that, despite the best intentions, the understandings of poverty that are adopted (and consequent policy responses) are ultimately flawed because the implicit spatiality of urban poverty (e.g., inherited social/power relations) are overlooked. Ignoring the ways in which the spaces of the city contribute towards urban poverty causality is, in our opinion, a serious oversight in need of urgent redress. The three themes that underpin this concern relate to the multi-sitedness of urban poverty, the spatiality of impoverishing processes, and the spatial positionality of poverty scholars and policy makers.

The multi-dimensional, multi-sited nature of urban poverty

It is now well established that poverty is a multi-dimensional phenomenon. As elaborated in the review of urban poverty in the introduction, much of the purpose of defining urban poverty has been to draw attention to its multi-dimensional nature because the diversity and multiplicity of urban lives means that impoverishment is produced and experienced in multiple ways. As part of this, it is largely recognised that a definition of urban poverty which rests solely on a definition of income is seriously deficient and must include other factors such as low quality and quantities of housing, health care, educational opportunities, employment and feelings of disempowerment and humiliation. Although the multi-sited nature of urban poverty (see, for example, Yapa's 1998 analysis of how poverty is materially and discursively produced at multiple sites) has received less traction, interventions to address poverty now increasingly recognise the need to adopt a multi-sectoral and multi-dimensional aspect if they are to have any chance of success (see also Mitlin and Satterthwaite, 2013).

It is Chant and Datu who first draw attention to the ways in which urban poverty is multi-sited as well as multi-dimensional in this book. That is, it is not that urban poverty is only multi-sited because it is multi-dimensional: that urban poverty emerges because of processes related to the different places that people access shelter, education and health, for example. Instead, urban poverty emerges in different spaces and can be multi-dimensional in these spaces. If, repeating an insight from human geography, the urban is the 'co-presence of multiple spaces, multiple times and multiple webs of relations tying local sites, subjects and fragments into globalising networks of economic, social and cultural change', then urban poverty can only be multi-sited and multi-dimensional (Amin and Graham, 1997: 417–418). At the same time, it is worth heeding Chant and Datu's caution that a plethora of intervention points afforded by a multi-dimensional understanding of urban poverty means that the possibilities of effectively addressing urban poverty may remain elusive. It remains to be seen whether considering urban poverty as both multi-dimensional *and* multi-sited compounds or overcomes the elusiveness of poverty reduction.

Although a multi-sited approach to urban poverty is most explicit in Chant and Datu's chapter, it emerges in different ways in the approaches of several other authors in this volume. Levy shows how an initiative to reduce poverty in an urban slum in India required co-ordinated production of an understanding of urban poverty and actions across multiple institutional and physical spaces: in the slum itself, other slums in Mumbai, the city of Mumbai, London, and Coventry. Goswami reveals how action to reduce poverty in New Delhi must take into account physical spaces of the street, juridical spaces of constitutional courts and shifting spaces of politics, as well that street vendors are typically voiceless, working informally, and characterised by gender dynamics. Baud shows how a multi-dimensional understanding of urban poverty is also associated with multi-sited political initiatives that cross the patchwork of regulatory boundaries to characterise poverty. Sanyal discusses another variation of multi-sitedness by drawing attention to how urban spaces of poverty in Calcutta were born out of spaces and experiences that people migrated from and to. Frediani illustrates how claims, entitlements and capabilities have different spatialities. Jones and Rodgers' demonstration of the ways in which identical spaces of the city are paradoxically displayed as both repellent (due to violence) and attractive (due to aspirations of prosperity), implicitly highlights the importance of combining multi-sitedness with multi-dimensionality when addressing urban poverty in the Global South. In fact, all the chapters highlighted above indicate that an important way of taking forward the spatial agenda in relation to urban poverty is to bring together analyses of the multi-dimensional aspects of poverty with different dimensions of the multi-sitedness of poverty.

One immediate way in which this could be addressed would be to focus on the way in which data on urban poverty is generated: urban poverty is experienced multi-dimensionally across multiple sites and analysed across multiple sites and produced across multiple sites. One of the possible reasons why the multi-sitedness of poverty has gained so little traction is because of the household focus of typical poverty surveys and analyses which means that no matter how hard researchers try, they are always only 'seeing' poverty from a single urban site. Developing methodologies that simultaneously generate data at multi-sites on multi-dimensional criteria is surely one of the next challenges.

Going beyond redistribution

Current spatial conceptions of poverty are extremely good at mapping the location of deprivation and poverty. For example, most cities have developed some way in which to record standards of living, income levels, access to services and the like. The consequences of this mapping are significant because it provides policy makers with a clear indication of where to target certain (limited) resources. And especially in relation to persistent areas of deprivation which are identified as 'spatial poverty traps'.

The distribution of deprivation is clearly important. However, maps indicating the distribution of poverty are fundamentally unable to capture the dynamics that impoverish people. As a snapshot of the distribution of resources, all the location of poverty can provide is the result of a series of processes of impoverishment (typically) in a certain space (usually the household and/or settlement). What would maps of poverty look like that depicted the processes of impoverishment? Baud picks up this challenge and shows how distributions of deprivation do not map onto the processes of impoverishment. Lombard shows how a relational sense of space challenges the dynamics that are associated with particular 'poor' spaces of informal settlements in cities. What kinds of governance changes would this invoke and how? Parnell implicates the institutional functioning of the city itself in perpetuating urban poverty and suggests that institutional changes are required in governance systems.

The consequences of focusing on the distribution of urban poverty and deprivation also impact on the people identified as poor because they provide the 'proof' to demand redress of some kind. The politics that ensue are those of redistribution and the extent that redistribution can take. It is important not to deny the need for redistribution. As Dikeç (2001) observes, in some circumstances, distributional issues are all that poor people may have to organise around. However, the main issue with redistributive approaches is that, in order to be considered legitimate and intelligible, they must make a claim on what is commonly accepted to be available for redistributive purposes. It is extremely difficult for 'the poor' to make any claims, let alone any on future resources that do not exist yet, despite this being the promise (and premise) of the dominant 'trickle-down' model of economic growth. Hence, working within the confines of existing allocations requires the focus to be on the struggle to increase the allocation to address poverty, understood as it is at a particular point in time. This leaves little space to also focus on the multiple sites and processes through which poverty is experienced, produced and analysed.

Despite this limitation, there is a need to maintain a balance between redistributional approaches and those that challenge the processes of impoverishment. Dikeç's (2001) distinctions between the injustice of spatiality and spatiality of injustice are instructive here. Considering poverty as a form of injustice, the notion of the spatiality of injustice provides a means of comprehending how injustice is produced in space, that is, its distribution. The injustice of spatiality, however, is produced through space and speaks to the elimination of the possibility to form a political response (Dikeç, 2001: 1792). Levy makes this point clearly in her articulation of urban planning agendas that must simultaneously engage with redistribution, recognition and participation in order to develop new frameworks to address the spaces of urban poverty.

Positionality

As we mentioned in the introduction, the spatial positionality of poverty scholars is important: who is writing about urban poverty and from what context does matter. Positionality is about space, but it is also about the resources, theoretical frameworks, values, relations, and perspectives that come with spaces. This point is well recognised in human geography (e.g., Rose, 1997). However, in studies of urban poverty it has tended to take a particular form. In studies of poverty more generally, there is a long tradition that argues that those who experience poverty have particular insights and that it would be foolish to ignore the location of such 'voices' if the intention is truly to address poverty. In the context of cities in the Global South, one of the best contemporary examples of this is the work related to Slum/Shackdwellers International (SDI) and their associated organisations and federations. Scholar/activists such as Satterthwaite, Mitlin, Patel, Boonyabancha[1] and others have worked strategically over many years to confirm the value of the positionality of urban poor women and men, girls and boys. This work is extremely important in assisting organisations representing the urban poor in making (political) space for their voices to be heard, and heard more clearly and decisively. However, the cumulative struggle to open spaces for other positionalities (of the urban poor themselves) to emerge in urban poverty discourses has tended to neglect an examination of the positionalities of urban poverty scholars themselves. The contributions to this collection highlight that while the positionalities of the urban poor themselves is now widely included (in some more or less effective forms than others), there needs to be much more critical debate surrounding urban poverty scholars' spatial positioning. Indeed, the absence of virtually any mention of who is writing, and from where, is a vast omission, particularly in a field so ostensibly in favour of hearing multiple 'voices'.

This positionality is important, not as a tick-box requirement, but because, as we have argued throughout this book, space and place matter in relation to claims about the universality of definitions and analyses of urban poverty. If we are interested in the role of city spatiality in perpetuating urban poverty, then we must surely also be interested in the roles played by the spaces of urban poverty scholarship. Indeed, while it is worrying that international experts spend more time adjusting expert per diem rates across different locations than they do adjusting poverty lines (Satterthwaite and Mitlin, 2014), this example implicitly highlights the importance of space and place that could be built on.

The significance of place is echoed in Lombard's chapter, which develops the notion of 'place-making' to describe the messy and complex ways in which 'place' is assembled by a broad range of players and strategies working in both cooperation and conflict. Although Lombard develops this analytical approach to explore the socio-spatial construction of informal settlements in the city, her argument could equally be applied to the relational and spatial ways in which scholars construct urban poverty concepts and approaches. Furthermore, ideas surrounding the production of knowledge are implicitly explored in both Baud's and Levy's contributions to this volume, who in different ways highlight how spatialised knowledge production plays a crucial role in highlighting previously overlooked arenas and voices in the construction of urban poverty concepts and approaches. In this sense, we extend our argument about the dynamic role played by the spaces of the city in creating and perpetuating urban poverty, to argue that that the spatial positioning of urban poverty scholars is equally influential in determining urban poverty concepts and approaches.

To conclude, where does this leave us? Throughout this book we have strongly argued the need to award urban spatiality a higher profile in the analysis of, and policy responses to, urban poverty. In particular, it is our intention to stimulate a debate about the relevance of the spatialities of cities (and towns) for gaining a greater insight into the dynamics of urban poverty causality. However, reflective of our own partialities, biases, locations, and experiences, it is beholden on us to note our uncertainties, insecurities and inabilities to provide definitive answers. So while we reassert the claim that 'space matters', we are as yet unclear about what types of new knowledge, new understandings and new policies might be produced by a spatialised approach to urban poverty. We do not hide this uncertainty, but acknowledge it as part of our role in highlighting the importance of space, and consequently opening the floor to others (including the authors in this volume) to speak up in a context where the solutions are not pre-determined. However, this uncertainty notwithstanding, it seems to us that the key questions that emerge, at this moment and from our vantage point, are: what would urban poverty be if it was considered as multi-sited and multi-dimensional, if it balanced distributional issues with the processes that impoverish and if the positionalities of the researchers were more transparent? What kind of politics would ensue, or be required, in order to create space for such a perspective?

Note

1. See, for example, Satterthwaite and Mitlin (2014), Mitlin and Satterthwaite (2007), Patel (2004) and Boonyabancha, Carcellar and Kerr (2012).

References

Amin, N. and Graham, S. (1997). The ordinary city. *Transactions of the Institute of British Geographers, 22*: 411–429.

Boonyabancha, S., Carcellar, N. and Kerr, T. (2012). How poor communities are paving their own pathways to freedom. *Environment and Urbanisation, 24*(2): 403–422.

Dikeç, M. (2001) Justice and the spatial imagination. *Environment and Planning A, 33*(10): 1785–1805.

Mitlin, D. and Satterthwaite, D. (2007). Strategies for grassroots control of international aid. *Environment and Urbanisation, 19*(2): 483–500.

Mitlin, D. and Satterthwaite, D. (2013). *Urban Poverty in the Global South*. Abingdon: Routledge.

Patel, S. (2004). Grassroots driven development: The alliance of SPARC, the National Slum Dwellers Federation and *Mahila Milan*, in: D. Mitlin and D. Satterthwaite (eds), *Empowering Squatter Citizens*. London: Earthscan Publications, 216–244.

Rose, G. (1997). Situating knowledges: Positionality, reflexivities and other tactics. *Progress in Human Geography,* 21(3), 305–332.

Satterthwaite, D. and Mitlin, D. (2014). *Reducing Urban Poverty in the Global South*. Abingdon: Routledge.

Yapa, L. (1998). The poverty discourse and the poor in Sri Lanka. *Transactions of the Institute of British Geographers, 23*: 95–115.

Index

CPSIA information can be obtained at www.ICGtesting.com
Printed in the USA
LVOW04*1230140515

438283LV00003B/4/P